HARDEN'S

Good Cheap Eats in London

James,

No chocolate for Easter for you this year, but lots of great places to eat in your new 'home' town. James and I thought you'd like this. Looking forward to trying out some of these when we visit you in London.

with love Susannah.

Easter 2004.

Other Harden's titles

London Restaurants
UK Restaurants
Hotel Guide – NEW!
London Party Guide
London Bars & Pubs
London Baby Book
London for Free

ISBN 1-873721-60-9

British Library Cataloguing-in-Publication data:
a catalogue record for this book is available from
the British Library.

Printed and bound in Italy by Legoprint

Production Manager: Elizabeth Warman
Editorial Assistant: Julia Lander
Research Manager: Frances Gill

Harden's Limited
14 Buckingham Street
London WC2N 6DF

CONTENTS

Ratings & prices

Page

Introduction **8**

Recommendations

Best all-round deals – A★★ 9
Best food – ★★ 9
Special deals at top restaurants 9
New openings 10
Most interesting ethnic places 10
The most stylish places 11
Best for romance 11
Best breakfast/brunch 11
Top pub grub 12
The best fun places 12

Directory **14**

Indexes

Breakfast 102
BYO 102
Children 103
Entertainment 105
Late 106
No-smoking areas 107
Outside tables 108
Pre/Post theatre 110
Private rooms 110

Cuisine indexes **114**

Area overviews **126**

Maps **142**

1 – London overview
2 – West End overview
3 – Mayfair, St James's & West Soho
4 – East Soho, Chinatown & Covent Garden
5 – Knightsbridge, Chelsea & South Kensington
6 – Notting Hill & Bayswater
7 – Hammersmith & Chiswick
8 – Hampstead, Camden Town & Islington
9 – The City
10 – South London (& Fulham)
11 – East End & Docklands

RATINGS & PRICES

RATINGS

Ratings are based both on our own experiences – we have visited all of the listed establishments at our own expense – and also on the views of the reporters who take part in our annual survey. We have given ratings as follows:

★★ Exceptional

London's top bargains. They offer a quality of cooking which is, given the price, worth travelling for.

★ Very good

Places where the cooking offers above-average value for money.

A Good atmosphere

Spots with particular "buzz", style or charm.

PRICES

So you can compare the costs of different establishments, we have tried to give a realistic estimate of the cost for a typical meal in each place.

For *restaurants, pubs and wine bars,* we have given an estimate of the cost for one (1) person of two courses with a drink and a cup of coffee.

For *cafés,* the price we show is the approximate cost of a sandwich, a cake and a cup of coffee.

These prices include service (we have included a 10% tip if there is no service charge), VAT and any cover charge.

* Where an asterisk appears next to the price, you can usually keep expenditure to £20 a head or less only at certain times of day (usually lunch), by sticking to a particular menu, or (in a few cases) by eating in a specified area, such as the bar. Eating at other times or from the à la carte menu may be much more expensive – see the text of the entry for details. In the area lists, the ratings for such restaurants appear in brackets, eg (A★).

Telephone number – all numbers should be prefixed with '020' if dialling from outside the London area.

Map reference – shown immediately after the telephone number. (Major coffee shop chains are not shown on the maps.)

Website – if applicable, is the first entry in the small print.

Last orders time – the first entry in the small print, after the website (if applicable); Sunday may be up to 90 minutes earlier.

Opening hours – unless otherwise stated, restaurants are open for lunch and dinner seven days a week.

Credit and debit cards – unless otherwise stated, Mastercard, Visa, Amex and Switch are accepted.

Dress – where appropriate, the management's preferences concerning patrons' dress are given.

Smoking – cigarette smoking restrictions are noted. Pipe or cigar smokers should always check ahead.

INTRODUCTION

This is the tenth edition of our guide for anyone who wants to enjoy eating out in London while keeping costs under control. It is less difficult than many people might think to find interesting and satisfying meals at modest cost. And it's not even as if you are restricted to a particular *type* of establishment. The coverage of this guide extends all the way from basic East End canteens to grand, 'big name' restaurants in the heart of fashionable London.

We have decided, once again, to maintain the £20 a head 'cut-off' price as we used for previous editions. For this amount, a qualifying establishment must provide two courses, a drink, coffee and service. (If there is no compulsory service charge, we have allowed for a 10% tip.) Many of the places listed can be visited for light meals or snacks at rather less cost than the 'formula' price we quote.

Diners on a budget, in particular, have to know *where* to go, of course – but it's often almost more important to know *when*. Many of the more interesting experiences are to be had at places where the price is asterisked* – see the previous page for an explanation. These are usually 'proper' restaurants which experience a shortage of custom at lunchtime (or, in some office areas, dinner time). They offer low-price set menus as loss leaders, hoping either to make up the difference through wine sales or to impress customers enough to guarantee a return visit. Whatever the restaurateurs' motives, there are some great bargains to be had – especially for those who do not need too much wine with their meal!

We wish you some excellent lunching and dining. Perhaps you would like to tell us about your successes (or any failures). Every spring, we conduct a detailed survey of restaurant-goers experiences. Those who participate – nearly 6,500 people in 2003 – receive a complimentary copy of the guide combined London & UK Restaurants guide.

We invite you, too, to register to take part in the survey by visiting www.hardens.com and following the 'Register' instructions. You will find on the site a wealth of information about restaurants and about Harden's guides and our other products and services.

Richard Harden **Peter Harden**

RECOMMENDATIONS

BEST ALL-ROUND DEALS A★★

Frederick's *(N1)*
Lundum's *(SW7)*
Moro *(EC1)*
Real Greek Souvlaki *(EC1)*
J Sheekey *(WC2)*
The Stepping Stone *(SW8)*
Vama *(SW10)*
Yming *(W1)*

BEST FOOD ★★

For £15 & under:

Beirut Express *(W2)*
Faulkner's *(E8)*
Geeta *(NW6)*
Inaho *(W2)*
Kastoori *(SW17)*
Lahore Kebab House *(E1)*
Mandalay *(W2)*
Mirch Masala *(chain)*
Sabras *(NW10)*
Sakonis *(HA0)*
Sree Krishna *(SW17)*
Talad Thai *(SW15)*
El Vergel *(SE1)*
Vijay *(NW6)*

For over £15:

The Anglesea Arms *(W6)*
Basilico *(chain)*
Blah! Blah! Blah! *(W12)*
Café Japan *(NW11)*
Chez Liline *(N4)*
Chiang Mai *(W1)*
Chowki *(W1)*
Deca *(W1)*
Frederick's *(N1)*
The Gate *(chain)*
Incognico *(WC2)*
Jin Kichi *(NW3)*
Kennington Lane *(SE11)*
Konditor & Cook *(SE1)*
Kulu Kulu *(chain)*
Lundum's *(SW7)*
Mandarin Kitchen *(W2)*
Moro *(EC1)*
The Parsee *(N19)*
Rasa *(chain)*
The Rôtisserie *(chain)*
Royal China *(chain)*
Sarkhel's *(SW18)*
J Sheekey *(WC2)*
The Stepping Stone *(SW8)*
Yming *(W1)*
Yoshino *(W1)*

SPECIAL DEALS AT TOP RESTAURANTS

Bank Aldwych *(WC2)*
Bank Westminster *(SW1)*
Blue Elephant *(SW6)*
Butlers Wharf Chop-house *(SE1)*
Carpaccio's *(SW3)*
Deca *(W1)*
Incognico *(WC2)*
Lou Pescadou *(SW5)*
Mon Plaisir *(WC2)*
Quality Chop House *(EC1)*
J Sheekey *(WC2)*
Sherlock's Grill *(W1)*
Vama *(SW10)*
Veeraswamy *(W1)*
ZeNW3 *(NW3)*

RECOMMENDATIONS

NEW OPENINGS

The Abbeville *(SW4)*
Apium *(EC1)*
Aziz *(SW6)*
Balham Kitchen & Bar *(SW12)*
Bar Mezé *(chain)*
Cristini *(W1)*
Don Pedro *(EC1)*
Eagle Bar Diner *(W1)*
The Easton *(WC1)*
The Endurance *(W1)*
Exotika *(WC2)*
Giá *(SW3)*
The Green *(NW2)*
Haz *(E1)*
Kaslik *(W1)*
Kazan *(SW1)*
Khew *(W1)*
Kulu Kulu *(chain)*
Little Basil *(NW3)*
Ma Cuisine *(TW1)*
The Mall Tavern *(W8)*
Nicolas Bar à Vins *(SW10)*
Opera *(NW3)*
The Pepper Tree *(chain)*
The Phoenix *(SW3)*
Real Greek Souvlaki *(EC1)*
Rocket *(chain)*
Running Horse *(W1)*
Sagar *(W6)*
Segafredo Zanetti *(W1)*
Sherlock's Grill *(W1)*
Smithy's *(WC1)*
So.uk *(chain)*
The Station *(W10)*
The Swan *(W4)*
Taro *(chain)*
Tas Pide *(SE1)*
Thai Canteen *(W6)*
Zimzun *(SW6)*

MOST INTERESTING ETHNIC PLACES

Abeno *(WC1)*
Alounak *(chain)*
Babur Brasserie *(SE23)*
Brilliant *(UB2)*
Busaba Eathai *(chain)*
Café de Maya *(NW3)*
Chez Liline *(N4)*
Chiang Mai *(W1)*
Chowki *(W1)*
Coromandel *(SW11)*
Gaby's *(WC2)*
Hakkasan *(W1)*
Huong-Viet *(N1)*
Ikkyu *(W1)*
Inaho *(W2)*
Jashan *(chain)*
K10 *(EC2)*
Kandoo *(W2)*
Kastoori *(SW17)*
Kasturi *(EC3)*
Lahore Kebab House *(E1)*
Lan Na Thai *(SW11)*
Ma Goa *(SW15)*
Mandarin Kitchen *(W2)*
Mangal *(E8)*
Mela *(WC2)*
Mirch Masala *(chain)*
Opera *(NW3)*
Ophim *(W1)*
Ozer *(W1)*
The Parsee *(N19)*
Poons, Lisle Street *(WC2)*
Ranoush *(chain)*
Rasa *(chain)*
Real Greek Souvlaki *(EC1)*
Royal China *(chain)*
Sagar *(W6)*
Sakonis *(HA0)*
Shish *(chain)*
Sree Krishna *(SW17)*
Tajine *(W1)*
Tas *(chain)*
Thai Noodle Bar *(SW10)*
Tsunami *(SW4)*
Uli *(W11)*
Vama *(SW10)*
Viet-Anh *(NW1)*

THE MOST STYLISH PLACES

The Abingdon *(W8)*
Aperitivo *(W1)*
Baltic *(SE1)*
Bam-Bou *(W1)*
Bank Aldwych *(WC2)*
Bank Westminster *(SW1)*
Benihana *(chain)*
Busaba Eathai *(chain)*
Bush Bar & Grill *(W12)*
Butlers Wharf
Chop-house *(SE1)*
Carnevale *(EC1)*
Carpaccio's *(SW3)*
Deca *(W1)*
Eco *(chain)*
Fortnum's Fountain *(W1)*
Giá *(SW3)*
Gung-Ho *(NW6)*
Hakkasan *(W1)*
Incognico *(WC2)*
Kennington Lane *(SE11)*
Lansdowne *(NW1)*
Mango Room *(NW1)*
Opera *(NW3)*
PizzaExpress *(chain)*
Raks *(W1)*
Real Greek Souvlaki *(EC1)*
Rocket *(chain)*
Sarastro *(WC2)*
Smiths (Ground Floor) *(EC1)*
So.uk *(chain)*
Sosho *(EC2)*
The Stepping Stone *(SW8)*
Tate Modern (Café 7) *(SE1)*
Tom's *(W11)*
Vama *(SW10)*
Veeraswamy *(W1)*
ZeNW3 *(NW3)*

BEST FOR ROMANCE

Anglo Asian Tandoori *(N16)*
Arancia *(SE16)*
Aurora *(W1)*
Bam-Bou *(W1)*
The Depot *(SW14)*
Frocks *(E9)*
Giá *(SW3)*
Gordon's Wine Bar *(WC2)*
Hakkasan *(W1)*
Incognico *(WC2)*
Lundum's *(SW7)*
Ma Cuisine *(TW1)*
Maggiore's *(WC2)*
Mon Plaisir *(WC2)*
Osteria Basilico *(W11)*
Patio *(W12)*
Sarastro *(WC2)*
So.uk *(chain)*
Vama *(SW0)*
Yum Yum *(N16)*

BEST BREAKFAST/BRUNCH

Aurora *(W1)*
Balans *(chain)*
Bank Aldwych *(WC2)*
Banners *(chain)*
Brick Lane Beigel Bake *(E1)*
Café 206 *(W11)*
Café Laville *(W2)*
Café Mozart *(N6)*
Chamomile *(NW3)*
Chelsea Bun Diner *(chain)*
Fortnum's Fountain *(W1)*
Fox & Anchor *(EC1)*
Frocks *(E9)*
Gastro *(SW4)*
Giraffe *(chain)*
Hope & Sir Loin *(EC1)*
Hudson's *(SW15)*
Konditor & Cook *(SE1)*
Maison Bertaux *(W1)*
Pâtisserie Valerie *(chain)*
Pizza on the Park *(SW1)*
Tapa Room (Providores) *(W1)*
Segafredo Zanetti *(W1)*
Smiths (Ground Floor) *(EC1)*
Star Café *(W1)*
Tom's *(W11)*
Troubadour *(SW5)*
Vingt-Quatre *(SW10)*

RECOMMENDATIONS

TOP PUB GRUB

The Anglesea Arms *(W6)*
The Atlas *(SW6)*
The Builder's Arms *(SW3)*
The Castle *(SW11)*
Churchill Arms *(W8)*
Dartmouth Arms *(NW5)*
The Eagle *(EC1)*
Ebury Street Wine Bar *(SW1)*
The Endurance *(W1)*
The Fox *(EC2)*
The Havelock Tavern *(W14)*
The Highgate *(NW5)*
Hope & Sir Loin *(EC1)*
The Ifield *(SW10)*
The Lord Palmerston *(NW5)*
Lots Road *(SW10)*
Queen's Pub & Dining Rm *(NW1)*
The Station *(W10)*
Stone Mason's Arms *(W6)*
The Sun & Doves *(SE5)*
The Swan *(W4)*
White Cross *(TW9)*
White Horse *(SW6)*
William IV *(NW10)*
The Windsor Castle *(W8)*

THE BEST FUN PLACES

Balans *(chain)*
Bam-Bou *(W1)*
Bar Italia *(W1)*
Benihana *(chain)*
Buona Sera *(chain)*
Busaba Eathai *(chain)*
Bush Bar & Grill *(W12)*
Café Emm *(W1)*
Cantaloupe *(EC2)*
The Depot *(SW14)*
don Fernando's *(TW9)*
Don Pepe *(NW8)*
Eco *(chain)*
Efes Kebab House *(chain)*
Gordon's Wine Bar *(WC2)*
Gourmet Burger Kitchen *(chain)*
Hakkasan *(W1)*
Hard Rock Café *(W1)*
Itsu *(chain)*
Lemonia *(NW1)*
Levant *(W1)*
Little Bay *(chain)*
Mango Room *(NW1)*
Mediterraneo *(W11)*
Meson don Felipe *(SE1)*
Ophim *(W1)*
Osteria Basilico *(W11)*
Pappa e Ciccia *(chain)*
Patio *(W12)*
La Piragua *(N1)*
Pizzeria Castello *(SE1)*
Porchetta Pizzeria *(chain)*
Pucci Pizza *(SW3)*
Real Greek Souvlaki *(EC1)*
Rebato's *(SW8)*
Sarastro *(WC2)*
So.uk *(chain)*
Souk *(WC2)*
The Sun & Doves *(SE5)*
Tartuf *(N1)*
Tsunami *(SW4)*
Vingt-Quatre *(SW10)*
Wagamama *(chain)*
Wong Kei *(W1)*
Yum Yum *(N16)*

DIRECTORY

A Cena TW1 £18* A★

418 Richmond Rd 8288 0108 1–4A

Chic and understated decor dominated by a sizeable bar lends a classy feel to this St Margaret's brasserie (just south of Richmond Bridge). Its Italian-based cooking can only really be enjoyed by the budget diner for lunch, when, for £10, you might have the likes of broad bean, Pecorino and mint bruschetta followed by roast duck with cherries, Valpolicella, olive oil mash and green beans. If you fancy a pudding, that will add just a couple of pounds to the bill. The house wine is £12.50 a bottle. / 10.30 pm; closed Mon & Sun D; booking: max 6, Fri & Sat.

The Abbeville SW4 £ 18 ★

67-69 Abbeville Rd 8675 2201 10–2D

Simple dishes, often with a Mediterranean twist are the stock in trade of this new Clapham gastro-bar. Tagliatelle with smoked salmon, chives and lemon (£4.50) followed by chargrilled chicken breast with portobello mushrooms and roast potatoes (£9) would be a typical selection, and dishes are done well and reasonably priced. The house wine is £9.95 a bottle. / www.theabbeville.co.uk; 10.30 pm; no Amex; no booking.

Abeno WC1 £12* ★

47 Museum St 7405 3211 2–1C

This friendly Japanese outfit, handy for the British Museum, offers a very reasonable 2-course set lunch menu (£6.50). The speciality is okonomi-yaki (a cross between a pancake and an omelette, cooked at your table) – and a typical meal à la carte would be squid and soya bean pancakes (£5.20), followed by a Shinsu mix (a topping of chicken, asparagus and cheese, £9.80). Such prices test our limit, however, especially with house wine at a hefty £14.50 a bottle. / www.abeno.co.uk; 11 pm.

The Abingdon W8 £20* A

54 Abingdon Rd 7937 3339 5–2A

It's only a couple of minutes' walk from the High Street, but this intimate Kensington pub-conversion is rather hidden away and doesn't get much passing trade. Shoppers in the know, however, can seek out the 2-course set lunch for £13.95 (Mon-Sat), from which your selection might be crispy fried squid, followed by marinated tiska (Javanese-spiced) pork with mash and spring greens. There's also a 2-course Sunday lunch (£13.95). The house wine is £10.75 a bottle. / 11 pm.

Abu Zaad W12 £ 10 ★

29 Uxbridge Rd 8749 5107 7–1C

If you're really looking to dine on a budget, this Syrian café/takeaway near Shepherd's Bush Market makes an ideal destination, as most dishes are under a fiver. There's quite a diverse menu and it's all tasty stuff, with kebabs a highlight – wash 'em down with Aryan (drinking yoghurt) or Arabic tea or coffee. / 11 pm; no Amex; no smoking area.

Adams Café W12 £ 19

77 Askew Rd 8743 0572 7–1B

This friendly Shepherd's Bush spot (named for the owners' son) is a popular oddity – by day it's a greasy spoon, but by night it's well known for its Tunisian and Moroccan specialities. Prix-fixe menus, which all include complimentary appetisers and mint tea or coffee, range from the 1-course "menu rapide" (£10.50), to the 2-course "menu gourmet" (£13.50), and up. You might choose 'brik au thon' – crispy filo filled with tuna, egg and fresh herbs – followed by a lamb couscous. BYO (corkage £3), or indulge in a Tunisian digestif made from figs (£2). / 11 pm; D only, closed Sun.

Afghan Kitchen N1 £ 13 ★

35 Islington Grn 7359 8019 8–3D

It offers little in the way of creature comforts, but it you're looking for cooking that's rather unusual, as well as filling and good value, you won't do much better than this tiny café, overlooking Islington Green. There are eight main dishes on offer – four meat, which are all £6 apiece, and four veg which are around a fiver. All are served in portions to satisfy the hungriest punter. Rice or a large chunk of bread add £2 to the cost, and house wine is £10 a bottle. / 11 pm; closed Mon & Sun; no credit cards.

Aglio e Olio SW10 £ 20 ★

194 Fulham Rd 7351 0070 5–3B

This nice but noisy Italian diner is a continuing success with the trendy crowd which hangs out on Chelsea's 'Beach' (as this fashionable 800-yard strip of the Fulham Road is known). Little wonder, as the food's of good quality and pleasantly served. Your selection might be aubergine with goat's cheese (£5.20), followed by fusilli with meatballs and herbs (£7.20), or you might skip the starter and finish with a panna cotta (£3.50). The house wine is £11.50 a bottle. / 11.30 pm.

Alba EC1 £20* ★

107 Whitecross St 7588 1798 9–1B

This rather stark regional Italian, not far from the Barbican, makes a good place for a reasonably priced meal on the fringes of the City. A 2-course set dinner (£12) is available, and offers Piedmontese specialities alongside the likes of asparagus with mayonnaise and vinaigrette, and grilled poussin with lemon and herb sauce. With house wine at £11.50 a bottle, the place is rather outside our price range à la carte. / 10.30 pm; closed Sat & Sun.

Ali Baba NW1 £ 15 ★

32 Ivor Pl 7723 5805 2–1A

They haven't wasted any money on the décor of this long-established, living room-style BYO café, located at the back of an Egyptian takeaway near Marylebone Station. Prices are low, so if you go in a small party you can sample a good range of the specialities, such as tabbouleh salad (£3) and cabsa (red rice and lamb, £6). BYO (no corkage). / 11.30 pm; no credit cards.

Alma SW18 **£ 20** 𝔸

499 Old York Rd 8870 2537 10–2B

This large and characterful Wandsworth pub – which is particularly popular with rugby-playing locals – offers the bargain-seeker plenty of scope. Eat in the bar, or head to the rear dining room for a meal which might combine smoked salmon fishcakes (£4.95) with a homely choice such as grilled lamb cutlets with minted pea mash (£9.55). Drink bitter at £2.30 a pint, or the house wine at £10.40 a bottle. / www.thealma.co.uk; 10.30 pm.

Alounak **£ 16** ★

10 Russell Gdns, W14 7603 1130 7–1D

44 Westbourne Grove, W2 7229 0416 6–1B

These welcoming Olympia and Bayswater Iranians offer real, meaty cooking at modest cost, and the BYO policy helps keep costs low. Lamb is the speciality (though there are also chicken options), and most main dishes cost somewhere between £6 and £10. Iranian tea costs just 80p per cup. / 11.30 pm; no Amex.

Amaranth SW18 **£ 14** 𝔸★

346 Garratt Ln 8871 3466 10–2B

There may be nothing particularly remarkable about its aims, but this intimate BYO Thai restaurant has become world famous in Earlsfield by doing what it does very well. Cheery service adds much to the experience. With starters, such as prawns in a blanket (£4.20) and main courses such as green chicken curry (£5.50), this is one of those places where you'd really have to try quite hard to spend beyond our price-limit. / 10.30 pm; D only, closed Sun; no Amex; no smoking area.

Anarkali W6 **£ 14**

303-305 King St 8748 6911 7–2B

It may look like a standard curry house, but this Hammersmith spot has been an above-average performer since the '70s. Starters, such as kebabs, are around the £4 mark, and main courses – which include some unusual specials – are in the £5-£9 range. House wine is £7.95 a bottle, or a pint of Carlsberg is £2.50. / midnight.

The Anglesea Arms W6 **£ 20** ★

35 Wingate Rd 8749 1291 7–1B

There's a lot of competition around Hammersmith and Shepherd's Bush for the title of top gastropub, but this place has as stronger claim than most. It's cosy and no-frills and yet stylish too, and its modern British cooking (of a standard much higher than most gastropubs) can hit real heights. With dishes such as escalopes of wild salmon (£11.25), prices can easily test our limit, but, with house wine at £10.50 a bottle, you can just about fit a pudding (say, panna cotta, £4.25) within our budget. / 10.45 pm; no Amex; no booking.

Anglo Asian Tandoori N16 **£ 15** ★

60-62 Stoke Newington Church St 7254 9298 1–1C

You don't usually think of Indian restaurants as romantic, but this low-lit Stoke Newington spot is the exception which proves the rule. It offers all the traditional dishes at reasonable prices. A meat thali (set meal), for example, is £9.50. On Sundays, the all-you-can-eat buffet lunch (£6.95) is particularly good value. House wine is £8.95 a bottle. / www.angloasian.co.uk; 11.30 pm, Fri & Sat 11.45 pm; no smoking area.

Antipasto & Pasta SW11 £ 18

511 Battersea Park Rd 7223 9765 10–1C

Sunday, Monday, or Thursday nights are the times to seek out this good-quality Battersea Italian. On those days, all starters (usually between £5.90 and £8.50) and main dishes (usually £6-£10) are half-price. You might start with antipasti such as Parma ham & melon or fried Mozzarella, followed by pasta carbonara, washed down with house wine at £10.50 a bottle. / 11.30 pm; no Amex; need 4+ to book.

Antipasto e Pasta SW4 £16* ★

31 Abbeville Rd 8675 6260 10–2D

This good-quality Italian restaurant in Clapham is rather out of our price-range à la carte, but there are top-value 3-course set menus available at lunch (£9.95, including coffee) and dinner (£12.95, Sun-Thu, also including coffee) from which you might have Caesar salad followed by sautéed chicken with peppers and wine sauce, and then crème caramel. A bottle of the house vino is £11.65. / 11.30 pm.

Aperitivo W1 £ 19 A

41 Beak St 7287 2057 3–2D

This chic Italian tapas bar in the heart of Soho offers a range of interesting dishes. Your selection (to share) might be fried polenta with Gorgonzola and truffle cheese (£4.95), prawns wrapped in bacon (£6.75), walnut salad (£4.95) and some fries (£2.95), washed down with the house wine, at £12.50 a bottle. Traditional desserts, maybe tiramisu or panna cotta (both £3.50) are also available. / www.aperitivo-soho.com; 11 pm; closed Sun.

Apium EC1 £ 14

50-52 Long Ln 7796 4040 9–1B

Busy, cramped and rather smoky, this large and noisy new noodle bar has found a ready following, down Farringdon way (and makes a handy destination before a trip to the Barbican). The food is nothing remarkable, but the rendition of a meal such as spring rolls (£3.50) and roast duck noodle (£6.95) is perfectly acceptable. The house wine is £8.95 a bottle. / www.apium.co.uk; 11 pm; closed Sun; no Amex; no smoking.

Arancia SE16 £ 19 A

52 Southwark Park Rd 7394 1751 11–2A

This tiny Bermondsey Italian has rightly been extremely successful, thanks to its down-to-earth approach and its quality cooking (which can be sampled within our budget at any time) Starters are around £4, and most main courses are £9. For top value, however, opt for the set lunch, which offers two courses – minestrone soup, say, followed by seared tuna steak – for only £7.50. The house wine is £9 a bottle. / www.arancia-london.co.uk; 11 pm; closed Mon & Sun; no Amex.

Arkansas Café E1 £ 15

107b Commercial St 7377 6999 9–1D

Amid the hustle and bustle of Spitalfields Market, chef-patron Bubba presides over his grill, and serves up basic, but tasty and filling fare to shoppers and stockbrokers alike. The BBQ platter – including ribs, sausages, chicken and all the trimmings – will set you back £13.50. Puddings, if you're still game, are all around the £2.50 mark, and the extensive American beer list includes bottled Anchor Steam at £2.50 a throw. A bottle of the house wine costs £8.95. / L only, closed Sat; no Amex; no smoking; booking essential at D.

Ask! Pizza **£ 16**

160-162 Victoria St, SW1 7630 8228 2–4B
121-125 Park St, W1 7495 7760 2–2A
14-16 Quadrant Arc, Air St, W1 7734 4267 3–3D
48 Grafton Way, W1 7388 8108 2–1B
56-60 Wigmore St, W1 7224 3484 3–1A
300 King's Rd, SW3 7349 9123 5–3C
345 Fulham Palace Rd, SW6 7371 0392 10–1B
23-24 Gloucester Arc, SW7 7835 0840 5–2B
145 Notting Hill Gate, W11 7792 9942 6–2B
17-20 Kendal St, W2 7724 4637 6–1D
41-43 Spring St, W2 7706 0707 6–1C
Whiteley's, 151 Queensway, W2 7792 1977 6–1C
219-221 Chiswick High Rd, W4 8742 1323 7–2A
222 Kensington High St, W8 7937 5540 5–1A
52 Upper St, N1 7226 8728 8–3D
197 Baker St, NW1 7486 6027 2–1A
30 Hawley Cr, NW1 7267 7755 8–2B
216 Haverstock Hill, NW3 7433 3896 8–2A
34 Shad Thames, SE1 7403 4545 9–4D
Station Rd, SW13 8878 9300 10–1A
103 St John St, EC1 7253 0323 9–1A

This ever-expanding Italian chain, with its modishly cool interiors, continues to outscore that benchmark-veteran PizzaExpress for both décor and service, if not for food. Most starters are around £4 and most pasta and pizza dishes around £6.50, with house wine at £11.50 a bottle. / www.askcentral.co.uk; 11.30 pm; some booking restrictions apply.

The Atlas SW6 **£ 19** A

16 Seagrave Rd 7385 9129 5–3A

Appearances can be deceptive. From the outside, one might be forgiven for getting the impression that this is a rather grotty old boozer, but the good quality Mediterranean dishes on offer within prove it to be quite the opposite. To start you could share an antipasti plate (£6) with a friend, followed by fillet of roast salmon (£9.50). The house wine is £10 a bottle, or a pint of bitter will set you back £2.40. / 10.30 pm; no Amex; no booking.

Aurora W1 **£20*** A

49 Lexington St 7494 0514 3–2D

This sweet and cosy Soho spot is notable for Saturday brunch (£7.95) or a coffee-and-cake break, especially in summer particularly if you can nab a seat in the tiny rear courtyard. In the evenings, it's dimly-lit and romantic, but the 2-course pre-theatre menu (£15, including coffee) is sadly the only budget option (6pm-7pm) these days. You might try the likes of teriyaki mackerel, followed by pork with spiced red cabbage, with a bottle of the house wine (£11.90). / 10.30 pm; closed Sun; no Amex.

Aziz SW6 **£ 14** ★

24-32 Vanston Pl 7386 0086 5–4A

The minimalist styling of this recent newcomer near Fulham Broadway is a bit boring. The Moroccan/Middle Eastern cooking it offers, however, is some of the most exciting food to arrive in the area for a long time. Normally it's out of our budget, but they do a good deal on weekday lunches starting from £12.50, including a glass of wine (with further supplies at £12 a bottle). Or you can snack at the very popular neighbouring deli. / 10.30 pm.

Azou W6 **£ 20**
375 King St 8563 7266 7–2B
North African cuisine has been one of the more fashionable cuisines of recent times, but no hint of trendiness attaches to this family-run Hammersmith destination, which offers a short menu of specialities from Morocco, Algeria and Tunisia. Starters include 'Foules Mesdames' (hot broad bean salad) and brik (pastry filled with tuna and egg), both at £3.95. Main courses generally involve a choice between couscous and tajines (stews), most of which cost around £9, about one pound less than a bottle of the house wine. / 11 pm; no Amex.

Babur Brasserie SE23 **£ 20** ★
119 Brockley Rise 8291 2400 1–4D
Fans of Indian cooking will find ample reward in a visit to this Forest Hill subcontinental, where friendly staff help you through a menu of much above-average interest. Masala dosa (£3.95) followed by chicken chettinad (£7.95) might be a typical choice, or select from the rolling menu of regional specialities, or the numerous veggie options (all under a fiver). There's also a Sunday lunch buffet for £8.95 (children under seven eat free). The house wine is £8.95 a bottle. / www.babur-brasserie.com; 11 pm; closed Fri L; no smoking area.

Balans **£ 20**
60 Old Compton St, W1 7439 2183 4–3A
239 Old Brompton Rd, SW5 7244 8838 5–3A
187 Kensington High St, W8 7376 0115 5–1A
Flirting with the waiter – if you're a man, that is – is all part of the experience at these breezy, gay-friendly diners (which also have an offshoot in Miami's fashionable South Beach). A good range of breakfasts, including the Full Monty (relatively pricey, at £7.75) and eggs Benedict with smoked salmon (£6.50) are served until the wee hours. Otherwise, a typical meal might be thyme & onion tart (£4.25) followed by Cumberland sausage & mash (£7.95), washed down by house wine at £10.25 a bottle. / www.balans.co.uk; midnight, SW5 2am Fri & Sat, W1 Mon-Fri 5 am, Sat 6 am, Sun 2 am; W1 no booking, SW5 Sun L no booking.

Balham Kitchen & Bar SW12 **£ 20**
15-19 Bedford Hill 8675 6900 10–2C
After Notting Hill and New York, the Soho House people chose … Balham for the latest of their trendy outlets. It's already outrageously popular with the beau monde south of the river, but – by choosing carefully – still accessible to the budget diner. You might start with pea soup (£5) with perhaps a beefburger and fries (£8) for the main course. Wines – and there's quite a good selection – start at £12.50 a bottle. / www.sohohouse.com; 11 pm; booking: max 6.

Baltic SE1 **£18*** A
74 Blackfriars Rd 7928 1111 9–4A
This impressively-converted former carriage-making factory opened as a restaurant pretty soon after the opening of Tate Modern put Borough 'on the map'. It's been a great success, as both a bar and a restaurant. The top-value choice – ideal after a morning in the Tate – is the 2-course set lunch and pre-theatre menu (£11.50), which might be gravadlax with potato latkes followed by chargrilled chicken with bulgar wheat and garlic yoghurt, washed down by house wine at £11.50 a bottle (or a Polish beer at £3). You'd have to choose pretty carefully à la carte to stay within our price limit. / www.balticrestaurant.co.uk; 11 pm; closed Sat L.

Bam-Bou W1 £18* 𝔸★

1 Percy St 7323 9130 2–1C

The set lunch at this townhouse restaurant, just north of Oxford Street, allows you to check out a very cool scene at modest cost – at night this is sort of place you could easily spend our budget on a couple of cocktails. For £7.50, your two courses might be fishcakes with cucumber cham followed by caramelised ginger chicken. Beware the wine though – at £14.50 a bottle, it's very much at the place's 'normal' price-levels. Heck, you may as well have one of those cocktails! / www.bam-bou.co.uk; 11.30 pm; closed Sat L & Sun.

Bangkok SW7 £ 20 ★

9 Bute St 7584 8529 5–2B

The menu's pretty much the same as ever – the locals just wouldn't have it any other way – at the UK's longest-established Thai restaurant, near South Kensington tube. Satay (£5.95) followed by a Thai green curry (£7.70) are the sorts of dishes which have kept the punters coming back for over thirty years now. House wine is surprisingly pricey at £14 a bottle. / 10.45 pm; closed Sun; no Amex or Switch.

Bank Aldwych WC2 £20* 𝔸★

1 Kingsway 7379 9797 2–2D

Readers with long memories may recall that, in the late-'90s, we were – or so it was said – entering a new era when we would all eat in big and noisy 'modern British' brasseries. This was one of the best, and it still is. It's quite pricey à la carte, but there's nearly always a budget option available – the breakfast menu will set you back £12.95 including juice and a coffee, and at lunch, pre- and post-theatre (5.30pm-7.30pm, 10pm-11.30pm) there's a 2-course set menu (£12.50), from which you might choose sautéed chicken livers followed by roast chicken with grilled Mediterranean vegetables and black olive tapénade. The house wine is £13 a bottle. / www.bankrestaurants.com; 11 pm.

Bank Westminster St James Court Hotel SW1 £20* 𝔸★

45 Buckingham Gate 7379 9797 2–4B

Boasting one of the longest bars in Europe, this large and would-be trendy restaurant seems rather oddly situated in the businessy no-man's-land near St James's Park tube. A la carte, it's clearly out of our price bracket, so it's all the more worth availing yourself of the £12.50 lunch and evening (5.30pm-7pm and 10pm-11.30pm) set menus, which might offer you the likes of salmon satay followed by spiced polenta cake with grilled goat's cheese and oven-dried tomatoes. House wine is £13 a bottle. / www.bankrestaurants.com; 11 pm; closed Sat L & Sun.

Bankside SE1 £ 19

32 Southwark Bridge Rd 7633 0011 9–4B

There's nothing especially cutting-edge or hip about this new basement brasserie-cum-restaurant near Tate Modern, but if you're looking for somewhere reasonably priced to eat in that vicinity it's one of the few tolerable choices, and handily open all day at weekends. All starters (such as potted ox tongue) are £4, and all mains are either £7 (Cumberland sausages, mash and onion gravy, for example) or £9 (chargrilled ostrich liver), and come with a guaranteed service time (largely for business customers – the FT's office is nearby). The house wine is £10.50 a bottle. / www.banksiderestaurants.co.uk; 10.30 pm; no smoking area.

Banners £ 20

83 Hazelville Rd, N19 7686 2944 1–1C
21 Park Rd, N8 8348 2930 1–1C

It's as a weekend venue for all the family that these funky Crouch End (and now also Upper Holloway) bar/diners are best known, so brunch (£6.25) is a natural forte (although the 2-course set weekday lunch (£5.95) is a pretty special feature, too). A la carte, starters (perhaps Thai fishcakes or calamari) are around £4.50 and main courses (such as Jamaican jerk chicken or grilled swordfish) around £9. The house wine is £10.95 a bottle.

Bar Capitale £ 18 ★

The Concourse, 1 Poultry, EC2 7248 3117 9–2C
Bucklersbury Hs, 14 Walbrook, EC4 7236 2030 9–3C

The City is sparsely provided with places for a speedy but satisfying lunch. The number of Italian customers, however, hints at the good quality of the simple fare – mainly pizza and pasta (around £8) – on offer at these fast and friendly spots near Bank. The house wine is £11.50 a bottle. / www.mithrasbars.co.uk; 10 pm; closed Sat & Sun.

Bar Estrela SW8 £ 14 ★

111-115 South Lambeth Rd 7793 1051 10–1D

A rallying point for the local Portuguese community – especially when the national team is competing in major sporting events – this South Lambeth café is a remarkably 'authentic' destination, not least thanks to its very low prices. The menu is so long it would be simpler to list what's not available – a recent meal included oysters followed by beef stew (both 'specials'), giving rise to a total bill well within our budget. The house wine is £8.50 a bottle. / 11 pm.

Bar Italia W1 £ 8 A

22 Frith St 7437 4520 4–2A

A cult venue for Soho trendies, this long-established, very Italian coffee bar (open 23 hours a day and non-stop at weekends) is the quintessential post-clubbing hang-out. Though culinary delights are not the main attraction, the food runs to the likes of sandwiches and light pasta dishes (around the £2-£4 mark). No alcohol – wash down your snack with an espresso or cappuccino (£1.60), or fresh juices (from £2.50). / open 24 hours Mon-Sat, Sun 4 am; no booking.

Bar Japan SW5 £17* ★

251 Old Brompton Rd 7370 2323 5–3A

Fun, if basic, this Earl's Court café is always a good place to pop in for a quick and interesting bite. Service is friendly, and the sushi is decent. Bigger meals may stretch the budget a little, with starters costing from £3 and main courses, for example a chicken teriyaki set, setting you back around a tenner. House wine is £10 a bottle. / 10.45 pm; no Amex.

Bar Mezé **£14***

462 Muswell Hill Broadway, N10 8442 2661 8–1C
55-57 Exmouth Mkt, EC1 7833 2026 9–1A
64 Northcote Rd, SW11 7228 5010 10–2C

This small but ambitious new chain offers simple Cypriot fare in surroundings rather like a '60s (English) kitchen. It might stretch our budget if you chose the individual dishes, but the top choice for groups is the meze (£7.95). This offers ten cold meat-free dishes and dips, with hot pitta bread – wash it down with house wine at £10.95 a bottle, and you can stay comfortably within our price-limit. / www.barmeze.com; 11 pm, SW11 10.30 pm; no smoking area.

Basilico **£ 19** ★★

690 Fulham Rd, SW6 0800 028 3531 10–1B
515 Finchley Rd, NW3 0800 316 2656 1–1B
175 Lavender Hill, SW11 0800 389 9770 10–2C
178 Upper Richmond Rd, SW14 0800 096 8202 10–2B

Take-outs are what these pukka pizzerias are really all about, but devotees are willing enough to fight for elbow room to 'eat in' – both branches are quite cramped. The pizzas come in two sizes, 13" (£8.75-£12.75) and 18" (£11.95-£15.75) and may be accompanied by a Caesar salad (£2.95) or followed by tiramisu (£3.75), and washed down with house wine at £7.90 a bottle. / www.basilico.co.uk; 11pm; no Amex; no booking.

Beirut Express W2 **£ 15** ★★

112-114 Edgware Rd 7724 2700 6–1D

A less expensive option from the glitzy-but-good Maroush group, this Bayswater café offers quality snacks at reasonable cost. Starters, such as tabbouleh and houmous (both around £4) are of high quality, or you can make a meal of a plate of mixed starters for £9. There are main-course dishes, but you would find yourself testing our price limit. No alcohol is served, so enjoy a freshly-squeezed juice (from £1.75). / www.maroush.com; 1.45 am; no credit cards.

Ben's Thai W9 **£ 16**

93 Warrington Cr 7266 3134 8–4A

Above a palatial Victorian pub (The Warrington Hotel) in Maida Vale, this first-floor dining-room provides the rather unlikely setting for one of the more characterful Thai eateries in town – it's best to book. Starters such as spring rolls are around £3, and main courses are all under £7 (which is the price of a 'house special', such as salmon in chilli sauce). The house wine is £9.50 a bottle. Tipping is discouraged. / 10 pm; D only; no Amex; no smoking area.

Bengal Clipper SE1 **£18*** ★

Shad Thames 7357 9001 9–4D

It tends to be eclipsed in public consciousness by Conran's collection of riverside restaurants by Tower Bridge, but this neighbouring Indian is a smart and airy place with much to offer the budget diner – namely a 2-course set lunch and dinner for £8. A la carte, the menu is quite pricey, with starters generally around £4.50 and main courses around £11. The cover charge of £1.50 includes poppadoms and chutneys. House wine is £11.50, or drink Cobra beer at £4.95 a pint. / www.bengalrestaurants.co.uk; 11.30 pm.

Benihana £18* A★

37 Sackville St, W1 7494 2525 3–3D
77 King's Rd, SW3 7376 7799 5–3D
100 Avenue Rd, NW3 7586 9508 8–2A

You might think this swanky (Americo-)oriental chain of eateries an odd choice for a budget guide, but they make a handy and quite comfortable place for the rather enthusiastically described "5-course" set lunch – california roll, hibachi chicken with vegetables, rice, benihana salad and green tea. Wine with your lunch, starting at £15 a bottle, is best avoided. / www.benihana.co.uk; 10.30 pm; smoking restricted during cooking.

Bersagliera SW3 £ 17 A

372 King's Rd 7352 5993 5–3B

It has had a bit of a refurbishment in recent times, but the attractions of this World's End trattoria/pizzeria are pretty much as they always were – it offers tasty pizza and pasta dishes (mainly around £6.20-£8.80) in a friendly but noisy environment. The house wine is £10.80 a bottle. / 11.30 pm; closed weekday L; no Amex.

Bistro 1 £ 14

50 James St, W1 7486 9185 3–1A
75 Beak St, W1 7287 1840 3–2D
33 Southampton St, WC2 7379 7585 4–3D

There are now three of these admirable bistros in central London, and we hope they continue to flourish. It's not that they offer anything remarkable in the way of cooking, but they are simple, honest and homely places – with the emphasis on the food, not the décor – of a type that's all too rare. It's practically impossible to bust our price limit – a 3-course menu is £6.90 at lunch, and just £2 more in the evening, and house wine is £10.50 a bottle. A typical meal might comprise grilled sardines followed by Cumberland sausages & mash, with stuffed apricots for pudding. / 11.30 pm; no smoking area Southampton St & James St.

Blah! Blah! Blah! W12 £ 19 ★★

78 Goldhawk Rd 8746 1337 7–1C

This Shepherd's Bush spot has proved itself to be a veggie with staying power, and it's quality rather than rock-bottom prices which keeps the punters coming back. Starters are under a fiver and mains are around the £9.50 mark. You might have kung-po shiitake mushrooms on chow mein noodles followed by roast vegetable tart. BYO (£1.25 corkage) helps keep costs under control. / 11 pm; closed Sun D; no credit cards.

Blue Elephant SW6 £19* A★

3-6 Fulham Broadway 7385 6595 5–4A

London best Thai restaurant of long-standing, this Fulham establishment, decorated in OTT jungle style, offers a top-value, loss-leading set weekday lunch for £10. Choose any two courses from a choice of four (starter, soup, main or dessert) – you might have chicken satay with tom yam koong soup, or lamb Massaman curry followed by ice cream (maybe black pepper or honey and ginger), washed down with house wine at £13 a bottle. / www.blueelephant.com; midnight; closed Sat L.

Blue Jade SW1 **£ 20**

44 Hugh St 7828 0321 2–4B

It's not what you'd call an exciting place, but this backstreet Pimlico Thai is a pretty consistent performer. You could eat here at any time within our budget, as most starters, such as chicken satay, are around the £5 mark, and most main courses around £7-£8 – or there's a 2-course set lunch, including coffee, for £11.95. House wine is £11.25 a bottle. / 11 pm; closed Sat L & Sun.

Blue Lagoon W14 **£14***

284 Kensington High St 7603 1231 7–1D

The extensive menu of this spacious but slightly tackily furnished oriental includes all the familiar Thai staples. It's a touch out of our price range à la carte, but a couple of set-price meals, including a vegetarian dinner (£13.99) and a 3-course set lunch (£7.99, available all week) offer especially good value. A typical selection might comprise satay or fishcakes to start, yellow curry or Pad Thai to follow, and lychees to finish. House wine is £9.50 a bottle. / www.blue-lagoon.co.uk; 11 pm; no smoking area.

Boiled Egg & Soldiers SW11 **£ 14**

63 Northcote Rd 7223 4894 10–2C

During weekdays, this celebrated café at the heart of Wandsworth's 'Nappy Valley' is the official gathering-point for the local nannies and their charges. At weekends, however, it's known for the hangover cure offered by its popular fry-ups – the full English works will set you back £5.50. The menu has recently been boosted by the addition of few more bistro-style items, such as steak sandwich (£6.95). / 6 pm; L & afternoon tea only; only Switch; no booking.

La Bouchée SW7 **£12*** A

56 Old Brompton Rd 7589 1929 5–2B

Improving standards are making this ever-popular, younger-scene South Kensington bistro again worth seeking out, especially before 7pm, when there's a £6.95 set menu. You might choose mixed salad followed by Toulouse sausages with mashed potato and red onion gravy, washed down by house wine at £9.95 a bottle. There's a wider choice on the 3-course menu (£10.95), but you'd really have to scrimp (or go veggie) to dine here à la carte within our price range. / 11 pm; no Amex.

Boulevard WC2 **£17***

40 Wellington St 7240 2992 4–3D

The variety of set menus available makes this unpretentious Covent Garden bistro a useful central stand-by, at any time of day. At lunch (all week) and pre- and post-theatre, two courses cost £9.95 (three courses, £12.50). You might have pâté of chicken livers, apricot chutney and brioche followed by asparagus, parmesan and truffle oil risotto. A la carte, prices may slightly stretch our budget, but there's an interesting choice of lighter dishes, such as tuna steak or blackened goat's cheese salad, at £7-£8. House wine is £11 a bottle. / www.boulevardbrasserie.com; midnight; no smoking area.

The Brackenbury W6 £18* A★
129-131 Brackenbury Rd 8748 0107 7–1C
This perennially popular spot in a Hammersmith backwater keeps locals and BBC regulars coming back and back with its friendly attitude and simple but tasty modern British grub at reasonable prices. Another plus is its small pavement terrace which is great for al fresco eating in summer. Choices from the 2-course set weekday lunch menu (£10.50) might include chilled pea and mint soup followed by pan-fried calves liver with mash and onion rings. Add a pudding for just £2 more, and drink the house wine at £11 a bottle. / 10.45 pm; closed Sat L & Sun D.

Bradley's NW3 £20* ★
25 Winchester Rd 7722 3457 8–2A
Excellent seafood is a menu highlight at this friendly local restaurant in St John's Wood. No great surprise then that it's rather out of our price range in the evening, but there is a good value 2-course set lunch – your £12 might buy you the likes of fish soup, followed by cod with cabbage, mash and mussel sauce, washed down with house wine at £13.50 a bottle. / 11 pm; closed Sat L.

Brady's SW18 £ 16 ★
513 Old York Rd 8877 9599 10–2B
One of the sadly few places which do some sort of justice to our great national dish of fish 'n' chips, this Wandsworth bistro has a devoted local following. You could start with potted shrimps (£2.95), followed by a large order of haddock 'n' chips (£6.50), washed down with house wine at £8.75 a bottle. You could even squeeze some apple crumble (£1.95) in to our budget! / 10.30 pm; D only, closed Sun; no credit cards; no booking.

Brahms SW1 £ 14
147 Lupus St 7233 9828 5–3D
For top value at this budget Pimlico bistro, opt for the 2-course £5 set meal (available until 7pm), or choose three courses for £7.50. Starters include avocado with crispy bacon or soup, and for a main course you might have duck with Grand Marnier sauce or Mediterranean pork, with crème brûlée for pudding. Even à la carte – with the starters at £2.50 and main courses around £5.50 – you would have difficulty stretching our budget. The house wine is £9.65 a bottle. / 10.45 pm; no Amex.

La Brasserie Townhouse WC1 £17* ★
24 Coptic St 7636 2731 2–1C
Despite its handy location near the British Museum, this side street townhouse restaurant never seems to get quite the following it deserves. Bad luck for the owners, but good luck for the budget-conscious luncher, who should seek out the £9.95 3-course set lunch menu – which might comprise feta and tomato salad with basil dressing followed by ribeye steak with garlic butter and fries, and then chocolate tart – washed down with house wine at £10.50 a bottle. / www.townhousebrasserie.co.uk; 11 pm; closed Sun L; no smoking area.

Bread & Roses SW4 £ 18 A

68 Clapham Manor Street 7498 1779 10–1D

This Clapham boozer – with its nice decked garden – makes an especially pleasant sunny-day destination. The fare on offer is the likes of houmous and taramasalata with grilled bread (around £4) followed, perhaps, by penne with a goat's cheese and roast pepper sauce (£7.50). At weekends, it tends to be more adventurous, and on Sunday 'Family Days', there's a varying ethnic selection that makes an interesting alternative to a traditional roast. Desserts, such as chocolate cake with ice cream and q strawberry coulis are £4, and a bottle of the house wine is £9.75.

/ www.workersbeer.co.uk; 9.30 pm; no Amex; no smoking area; no booking.

Brew House Kenwood House NW3 £ 14 A

Hampstead Ln 8341 5384 8–1A

A steady stream of local fans and passing tourists ensure that this popular cafe, attached to Hampstead Heath's magnificent Kenwood House, is always buzzing. In the mornings you can fill up on a top quality full breakfast (£5.95) before visiting the house's impressive art collection, or take an afternoon break from a stroll on Hampstead Heath for a pot of tea (£1.15) and a treacle tart (£1.75). A lunch dish from the buffet selection – perhaps free-range sausages with vegetables of the day – will not set you back more than £8: on a sunny day, settle down in the walled garden to enjoy it with a bottle of the house vino (£10.75).

Brick Lane Beigel Bake E1 £ 3 ★★

159 Brick Ln 7729 0616 1–2D

You might find a queue at any time of the day (or night) at this all-hours East End institution, which is almost as well known as the famous street in which it is situated. The attraction? – delicious filled bagels, such as tuna (75p) or cream cheese (60p), washed down with a large tea (40p) or coffee (40p). Plain beiges to take home will cost you 12p each! / open 24 hours; no credit cards; no smoking; no booking.

Brilliant UB2 £ 19 ★

72-76 Western Rd 8574 1928 1–3A

It may occupy a site which is not exactly obvious (in a residential area ten minutes' walk from Southall BR), but this large curry house has long enjoyed a stellar reputation. Perhaps that's why prices are now well above 'bargain' level – seek kebab to start will set you back a couple of pounds, and Karahi lamb with pilau rice is about a tenner. House wine is £12 a bottle, or drink Cobra at £3.50.

/ www.brilliantrestaurant.com; 11 pm; closed Mon, Sat L & Sun L; no smoking area; booking: weekends only.

La Brocca NW6 £ 19 A

273 West End Ln 7433 1989 1–1B

This West Hampstead Italian isn't much to look at, but it's a popular local destination, thanks to the quality of its pizza and pasta dishes (mainly in the £7-£10 range), washed down with house wine at £9.50 a bottle. / 11 pm; booking: max 8.

Bu San N7 £ 15 ★

43 Holloway Rd 7607 8264 8–2D

This lesser-known Korean – just round the corner from Highbury & Islington tube – may look inauspicious, but it serves up some tasty, inexpensive fare. Veggies are well catered for, with starters including deep-fried aubergine (£2.80), spiced cucumber (£2.20) and fried marrow (£2.60), which could be followed by a more carnivorous main course, such as sizzling marinated ribs (£7.90). If you are in the area for lunch, there's a selection of one-course menus for £4.20-£6.70, including rice and tea. House wine is £9.75 a bottle. / 11 pm, Fri & Sat 11.30 pm; closed Sat L & Sun L; no Amex.

The Builder's Arms SW3 £ 20 A

13 Britten St 7349 9040 5–2C

'Gastropubs' have been a great and positive development in eating out over the past ten years. This Chelsea spot is a good example of the breed, offering enjoyable food (that sadly tends towards the top end of our budget). You might have watercress and mint soup (£4.25) followed by chicken breast stuffed with goat's cheese, pesto, lemon couscous and red onion relish (£9.95) – and it's quite a congenial and handily located spot. The house wine is £11 a bottle, or drink Castlemaine XXXX at £2.60 a pint. / 9.30 pm; no Amex; no booking.

Buona Sera £ 17 A

289a King's Rd, SW3 7352 8827 5–3C

22 Northcote Rd, SW11 7228 9925 10–2C

Though there are two branches of this jolly Italian chain, it's the family-friendly Battersea one which is the more truly 'budget' destination (and whose prices are included below). Here, pizza and pasta (sub-£7) are the most popular choices, although there's also meatier fare for around a tenner. Antipasti, such as octopus salad, are around the £6 mark, and the house wine is £8.90 a bottle. (The novelty at the Chelsea branch is wierd 'double decker' seating inherited from its previous incarnation as 'The Jam'). / midnight; SW3 closed Mon; no Amex.

Busaba Eathai £ 17 A

106-110 Wardour St, W1 7255 8686 3–2D

22 Store St, WC1 7299 7900 2–1C

As the regular queues attest, if you're looking for glamour on a budget, you won't do much better than these stylish low-lit noodle canteens in Soho and Bloomsbury. Phad thai (£6.10) followed by green chicken curry (£6.90) might be a typical meal, washed down by house wine at £11.30 a bottle, or Thai beers at £3.30. / 11 pm, Fri & Sat 11.30 pm; no smoking; no booking.

Bush Bar & Grill W12 £ 19 A

45a Goldhawk Rd 8746 2111 7–1C

This Shepherd's Bush bar/restaurant – an 'atmosphere' destination, rather than one where the cooking is a great attraction in its own right – has established itself as a cool hang-out for west London media types. It's worth checking out for lunch, though, when £10.50 might buy you tuna tartare followed by wild mushroom risotto. In the early evening (6.30pm-7.30pm), you can have a pudding too, for only £1.50 more (and a happy-hour cocktail for only £3). A bottle of the house wine is £11. / www.bushbar.co.uk; 11.30 pm.

Butlers Wharf Chop-house SE1 £18* A★

36e Shad Thames 7403 3403 9–4D

As house wine at £14.50 a bottle suggests, this riverside English restaurant, which boasts great views of Tower Bridge, is hardly a budget establishment in any normal sense. This makes a light 2-course meal in the bar all the more attractive – for £9, you might enjoy the likes of chilled leek and potato soup followed by slow roast duck leg, and a pudding, such as iced raspberry mousse, adds a mere £2 to the bill. / www.conran.com; 10.45 pm; closed Sun D.

Cabanon W1 £ 19 ★

35 Great Portland St 7436 8846 3–1C

Not far from Oxford Circus, this rather odd continental-style café/bar is a handy destination for a shopping lunch, where the cooking often surprises with its quality. For £12.50 – also the price of a bottle of the house wine – you might order a pancake with vegetables and goats cheese, followed by lemon sole with cauliflower and broccoli. / www.trpplc.com; 10.30 pm; closed Sat L & Sun.

Café 206 W11 £ 18 A

206 Westbourne Grove 7221 1535 6–1B

This isn't a seriously foodie destination, but if you're looking for a light bite while hanging out with the Notting Hill set, this popular café is an excellent location. It's perhaps at its best for breakfast (full English, £7), but later in the day you might have the likes of pasta (£7-8) or scallopini with mushrooms (£9), followed by a cake (£2.75), washed down with house wine at £11.95 a bottle. / 6.30 pm; L only; no booking.

Café 209 SW6 £ 13 A

209 Munster Rd 7385 3625 10–1B

If you're looking for a decent dinner with a bit of a laugh thrown in, you won't do much better than this BYO Chinese/Thai café in deepest Fulham, presided over by the ever-present owner/chef Joy. Chicken satay (£3.25) followed by pad Thai (£4.55) is the sort of fare which ensures a great crush nightly, and economy is aided by the fact that this is strictly a BYO spot (corkage £1). Minimum charge, £8. / 10.30 pm; D only, closed Sun; no credit cards.

Café Crêperie de Hampstead SW7 £ 15

2 Exhibition Rd 7589 8947 5–2C

Especially handy for those seeking fortification before a trip to one of the South Kensington museums, this oddly-named small bistro – it is in fact an offshoot of a stall in the middle of Hampstead – offers truly budget fare at any time. A top choice would be one of the sweet or savoury crêpes (£3-£6), accompanied by wines starting at £10.50 a bottle. Beware, though – the setting really is very cramped. / 11pm; no credit cards; no smoking; no booking.

Café de Maya NW3 £ 13

38 Primrose Hill Rd 7209 0672 8–3B

By night, this cheap and cheerful spot, a few steps from Primrose Hill's main drag, serves up interesting Thai and Malay dishes, such as Thai fishcakes (£3.80) and chicken with sweet basil (£4.45) – by day, what claims to be the first 'herbal tea house' in London is planned at the time of going to press. Puddings for £2.50 and a bottle of house wine for a mere £7.50 add to the place's charms. / 11 pm; D only, ex Sun open L & D; no Amex; no smoking area.

Café du Jardin WC2 £18* A★

28 Wellington St 7836 8769 4–3D

This modern British restaurant would be a boon to any area, but in tourist-trap Covent Garden its set menu is a positive value-beacon. It offers two courses, plus coffee, for £10.95 (three courses, £14.50), and is available at lunch and pre- and post-theatre (5.30pm-7.30pm; 10pm-midnight; all day Sun), The menu typically includes a soup, salad or pasta, followed by grilled meat or fish, with rice pudding or chocolate mousse to finish. House wine is £10.50 a bottle. / www.cafedujardin.com; midnight.

Café Emm W1 £ 15 A

17 Frith St 7437 0723 4–2A

This popular Soho brasserie would probably not be first choice for a romantic assignation, but the range of reasonably-priced meals – including the 'Lunchtime Snack' menu of toasted giant baps or jacket potatoes with a variety of fillings (£4.90) – makes it hugely popular nonetheless. The £5.95 dishes include the likes of sausage & mash, burgers & lentil rissoles, while the £7.95s include jerk chicken, blackened Cajun salmon and rump steak. The house wine is £9.90 a bottle. / www.cafeemm.com; 10.30 pm, Fri & Sat 11.30 pm; no booking at D.

Café Japan NW11 £ 20 ★

626 Finchley Rd 8455 6854 1–1B

Near Golders Green Station, this cheerful Japanese fixture has made quite a name for itself. It used to offer hot dishes, but these days restricts itself to sushi, which starts from £2 a plate. Wash it all down with house wine at £8.50 a bottle, a glass of hot sake (£2.80) or a Japanese beer (around £3). / 10 pm; closed Mon, Tue & Sat D; no Amex; no smoking area.

Café Laville W2 £ 20 A

453 Edgware Rd 7706 2620 8–4A

Let's be honest, dining out is never just about food, and sometimes it isn't even mainly about food. That's certainly the case at this diner whose whole point is a setting of almost Venetian charm, above a canal. Breakfast (on a sunny day) is the best time to go – the full works will set you back about £8.50 – or you could fit a light lunch or dinner comfortably within our price limit. The house wine is £13.50 a bottle. / www.cafelaville.co.uk; 10.30 pm; no Amex; no smoking area.

Café Mozart N6 £ 17 A

17 Swains Ln 8348 1384 8–1B

If you're planning a walk on Hampstead Heath (or if you've just completed one), this pâtisserie/bistro is well worth knowing about. You can kick the day off with a good English breakfast (from £5.25). As the day progresses, there's a Mitteleuropean flavour to most of the dishes, so the special of the day might be schnitzel Holstein (£7.95), and there are salads and fancy sandwiches (£3-£6) as well. The house wine is £9.95 a bottle. / 10 pm; no Amex; no smoking; no booking at L.

Café Portugal SW8 £ 17 A

5a-6a Victoria Hs, South Lambeth Rd 7587 1962 10–1D

For a Portuguese dinner without ceremony or pretence, it's worth seeking out this family-run Vauxhall spot (which, by day, is a café). Prices are not demanding – you might start with melon with Parma ham (£3.60), and follow it up with grilled squid in garlic (£8.50). The house vino is £8.20 a bottle. / 11 pm; no Amex; no smoking area.

Caffè Nero £ 8

Branches throughout London

The Americans continue to throw money at buying up the best coffee house sites, but they still don't know much about making coffee. This group, however, draws its inspiration from the right place – Italy – and the result is by far the best of the bigger coffee chains. A really good double espresso will set you back £1.30, and there are nice panini (around £2.50), and other cakes and snacks (80p-£2). / 8 pm-11 pm, City branches earlier; most City branches closed all or part of weekend; no credit cards; no booking.

Calzone SW10 £ 18

335 Fulham Rd 7352 9797 5–3B

The sole remnant of what was once a small chain of smart pizzerias, this Chelsea site is a pleasant place for a light bite – calzone (folded-over pizza, £5.50-£8.50) is, naturally, the house speciality, or you could have salads or pasta dishes (around the £7.50 mark). The house wine is £11.95 a bottle.

Cantaloupe EC2 £16*

35-42 Charlotte Rd 7613 4411 9–1D

There is a restaurant at the rear of this large Clerkenwell bar – the original trendy place to drink in this now ever-so-trendy area – but the large main space is a more fun and more budget-friendly place for a snack. There is a wide selection of bar snacks and tapas to choose from, such as char-grilled peri peri pork skewers (£4), or you could make life simple by ordering a platter (£6.50-£15). There's a huge range of alcoholic beverages, including house wine at £9.90 a bottle. / www.cantaloupe.co.uk; 11.30 pm; bar menu only Sat L & Sun.

Cantina Italia N1 £20*

19 Canonbury Ln 7226 9791 8–2D

The name says it all about this Islington side street spot (and the downstairs area may indeed seem a bit too canteen-like for some tastes). For about £7 you can choose from all the usual pizzas and pastas, pretty well done. If you felt like a starter, too, you might perhaps have mussels (£5.50). The house wine is £11.90 a bottle. / 11 pm, Fri & Sat 11.30 pm; closed weekday L; no Amex; no smoking area.

Cantinetta Venegazzú SW11 £14* ★

31-32 Battersea Sq 7978 5395 5–4C

This small Battersea spot is unusual in specialising in Venetian cuisine. Some people like it a lot, and others can't quite see the point. Fortunately checking the place out yourself is not ruinously expensive, especially if you seek out the 2-course weekday lunch (£6.90) from which a typical selection might be a mixed salad, followed by chicken in spicy tomato sauce. A la carte, you'd have to choose pretty carefully to stay within our price limit. The house wine is £9.95 a bottle. / 11 pm; Oct-Mar closed Sun.

Carluccio's Caffè £ 17

3-5 Barrett St, W1 7224 1122 3–2B
8 Market Pl, W1 7636 2228 3–1C
St Christopher's Pl, W1 7935 5927 3–1A
5-7 The Grn, W5 8566 4458 1–3A
305-307 Upper St, N1 7359 8167 8–3D
2 Nash Court, E14 7719 1749 11–1C
12 West Smithfield, EC1 7329 5904 9–2A

Avuncular TV chef Antonio Carluccio's chain of traditional Italian caffès seems to have made a better stab than most at maintaining quality during growth, and goes from strength to strength. It offers delights such as Sicilian deep-fried rice balls filled with Mozzarella (£3.95) and calzone (£4.95), as well as a few more pricey dishes. House wines start at £9.95. Pop in for a quick coffee or a full meal, but be warned that the 'no daytime booking' policy means lunchtime queuing (although as all branches double-up as Italian delis you can shop while you wait). / www.carluccios.com; 11 pm; no booking weekday L.

Carnevale EC1 £17* ★

135 Whitecross St 7250 3452 9–1B

This chic little veggie deli, near the Barbican, serves stupendous sandwiches (from £2.25) as well as a full menu of enterprising dishes. As the latter could rather stretch our budget, it's the set lunch menu (£12.50) which is of most interest – it offers three courses (or two, plus a glass of wine), from which you might have fresh figs with Pecorino followed by pennette with carrots, courgettes and goat's cheese, with strawberry and grappa sorbet to finish. The house wine is £9.95 a bottle. / www.carnevalerestaurant.co.uk; 10.30 pm; closed Sat L & Sun; no Amex.

Carpaccio's SW3 £19* A

4 Sydney St 7352 3433 5–2C

Ziani and Como Lario are two of the stalwarts of the SW3 Italian restaurant scene, and their younger sibling has similary established quite a local following. The place is out of our range in the evenings, but at lunchtimes – which are very jolly affairs in a rather Chelsea sort of way – you can sample the two courses for £12. Your choice may be grilled squid salad followed by grilled chicken kebab with a pepper sauce, washed down with a bottle of the house wine, also £12. / www.carpaccio.uk.com; 11.30 pm; closed Sun.

The Castle SW11 £ 18

115 Battersea High St 7228 8181 10–1C

It's rather lost among the backstreets of Battersea, but this revamped old boozer occupies quite a characterful building, and benefits from an unusually pleasant garden. The cooking – you might perhaps have Cobb salad (£4.75) followed by lamb kebabs (£8.50) – is well above average. House wine is £11.50 a bottle, or drink bitter at £2.25 a pint. / www.thecastle.co.uk; 9.45 pm; no Amex.

Chada £ 16 ★

16-17 Picton Pl, W1 7935 8212 3–1A
208-210 Battersea Park Rd, SW11 7622 2209 10–1C

It is only at the original, Battersea branch that you can visit this superior Thai mini-chain on a budget, and then only from 6.30pm-8pm. It is well worth it, though, to sample some innovative Thai cooking. While the starters on the £12 set menu are very standard (chicken satay, vegetable springs rolls and so on), the main courses offer much more inventive options such as stir-fried lean pork with fresh ginger and roast duck in a rich tamarind sauce. The meal also includes a glass of wine, but if you want to splash out a bottle will set you back £12.50. / 11 pm; closed Sat L & Sun, SW11 D only; no smoking area.

Chamomile NW3 £ 13

45 England's Ln 7586 4580 8–2B

With huge all-day breakfasts (£4.95) and homemade pastries (£1.50) to choose from, this busy little Belsize Park café is a great place to meet up with friends or to hang out with the weekend papers. There's also a wide selection of vegetarian fare available – most dishes are around £5. Wine is £2.75 for a miniature bottle, or drink Becks at £2.50 a bottle. / 6 pm; L & early evening only; no Amex; no smoking area; no booking.

The Chapel NW1 £ 20

48 Chapel St 7402 9220 6–1D

The fare at this lively gastropub near Edgware Road tube is nothing if not eclectic, and it comes at prices such that you'll need to choose pretty carefully to stay within our price-range – you might have braised chicken thighs with green peppercorns, celery, apple and white wine sauce (£11) followed by black cherry and vanilla mousse (£3.50) from the daily-changing blackboard menu. House wine is £9.90 a bottle. / 9.50 pm.

Chelsea Bun Diner £ 16

9a Lamont Rd, SW10 7352 3635 5–3B
70 Battersea Bridge Rd, SW11 7738 9009 5–4C

The Chelsea original is – for some – the only branch of this mini chain worth bothering with. It comes into its own as the ultimate hangover cure – for £7.95 you could work off the sins of the previous evening with the 'New York brunch' (pancakes, French toast, eggs and hash browns), or a more modest egg, bacon and toast for £2.20 (both served with tea or coffee). At other times, dishes such as lasagne (£6.50) provide suitable fodder for a quick bite. House wine is £8.90 a bottle. / SW10 10.45 pm, SW11 L only; SW10 closed Sun D; no Amex; no brunch bookings.

The Chelsea Ram SW10 £ 20

32 Burnaby St 7351 4008 5–4B

You know you're on the fringe of a smart area, as it's only with a modicum of care that it's possible to stay within our budget at this popular boozer. It can be done if you are careful, though, and the pay-off is a meal in very convivial surroundings. You need to stick to the likes of crab and saffron tart (£5.95) to start, and you could follow up with the house salad (chicken, bacon and avocado with a sour cream dressing, £8.95). The house wine is £9.95 a bottle. / www.chelsearam.com; 10 pm; no Amex.

Chez Liline N4 **£20*** ★★

101 Stroud Green Rd 7263 6550 8–1D

It may look rather grim, but this Mauritian fish restaurant in Finsbury Park really does offer some of the most interesting and best-value cooking in town. To stay comfortably within our price limit, choose from the 2-course set menu (£12.75) available at lunch and dinner (Sun-Thu) – your choice might be avocado and crab salad, followed by red snapper in Creole sauce. The house wine is £10.75 a bottle. / 10.30 pm; closed Mon & Sun L.

Chez Lindsay TW10 **£13*** A★

11 Hill Rise 8948 7473 1–4A

Breton crêpes and ciders, and good seafood, are menu highlights at this authentic Gallic café/bistro near Richmond Bridge. You'd have to be very careful to dine à la carte within our budget, so the 2-course lunch menu (£5.99) is especially worth seeking out – choices might include mixed salad, followed by a galette with a choice of fillings. House wine is £10.95 a bottle, or, for greater authenticity, opt for a large bottle of cider (£7.25). / 11 pm; no Amex.

Chiang Mai W1 **£12*** ★★

48 Frith St 7437 7444 4–2A

The 2-course set lunch (£7.90) served at this unprepossessing but highly regarded Thai in the heart of Soho is the main budget option. It does rather restrict your choice, but you'd need to choose very carefully to stay within our budget à la carte. The house wine is £10.90 a bottle, but Singha beer (£3) is a more popular option. / 11 pm; closed Sun L; no smoking area.

Chowki W1 **£ 18** ★

2-3 Denman St 7439 1330 3–2D

This comfortable and quite atmospheric Indian near Piccadilly Circus has quickly established a very big reputation as one of the (few) decent Indians in the heart of the West End, and one of the even fewer budget ones. The top deals are the £10.95, 3-course set menus, always available, each offering the cuisine of a different region, washed down with house wine at £9.90 a bottle. / www.chowki.com; 11.30 pm; no smoking area.

Chuen Cheng Ku W1 **£ 17**

17 Wardour St 7437 1398 4–3A

This gaudy behemoth offers the 'classic' Chinatown experience, and serves the familiar Cantonese repertoire. Dim sum (from £1.95 a dish, until 6pm) served from trolleys dashing between tables, are the highlight. In the evening, the place is no more than a stand-by, offering a series of set menus starting at £12 and house wine at £9.80 a bottle. / 11.45 pm; no smoking area.

Chula W6 **£ 18**

116 King St 8748 1826 7–2C

If you find yourself out and about on Hammersmith's un-lovely main drag, it's worth remembering this stark café – a somewhat trendier-looking alternative to nearby Saagar. Though arguably not quite as good as its rival, foodwise, its inventive nouvelle Indian fare is pretty good. You can sample a wide variety of the dishes at the lunchtime buffet, when £5.95 secures you no fewer than 15 choices. By prior arrangement, you can have quite a special dinner menu, including a glass of the house vino (generally £10.95 a bottle), for around £15. / www.chula.co.uk; 11.30 pm.

Churchill Arms W8 £ 12 A★

119 Kensington Church St 7792 1246 6–2B

The combination of real ale and Thai food would seem unlikely to be a happy one, but it's worked well for a good number of London pubs, and nowhere better than in the conservatory annexe of this unremarkable-looking Kensington boozer. Some 20 one-plate dishes are served, all priced at £5.85. You might have chicken with cashew nuts, followed by a hearty, non-Thai pud, such as apple pie (£1.95). The house wine is £10.50 a bottle.
/ 9.30 pm; closed Sun D; no smoking area; no booking at L.

Chutneys NW1 £ 15 ★

124 Drummond St 7388 0604 8–4C

Long a star performer in the 'little India' enclave behind Euston station, this jolly veggie is best known for its lunchtime buffet (£5.95, also served all day on Sunday). At other times, exceptional pooris (deep-fried, stuffed chapatis) cost only £2.80, and even the most expensive main courses are only around £5.40. A bottle of the house wine is £8.50. / 11 pm; no Amex; no smoking at L; need 4+ to book.

Cinnamon Cay SW11 £17* A★

87 Lavender Hill 7801 0932 10–1C

This place looks a bit like your regular Battersea local restaurant, but it's more ambitious than it might at first sight appear, and its fusion cooking has won quite a following. A la carte, you'd spend beyond our limit (if not by a great deal), but at lunch (Mon-Sat) and dinner (Mon-Tue) the 2-course set menu – for a very reasonable £10 – allows you free run of the full menu. So, for your tenner, you might have foie gras followed by springbok fillet with Parmesan gnocchi, washed down with house wine at £10.95 a bottle.
/ www.cinnamoncay.co.uk; 11 pm; closed Sun.

Le Colombier SW3 £20* A

145 Dovehouse St 7351 1155 5–2C

Hidden away on a Chelsea corner – and benefiting from one of the nicest terraces of any restaurant in town – this classic Gallic brasserie offers just the menu you'd expect. It's beyond our price-limit à la carte, but makes a splendid sunny-day lunching destination, when two courses will set you back £13. The house wine is £12.90 a bottle. / 11 pm.

Coopers Arms SW3 £ 17 A

87 Flood St 7376 3120 5–3C

This understated pub, in the heart of Chelsea, is a relaxed place to hang out, and it offers comforting cooking at reasonable prices – you might start with cream of mushroom soup (£3.95), for example, followed by chargrilled lamb chops with pumpkin mash (£8.25). Desserts, such as chocolate fudge cake, are all £3.50. A pint of Young's bitter will set you back £2.30, or there's a fair selection of wines, starting at £11.20 a bottle.
/ www.drinkatthecoopers.co.uk; 9.30 pm; closed Sun D; no booking, Sun.

Coromandel SW11 £ 20 ★

2 Battersea Rise 7738 0038 10–2C

Fans of south Indian cooking should certainly seek out this bright restaurant at the end of Battersea's restaurant strip, as it offers cooking of above-average quality. You'll need to exercise some care to stay within our price limit, but it's perfectly possible with starters such as deep fried dahl dumplings with chutney (£3.45) followed by Kerala chicken (£6.95), and washed down by the house wine at £12.95 a bottle. / 11.30 pm; no smoking area.

The Cow W2 £18* A

89 Westbourne Park Rd 7221 0021 6–1B

If you want to hang out with the Notting Hill set at reasonably modest cost, this packed and fashionable boozer – owned by Tom Conran, son of Sir Terence – is just the place. The restaurant upstairs is out of our price bracket, but in the Emerald Isle-style downstairs boozer you could have the 'Cow Special' – six rock oysters and a pint of the Black Stuff for £9.50, or sausages & mash for £8. The house wine is £12.50 a bottle. / 10.30 pm; no Amex.

Cristini W1 £ 19 ★

13 Seymour Pl 7724 3446 2–2A

Just north of Marble Arch, this sweet but cramped little Italian restaurant – which from the outside looks old-hat, but which is in fact run by a young and enthusiastic couple – is especially worth knowing about for its set lunch menu. At that time, £12.50 will buy you the likes of bruschetta followed by prawn risotto, and accompanied by house wine at £11 a bottle. Evening prices would rather stretch our budget. / www.cristini.co.uk; 10.30 pm; closed Sat L & Sun.

The Crown & Sceptre W12 £ 19

57 Melina Rd 8746 0060 7–1B

This boozer in the backstreets of Shepherd's Bush has been subtly trendified without losing the feel of a proper pub. The cooking, however, fortunately benefited from the revamp and – though simple – dishes are of good quality and come at reasonable prices. Smoked haddock risotto (£5.50) followed with pork escalope (£10) are typical items on the menu – so you should be able to dine easily within our price limit. House wine is £10 a bottle. / 10 pm; no Amex; no smoking area; no booking.

Dakota W11 £ 19

127 Ledbury Rd 7792 9191 6–1B

This Notting Hill eatery still aims to offer 'stylish modern American cuisine', but its trendy heyday when it numbered Madonna as a regular are well past. But while the food is not generally very remarkable these days, the budget opportunities offered by the set weekday lunch – two courses for £10, three for £12 – or for brunch (Sat, 11am-4pm) are well worth bearing in mind. For the latter, you might choose buttermilk pancakes with maple syrup and spiced apple (£5) with a side order of hash browns (£2). The house wine costs £12 a bottle. / www.dakotafood.co.uk; midnight; closed Sun D.

Daphne NW1 £ 15

83 Bayham St 7267 7322 8–3C

This humble Greek taverna in Camden Town – not to be confused with Daphne's at Brompton Cross, where ladies-who-lunch lunch – has long been renowned for offering good-value and filling nosh from a reliably well-produced menu of standard dishes, such as taramasalata (£2.60) and moussaka (£7.50), or houmous (£2.60) and kleftiko (lamb baked with lemon, £8.25). The house wine is £11.50 a litre. / 11.30 pm; closed Sun; no Amex.

Daquise SW7 £ 15

20 Thurloe St 7589 6117 5–2C

For a cosy, time-warp ambience, it's tough to match this unpretentious Polish restaurant and cafe (est 1947) which is handily situated by South Kensington tube (and provides a relaxing location for a break from a day at the nearby museums). The set lunch menu is great value – for £7.50 you might enjoy such specialities as borscht or blinis with smoked salmon, followed by meatballs or pancakes with mushrooms, accompanied by a Polish beer (around £2.50) or vodka (£2). Alternatively, wait until 3pm, when you could have an apple strudel (£1.80) or cheesecake (£2.20), washed down with a cup of tea. / 11 pm; no Amex; no smoking area.

Dartmouth Arms NW5 £ 15 A

35 York Rise 7485 3267 8–1B

Truly reasonable prices put this Dartmouth Park boozer well within the range of the budget diner at any time. You could even go for three courses within our price limit, say, terrine (£3.25) followed by sausages & mash (there is a different meat and vegetarian option everyday, £5 at lunch or £7 at dinner), with bread and butter pudding (£3) for desert. Wash it down with a pint of Carlsberg (£2.60), or the house vino (£10 a bottle). / 10 pm; no Amex.

Deca W1 £20* A★

23 Conduit St 7493 7070 3–2C

Budget dining experiences just don't come better than at the this grand restaurant, in the heart of Mayfair. So slip on your Savile Row suit – or go a touch more informal, if you prefer – to avail yourself of the £12.50, 3-course set lunch menu, which might comprise gnocchi with basil, then John Dory with chives and ginger, followed by raspberry cheesecake. Beware, though, that house wine is £14.50 a bottle, and that if you stray from this narrow path, you'll blow our budget big time. / 11 pm; closed Sun.

La Delizia SW3 £ 14 ★

63-65 Chelsea Manor St 7376 4111 5–3C

The only remaining remnant of what was a small Chelsea chain of pizzerias can still induce the occasional pang of nostalgia amongst old regulars for the days when its crisp, modernistic styling seemed to be very cutting edge. The place still does good pizzas (around £7) and other dishes such as asparagus risotto (£6.95), and it's very reasonably priced by local standards. A bottle of the house wine will set you back £8. / midnight; no Amex.

The Depot SW14 £18* A★

Tideway Yd, Mortlake High St 8878 9462 10–1A

The great views of the Thames are the highlight at this popular Barnes destination – perfect for a meal with the family. The prices are generally out of our range, but there is a £10.95 2-course set lunch, from which you might choose roast tomato and basil soup with garlic croutons followed by roast rainbow trout with Niçoise salad – fish dishes are something of a high point. The house wine is £10.95 a bottle. / 10.30 pm; no smoking area.

Le Deuxième WC2 £18* ★

65a Long Acre 7379 0033 4–2D

Under the same ownership as the nearby Café du Jardin, this bright modern Gallic restaurant is on a site which could hardly be more convenient for the Royal Opera House. It's out of our price range à la carte, but there's a 2-course lunchtime and pre/post -theatre (5-7pm and 10pm- midnight) menu for £10.95 including coffee. Your selection might be chicken breast with curried potatoes followed by a white and dark chocolate mousse, washed down with house wine at £11.50 a bottle. / midnight.

Diwana Bhel-Poori House NW1 £ 12 ★

121-123 Drummond St 7387 5556 8–4C

Even by the less than taxing local standards, this very '70s Indian behind Euston station isn't the smartest place. However, it's also laughably inexpensive and delivers good, tasty nosh. Go for the pooris (£2.50) and thalis (from £4.95), or really splash out on the lunchtime buffet (£5.95). The restaurant is unlicensed, but you're welcome to BYO in the evening (wine or beer only) and no corkage is charged. / www.diwanarestaurant.com; 11.15 pm; no smoking area; need 6+ to book.

don Fernando's TW9 £ 18 A

27f The Quadrant 8948 6447 1–4A

This large and lively tapas bar, just by Richmond station, dishes up some of the better grub in the area. It's a fun place for a get-together – they do a generous 2-course set menu for £14.95 per person (minimum 2 people) – or stick to the tapas, all priced at less than a fiver. House Rioja is £11.95 a bottle, or buoy the party spirit with a jug of sangria for £1 less. / www.donfernando.co.uk; 11 pm; no smoking area; no booking.

Don Pedro EC1 £ 19 A

70 Exmouth Mkt 7837 1999 9–1A

Amid all the cutting edge trendiness that is Clerkenwell, someone has – wittily? – opened a new tapas bar whose rather dated styling comes as quite a relief! The menu is similarly unfashionable, offering a large selection of tapas (£3-£5) which are each so substantial that a couple of them are likely to be sufficient. Alternatively, at lunchtime there's a set 2-course menu for £7.95. Wines, of which there's a reasonable selection, start at £10.95 a bottle. / midnight; closed Sat L; no Amex; no smoking area at L.

Don Pepe NW8 £ 19 A

99 Frampton St 7262 3834 8–4A

The oldest tapas bar in town, near Lords, is still a consistent performer. You can in fact dine in the restaurant within our budget at any time – the 3-course set menu is £13.95 – but it's much more fun to have tapas (mostly under a fiver) in the bar, especially when there's live music (most nights). The all-Hispanic wine list kicks off at £8.95 a bottle. / midnight; closed Sun.

The Eagle EC1 £ 16 A★

159 Farringdon Rd 7837 1353 9–1A

Good gastropubs are ten-a-penny nowadays, so it's easy to forget just how original this crowded Clerkenwell boozer (next to the Guardian's HQ) seemed when it was revamped at the start of the '90s. Gastronomically speaking it maintains its position in the front rank with some zesty Mediterranean dishes. They don't make much of starters or puds – for a main dish you might have marinated rump steak sandwich (£9). A good selection of wines starts from £10.50 per bottle. / 10.30 pm; closed Sun D; no Amex; no booking.

Eagle Bar Diner W1 £ 19 A

3-5 Rathbone Pl 7637 1418 4–1A

This bar and diner has quickly made itself quite a success, both as a cool bar (in the area known to some local trendies nowadays as North Soho) and as a burger-stop for those shopping in Oxford Street. It combines the two functions surprisingly well. A burger will set you back about £8. Wash it down with a bottle of beer (from £3) or a bottle of the house vino (£12.95).
/ www.eaglebardiner.com; 10.45 pm; closed Sun D; no Amex; need 6+ to book.

The Easton WC1 £ 17

22 Easton St 7278 7608 9–1A

The absence of any starters helps control the costs of eating at this large and basically revamped Clerkenwell boozer (which is visible from trendy Exmouth Market, which is its spiritual – if not its actual – address). The dishes, from an Aussie team, might be the likes of kangaroo and red wine sausages (£8.95) or charolais entrecote (£12.95). Puddings, such as baked honey and orange cheese cake, are on the menu more often than not. Wines start at £10.95 a bottle. / 10 pm; no Amex.

Ebury Street Wine Bar SW1 £19*

139 Ebury St 7730 5447 2–4A

Established in 1959, this wood-panelled restaurant has maintained a loyal local clientele for many years. If you find yourself in Belgravia and in need of a budget destination, this is a good place to enjoy some satisfactory cooking while observing the residents in their natural habitat. To squeeze within our budget, you will have to restrict yourself to the set 2-course lunch, however – for £12.50, you might choose spicy fishcakes followed by confit rabbit legs with shiitake dressing. The house wine is £12 a bottle. / 10.15 pm; closed Sun L May-August.

Eco £ 18 ★

162 Clapham High St, SW4 7978 1108 10–2D
4 Market Row, Brixton Mkt, SW9 7738 3021 10–2D

The tiny (and unlicensed) Brixton Market branch of this small chain remains many South Londoners' favourite pizzeria – the Clapham original has become too loud and possibly too popular for its own good. Still, the pizzas (all around £5.40-8.90) are pretty good and you can't argue with success (not unless you're prepared to shout at the top of your voice, that is). The house wine is £10.75 a bottle. / *SW4 11 pm, Fri & Sat 11.30 pm; SW9 L only, closed Wed & Sun; SW9 no booking.*

Efes Kebab House £ 17

1) 80 Gt Titchfield St, W1 7636 1953 2–1B
2) 175-177 Gt Portland St, W1 7436 0600 2–1B

Established in the early '70s, these Turkish restaurants have been twin beacons of value, up Marylebone way, for many years, and they continue to satisfy all comers with their impressive range of dishes. These include 22 kebabs (£6.95-£9.25), plus undemanding starters like houmous and taramasalata (£3.95), washed down with house wine at £11.90 a bottle. The Great Portland Street branch stays open until 3am at the weekends, and the nightly belly dancers add to the atmosphere. / *11.30 pm; Gt Titchfield St closed Sun.*

Elephant Royale
Locke's Wharf E14 £ 19

Westferry Rd 7987 7999 11–2C

Especially given the dirth of local dining opportunities – opposite Greenwich, at the tip of the Isle of Dogs – this Thai restaurant is certainly worth knowing about (not least for its impressive riverside terrace, which is much nicer than the glitzy interior). You'd spend a little outside our budget à la carte, so it's worth seeking out the £12.50 3-course set lunch. Your choice might be the 'Paradise Platter' of mixed starters, then lamb curry served with rice or noodles, and followed with a coconut crème brûlée. The house wine is £12 a bottle. / *www.elephantroyale.com; 10.30 pm; no smoking area.*

The Endurance W1 £ 20 ★

90 Berwick St 7437 2944 3–2D

Berwick Street, with its fruit market in the heart of Soho, is one of the more characterful thoroughfares in central London. Given the determinedly boozer-ish style of this pub in the heart of the street (right down to the dart board) it would be easy to miss its subtle retro makeover, although the trendy crowd is something of a give-away. It serves straightforward, traditional British grub at down-to-earth prices – perhaps a superior ploughman's (£4.50) followed by homemade pie and mash (£8.50), washed down by house wine at £10.90 a bottle. / *L only; no Amex; need 12+ to book.*

The Evangelist EC4 £ 20 A

33 Black Friars Ln 7213 0740 9–3A

This large modern bar/restaurant has an interesting layout, with lots of comfortable seating (and some nice alcoves, for those who get there early). It's established itself as a popular destination with local City workers, so if you're looking for a reasonably-priced lunch, it's safest to book ahead. Your choice might be Mexican salsa sausages with chilli mashed potato and guacamole (£9.95) – or a sandwich or salad (both around £7) followed by chocolate and espresso mousse (£4.50), washed down with house wine at £11 a bottle. / www.massivepub.com; 9 pm, Thu & Fri 8 pm; closed Sat & Sun.

Exotika WC2 £ 13

7 Villiers St 7930 6133 4–4D

If you're looking for a quick but proteinaceous meal in the immediate area of Charing Cross station, you might conclude that the local McDonalds (recently tastefully revamped) is the best choice. Fear not, however, this smart but barely furnished new diner – converted from what used to be the downstairs of the burgeria – now provides an alternative. It offers a disparate variety of dishes – from satay chicken with noodles (£4.50) to Parma salad (£3.50) – perfectly competently realised. Wine is BYO (£1 corkage), or you might opt for a smoothie (£2.10). / www.exotika.co.uk; 11 pm; no Amex; no booking.

Il Falconiere SW7 £17*

84 Old Brompton Rd 7589 2401 5–2B

The 3-course set lunch (£10) ensures that you'll stay well within budget at this well-worn and reassuringly old-school trattoria in South Kensington – at other times you'd spend rather over our price-limit (and we wouldn't especially recommend paying the premium anyway). Starters of cured beef with avocado or rocket and Parmesan salad and mains of pasta, veal, or grilled chicken are typical. Desserts are, of course, from a trolley, and the house wine is £11.50 a bottle. / 11.45 pm; closed Sun.

Faulkner's E8 £ 15 ★★

424-426 Kingsland Rd 7254 6152 1–1D

This East End chippy is justly renowned for dishing up some of the best fish 'n' chips in the capital. It's not especially cheap, with prices ranging from £8.50 for cod up to £13.50 for Dover sole, but the quality is high. You might start with scampi (£2.85) and you absolutely must finish with the sticky toffee pudding (£2.50). House wine is £7.95 a bottle. / 10 pm; no Amex; no smoking area; need 8+ to book.

Ffiona's W8 £20*

51 Kensington Church St 7937 4152 5–1A

Only a tiny number of restaurants in London offer cooking just like Mum's in cosily domestic surroundings, and this well-established Kensington bistro – where owner Ffiona is much in evidence – has many admirers. A la carte it just about fits within budget, but the top tip is the early evening menu (you must be out by 8.30pm) which offers three courses for £13.50. You might have onion & herb tart followed by coq au vin or steak & kidney pie and then apple crumble. There's also a 3-course set Sunday lunch menu, which, at £15.95, stretches our budget somewhat. The house wine is £11 a bottle. / 11 pm; closed Mon, Tue-Sat D only, Sun open L & D.

Fileric SW7 £ 7 ★

57 Old Brompton Rd 7584 2967 5–2B

Real French staff/customers/pastries – who needs the Eurostar? This South Kensington pâtisserie offers a top Gallic experience at modest cost. A croissant (70p) and a coffee (£1.50) is the perfect way to sample the fare, but they also do good snacks, such as croques messieurs and quiches – 2 courses plus a soft drink will set you back just £6.95. / 8 pm.

Film Café
National Film Theatre SE1 £ 16

Waterloo Rd 7928 5362 2–3D

If you're visiting the 'Eye', there are quite a few places nearby for a light meal, but this is one of the few which can be recommended, and it's especially good with kids. In summer, the outside seating is very popular. A wide range of dishes is offered, including quiches, pizza slices, stews and a few veggie alternatives, fairly priced from around £4 for salads and £6 for more substantial dishes. House wine is £10.80 a bottle. / 9 pm; no Amex; no smoking area; no booking.

Fish Hoek W4 £17* ★★

6-8 Elliott Rd 8742 0766 7–2A

It is not just the enthusiastic staff who make this tightly-packed Chiswick restaurant a place of notable interest – it offers many South African fish and seafood dishes which you are unlikely to find anywhere else in London. It's cracking stuff too. The option to order any dish (prices go up to £15) as a half-portion offers scope for the budget diner at any time. Alternatively, take advantage of the set 2-course menu (£9.95, lunchtime and 6pm-8pm), which includes delights such as stumpnose and snoek pâté. The house wine list, all South African, kicks off at £13 a bottle. / 10.30 pm; closed Mon (except Aug-Dec); no Amex; no smoking area.

Fish in a Tie SW11 £ 13 A

105 Falcon Rd 7924 1913 10–1C

Even à la carte, you can always eat within our budget at this cramped but very popular Battersea bistro – if you don't book, you'll do well to get a table. Top value of all, though, is to be had from the 3-course set menus – for £7.50, your choice might be deep fried gouda cheese to start, then chicken with brandy sauce followed by crunchy honey lime chocolate cake, washed down with house wine at £9.20 a bottle. / 11.45 pm; no Amex.

Food for Thought WC2 £ 11 ★

31 Neal St 7836 0239 4–2C

Even carnivores are happy to brave the wooden staircase down to this cramped, cave-like north-Covent Garden basement. It's a laid-back spot, offering a small and eclectic range of inexpensive and wholesome veggie fare, such as Thai vegetable curry (£4) and quiches and salads (both from £3). There's also a mouth-watering selection of cakes and puddings, perhaps an almond and coconut scone (£1.20). BYO – no corkage. / 8.15 pm; closed Sun D; no credit cards; no smoking; no booking.

Formosa Dining Room
The Prince Alfred W9 **£ 17** Ⓐ★

5a Formosa St 7286 3287 6–1C

Though built onto a rather elegant Victorian pub (The Prince Albert), this sleek, stripped down, new Maida Vale dining annex – with dark wooden tables and minimalist decor – fits in with the old, quirky bar brilliantly well. Sadly the good-quality cooking is generally rather out of our price-range, but at weekday lunchtimes there's a very good-value menu – for £10, you can choose the likes of foie gras parfait followed by pan fried sea bream with cherry tomatoes and new potatoes. The house wine, at £11 a bottle, is non too pricey either. / 11 pm.

Fortnum's Fountain W1 **£20*** Ⓐ

181 Piccadilly 7734 8040 3–3D

The Queen's grocers might seem an odd budget suggestion, but the grand ground-floor buttery (with a separate entrance from Jermyn Street) is a useful place to spoil yourself for breakfast (full works about £11.95), for lunch – when you might have Fortnum's Welsh rarebit (£8.95) followed by apple pie (£4.25) – or, perhaps best of all, for scones, clotted cream and jam (£4.95). Wines start at £13 a bottle. / www.fortnumandmason.co.uk; 7.45 pm; closed Sun; no smoking area; no booking at L.

The Four Seasons W2 **£ 15** ★

84 Queensway 7229 4320 6–1C

Although you never read about the area much in trendy magazines, Bayswater is in fact the best part of town to head for if you're looking for a quality Chinese meal. This particular place has all the brusque charms that generally characterise such experiences, but the food is consistently very good, and reasonably priced. Roast duck (£6.50) is a highlight. The house wine £9.50 a bottle. / 11.15 pm.

The Fox EC2 **£ 20** Ⓐ★

28 Paul St 7729 5708 9–1C

Michael Belben is still best known as the founder of the famous Eagle, but he's slowly winning quite a reputation for the cooking at this more recently acquired Shoreditch boozer. At £15 dinner risks putting you beyond our price-range, but you do get a real meal – perhaps split pea and ham soup followed by brill, spinach and hollandaise, and you can snack more inexpensively at the bar (and at lunchtime). Drink bitter (£2.50), or wines from £10.50 a bottle. / 11 pm; closed Sat & Sun; no Amex.

Fox & Anchor EC1 **£ 17**

115 Charterhouse St 7253 5075 9–1B

If breakfast is the Great British Meal, this Smithfield veteran, famous for its fry-ups, is the Great British pub. The meal is served all day, and your £7.95 buys you sausage, bacon, fried eggs, black pudding, fried bread, baked beans and grilled tomatoes. You might wash it down – thanks to a quirk in the local licensing laws, from breakfast onwards – with a pint of Guinness (£2.70), or the house wine at £9.95 a bottle. / breakfast (Mon-Fri) & L only; bar open in evening; closed Sat & Sun.

Frantoio SW10 £18* A★

397 King's Rd 7352 4146 5–3B

It's had something of a slow start, but this World's End trattoria is beginning to establish quite a local following. It's well outside our price-range à la carte, but offers a 2-course set lunch menu (£11), from which your selection might be cold veal with a tuna sauce, followed by salmon escalope in a potato crust, washed down with house wine at £11 a bottle. / 11.30 pm.

Frederick's N1 £20* A★★

106 Camden Pas 7359 2888 8–3D

You'd generally spend twice our budget dining at this smart and perennially popular Islington institution, whose special feature is its large and airy rear conservatory. The Gallic cooking's pretty good too, and quite affordable if you visit for the lunchtime and pre-7pm menu, when two courses – perhaps potted shrimps followed by Gruyere and broccoli quiche – will set you back just £12.50 (including coffee). The house wine is £12 a bottle.
/ www.fredericks.co.uk; 11.30 pm; closed Sun; no smoking area.

Frocks E9 £18* A

95 Lauriston Rd 8986 3161 1–2D

This cosy English bistro is a very popular destination, down Victoria Park way, especially for its all-day weekend breakfasts (11am-4pm, around £6.50). A la carte, it falls just outside our budget, but set lunches fall within it. A 3-course meal will set you back £13.50 – you might have goat's cheese and pea risotto with pesto, followed by Welsh lamb fillet with white beans and minted redcurrant jus, then poached nectarines and raspberry coulis for pudding. The house wine is £10.75 a bottle. / 11 pm; closed Mon & Sun D; no booking for Sun brunch.

Fryer's Delight WC1 £ 7

19 Theobald's Rd 7405 4114 2–1D

Inexpensive chippies don't come more 'Central Castings' perfect than this Formica-and-fluorescent-strip Bloomsbury parlour, and it offers what in our view is probably the best value eat-in food to be had in central London. With cod 'n' chips at £4.50 and a mug of tea at 35p, you really can have a filling one-course meal here, and still have change from a fiver. No puddings. / 10 pm; closed Sun; no credit cards; no booking.

Fujiyama SW9 £ 12

7 Vining St 7737 2369 10–2D

This buzzy, well-established noodle bar offers an ideal pit stop for those checking out the delights of Brixton. Main dishes – an example would be a big bowl of pork ramen (miso soup with noodles, topped with slices of grilled pork) – cost £5-£7.50, and the house wine is £10 a bottle. / www.newfujiyama.com; 10.45 pm, Sat & Sun midnight; no Amex; no smoking area.

Furnace N1 £ 17 ★

1 Rufus St 7613 0598 9–1D

For our money, this is the best inexpensive place to eat if you want to hang with the Hoxton trendies. Just off the Square, it's a buzzing, brick-lined establishment, where pizzas are around £8.50, or you can opt for other simple Italian fare such as the pasta of the day (£6.95). A bottle of house wine costs £9.45. / 11 pm; closed Sat L & Sun; no Amex.

Futures EC3 £ 8 ★

8 Botolph Alley 7623 4529 9–3C

We don't generally include take-aways, but we've always had a soft spot for this smart City veggie, hidden away in the lanes near the Monument. Good food is hard enough to find in that part of town, and the nosh here really is better than at most of the places where they sit you down with a knife and fork! Soups (£2.15/£2.95), salads (£3) and bakes (£4.10) are the sort of dishes which attract regular lunchtime queues. Top-quality, and inexpensive, breakfasting fare is also available. / www1e.btwebworld.com/futures1/; L only, closed Sat & Sun; no booking.

Gaby's WC2 £ 17

30 Charing Cross Rd 7836 4233 4–3B

For an interesting mix of Mediterranean and Middle Eastern dishes, check out this Formica-chic café in the heart of the West End. For £6.50 at lunchtime you could fill up on the 2-course set meal, which might include tuna salad, followed by goulash with rice. A la carte prices are just as reasonable – the very popular salt beef sandwich is £4.50. House wine is £8.50 a bottle. / www.gabys.net; 11.15 pm; no credit cards; no smoking area.

La Galette W1 £ 19

56 Paddington St 7935 1554 2–1A

Just off Marylebone High Street, this Gallic café can almost claim to be the capital's top destination for pancake-lovers. They also do simple dishes such as Breton country pâte with cornichons (£4), but it is the galettes (such as baked ham and brie, £5.90) and crêpes (lemon and sugar, £3.50) which are the star turn. For authenticity, drink Breton cider at £7.95 for a bottle, or wine at £11. / www.lagalette.com; 10.45 pm; no smoking; need 6+ to book.

Galicia W10 £ 18

323 Portobello Rd 8969 3539 6–1A

Benefiting from the proximity of one of London's largest Hispanic communities, this North Kensington tapas bar is strong on authenticity – including service whose warm heart can be hidden behind a rather gruff veneer – and high on atmosphere. The tapas (mostly £3-£5), washed down by house wine at £9.50 a bottle, can be pretty good, too. / 11.30 pm; closed Mon.

Gallipoli £ 18 A★

102 Upper St, N1 7359 0630 8–3D
120 Upper St, N1 7226 8099 8–3D

A few doors apart from each other, in the heart of Islington, these friendly Turkish bistros offer some of the best cheap eats in town, and they really are buzzing – from early evening till late, every day of the week. You could eat here à la carte within our budget – the lunch and dinner menus are pretty similar, but the lunch is cheaper with starters around £3.75 and main courses between £6 and £10. The house wine is £9.95 a bottle. / 11 pm, Fri & Sat midnight; no Amex.

Gastro SW4 £18* A

67 Venn St 7627 0222 10–2D

It's for the daytime attractions that this popular Gallic café by the Clapham Picture house is most worth knowing about – by night it's a bit pricey for our budget nowadays. Breakfast is served from 8am-3pm, or for lunch you might have the likes of ravioli (£5.80). Cakes (from £1.90) and coffee are available all afternoon. The house wine is £10.95 a bottle. / midnight; no credit cards; mainly non-smoking.

The Gate £ 20 ★★

51 Queen Caroline St, W6 8748 6932 7–2C
72 Belsize Ln, NW3 7435 7733 8–2A

Although it now has a worthy Belsize Park offshoot, it's the original branch of London's best vegetarian restaurant – off a church courtyard near Hammersmith Broadway – which remains the better-known location. Starters, such as feta cheese and couscous fritters, are under £6, while main courses, such as Caribbean curry, are between £10 and £11. Note that, with house wine at £10.50 a bottle,this place strains at the very limit of our budget. / www.gateveg.co.uk; 10.45 pm; W6 closed Sun & Sat L, NW3 closed weekday L; smoking restrictions at NW3; W6 booking: max 10.

Geeta NW6 £ 10 ★★

57-59 Willesden Ln 7624 1713 1–1B

You have to look below the surface, or at least past the exterior, of this grim-looking Kilburn Indian. For many years, it has delivered consistently good regional cooking at modest prices, with most starters under £2 and most curries around £5 (or less for the many veggie options). House wine is a modest £6.50 a bottle. / 10.30 pm, Fri & Sat 11.30 pm; no Switch.

Giá SW3 £ 19 A★

62 Fulham Rd 7589 2232 5–2C

A set 3-course lunch (£12.95) is available every day of the week at this new trattoria (which occupies the Brompton Cross site once home to the fabled San Frediano). The fare is not particularly exotic – you might have beef cannelloni and plaice in lemon sauce, followed by tiramisu – but prices like this are not to be sneezed at in these parts (and if you stray into à la carte territory you will spend very much more). The house wine is also £12.95 a bottle. / 11.15 pm.

Giraffe £ 19

6-8 Blandford St, W1 7935 2333 2–1A
270 Chiswick High Rd, W4 8995 2100 7–2A
7 Kensington High St, W8 7938 1221 5–1A
29-31 Essex Rd, N1 7359 5999 8–3D
46 Rosslyn Hill, NW3 7435 0343 8–2A
27 Battersea Rise, SW11 7223 0933 10–2C

Relaxed, jolly, child-friendly – it really is a mystery why more people don't set up informal diners along the lines of this all-day mini-chain. It's perhaps for brunch that they have a particular following, but you can eat here within our price limit at any time of day. Dinner, for example might be glazed chicken skewers (£4.95) followed by vegetarian moussaka with ricotta and oregano topping (£7.95), washed down with house wine at £10.50 a bottle. Even better, have a fresh fruit smoothie – maybe the 'giddy giraffe' (papaya, mint, orange, lime and banana, £3.25). / 11 pm; no smoking.

Golborne House W10 £20* A

36 Golborne Rd 8960 6260 6–1A

In the shadow of North Kensington's Trellick Tower, this is a gastropub destination of some note among local Bohos, and it can get quite crowded. An evolving menu offers starters such as bruschetta of marinated peppers and buffalo ricotta (£6.25). Lunchtime main course prices – perhaps salmon fishcakes (£8.75) – fit comfortably within our budget, but the dinner menu is such as to push the place towards and perhaps beyond our price-limit. The house wine is £10.95 a bottle. / www.golbornehouse.co.uk; 10.30 pm; booking: max 10.

Golden Dragon W1 £ 17

28-29 Gerrard St 7734 2763 4–3A

Dragons glare at you from every corner of this Chinatown spot, where a series of set meals (starting at £12.50 a head) are the cheapest and most straightforward budget options – as ever, though, the à la carte dishes (mostly around £6) will tend to be very much more interesting. The hectic atmosphere, buoyed by house wine at £9 a bottle, makes the place ideal for large parties.

/ 11.15 pm, Fri & Sat 11.45 pm.

Good Earth SW3 £18* ★

233 Brompton Rd 7584 3658 5–2C

As Knightsbridge is not exactly flush with budget lunching possibilities, it's particularly worth knowing about the 2-course set lunch (£9.95) at this smart and comfortable Chinese. Alternatively, try the one-bowl Japanese specials – for example, ramen noodles with seafood or chicken, from £7.50. Otherwise – as house wine at £13 a bottle might suggest – the place is outside our price range.

/ 10.45 pm.

Gopal's of Soho W1 £ 18

12 Bateman St 7434 1621 4–2A

Considering how many good Indian restaurants there are in London, and many of them inexpensive, it's a shame that those handily located in the West End are mostly pretty lacklustre. This Soho restaurant is a worthy exception, and it offers some unusual dishes, too – such as tandoori quail (£4.50), or Hyderabadi fish steamed in a banana leaf (£8.50). The house wine is £9.50 a bottle.

/ 11.15 pm; closed Sun.

Gordon's Wine Bar WC2 £ 17 A

47 Villiers St 7930 1408 4–4D

If it's Olde London character you're after (or, in summer, a large and leafy outside terrace), you won't do any better than this wonderfully scruffy wine bar, a few paces from Embankment tube. It's tremendously popular, thanks to its atmosphere and the modest prices of both food and drink. Wines start from £11.20 a bottle (with plenty of choice for a couple of pounds more) and the basic food includes well-kept cheeses, salads and hot 'dishes of the day' – all priced in the £7-£9 range. / 10 pm; no Amex; no booking.

Gourmet Burger Kitchen £ 14 ★

49 Fulham Broadway, SW6 7381 4242 5–4A

331 West End Ln, NW6 7794 5455 1–1B

44 Northcote Rd, SW11 7228 3309 10–2C

333 Putney Bridge Rd, SW15 8789 1199 10–2B

Burgers every possible way – including 'Jamaican' (with mango and ginger) and 'Kiwiburger' (with pineapple, beetroot and cheese), all around £5-£7 – have made this growing chain of diners the capital's key destination for burger-lovers. A side order of fat chips will set you back an extra £2, and house wine is £10.95 a bottle.

/ www.gbkinfo.co.uk; 11 pm; no Amex; no smoking; no booking.

Gourmet Pizza Company £ 19

7-9 Swallow St, W1 7734 5182 3–3D
56 Upper Ground, SE1 7928 3188 9–3A
18 Mackenzie Walk, E14 7345 9192 11–1C

Pizzas (typically about £9) more interesting than the norm – perhaps Chinese duck or grilled aubergine and goats cheese – make these basic pizzerias (now part of the PizzaExpress empire) a popular destination. The Gabriel's Wharf branch is particularly worth seeking out for its fine views of the City and St Paul's – expect to queue on a warm evening. The house wine is £12.95 a bottle. / www.gourmetpizzacompany.co.uk; 10.30 pm; no smoking area, E14; E14 & SE1, need 8+ to book.

Govinda's W1 £ 7 ★

9 Soho St 7437 4928 4–1A

For a filling West End snack at bargain prices, you won't do better that the cafeteria under the Hare Krishna temple, just off Soho Square. For religious reasons meat, onions and garlic don't feature in dishes, but that doesn't stop them from being plentiful and tasty and the place draws an enjoyably eclectic crowd. The best budget bets are the set meals (a fiver or less, served noon-8pm) which consists of two rices, steamed vegetables, dhal, salad, naan and popadoms. Alcohol and caffeine are also on the 'proscribed' list, so you will have to stick with the delicious lassis (£1.20) or herbal tea (60p). / 8 pm; closed Sun; no Amex; no smoking.

Great Nepalese NW1 £ 16

48 Eversholt St 7388 6737 8–3C

The popularity of this long-serving Euston-side Indian belies its inauspicious location. The simplest choice is a Nepalese set lunch or dinner (curry, pilau rice, relishes and dessert for £12.95) but, especially in a group, there are lots of interesting dishes to sample which will still leave you comfortably within our price limit, and the staff offer friendly and helpful advice. The house wine is £8.50 a bottle. / www.great-nepalese.co.uk; 11 pm.

The Green NW2 £ 20 A

110 Walm Ln 8452 0171 1–1A

The number of trendy places to eat in Willesden Green doubled last year on the opening of this stylishly converted billiards club – it's now a large gastopub, with a lofty and impressively designed rear dining room. You could easily spend beyond our price-limit, but with dishes such as fishcakes (£4.95) or a BLT sandwich with chips (£5.95), and house wine at £10.95 a bottle, it's quite possible to stay within it. / www.thegreen-nw2.co.uk; 10 pm; no Amex.

Grenadier SW1 £10* A

18 Wilton Row 7235 3074 5–1D

If you're looking for tradition by the bucket-load, you won't find a better place than this cutesy pub, hidden away in a Belgravia mews. Unfortunately it's in every guide-book so an appropriately Olde English clientèle is notable by its absence. The dining room is well out of our price range, but the bar is famous for its Bloody Marys (large, £4.50) and its sausages (£1 each) – what more nutritious a lunch could you want? / 9 pm.

Grumbles SW1 £17*
35 Churton St 7834 0149 2–4B
The scores of faithful locals who flock to this long-established Pimlico bistro prove that its rather '60s formula exerts a strong and unchanging appeal. Though you could just about squeeze an a la carte meal into our budget, best value is the 2-course lunch (£9.75, 3-courses for £12.25), washed down with the house wine at £9.95. / 11 pm.

Gung-Ho NW6 £ 18
328-332 West End Ln 7794 1444 1–1B
A local favourite, this stylish West Hampstead Chinese offers a friendly welcome, as well as decent fare. It would be easy to overspend, so choose carefully to keep within our budget – you might have lamb & spring onions (£6) with fried rice (£2.60) followed by toffee apple or banana (£2.80). House wine is £10 a bottle. / 11.30 pm; no Amex.

Hakkasan W1 £20* A★
8 Hanway Pl 7927 7000 4–1A
The undoubted style hit of 2001, this subterranean oriental has the most unlikely location, just off the Tottenham Court Road. Huge expenditure on the décor has partially been responsible for the success. No great surprise, then, that you won't have the opportunity to sample the restaurant in the evening within our price limit (or anything like). However, the lunchtime dim sum menu costs between £3.50 -£5 per plate, so head there to keep the costs down. You could drink the house wine, at a shocking £22 a bottle – or just quaff bottled beer at a trifling £4.50 a time instead! / 11 pm Mon-Wed, midnight Thurs-Sat; no smoking area.

Harbour City W1 £ 17
46 Gerrard St 7439 7859 4–3B
The décor may be rather understated by local standards, but this Chinatown spot still attracts a faithful following. It's at lunchtime that people seek the place out for it's notably interesting selection of dim sum, when nothing costs more than £2.80. House wine is £9.50 a bottle. / 11.30 pm.

Hard Rock Café W1 £ 20 A
150 Old Park Ln 7629 0382 3–4B
The famous queue has recently been not so much in evidence at the world's most famous theme-diner. That has more to do, though, with a decline in visitors than it does to a fall in standards, and the burgers (£7.55-£9.25) and other American fare continue to please such punters as there are. The house wine is £11.25 a bottle, or there's a wide range of cocktails, shakes and beers. / www.hardrock.com; midnight, Fri & Sat 1 am; no smoking area; no booking.

The Havelock Tavern W14 £ 20 A★
57 Masbro Rd 7603 5374 7–1C
If you want a table, you'd better arrive early at this fearsomely popular, trendified pub in the backstreets of Olympia. It's a packed, no-frills type of place whose staff sometimes leave you in no doubt as to how lucky you are to be there. The food is good, though, but is not amazingly cheap, so you'll need to pick carefully not to bust our budget – minestrone soup (£4) followed by butternut, leek, goat's cheese & tomato tart with salad (£7.50) would be economical choices, with house wine at £10 a bottle. / 10 pm; no credit cards; no booking.

Haz E1 £ 16 ★

9 Cutler St 7929 7923 9–2D

It may be a bit cramped and noisy, but this impressive-looking Turkish City newcomer is so popular simply because it has quickly developed a reputation for offering great value – book ahead, especially for a lunchtime table. Mezze is the obvious budget choice, but – with most main courses below £9 – you shouldn't find it too difficult to stay within our budget à la carte either. Wines kick off at a modest £7.75 a bottle. / 11.30 pm; no smoking area.

Hellenik W1 £19* A★

30 Thayer St 7935 1257 2–1A

If you were looking for a film set for London in the '60s, it would be hard to better this wonderfully unchanged Greek Marylebone institution, where charming service is a particular strength. You'll need to choose reasonably carefully to stay within our price limit – you might have houmous (£3.95) followed by moussaka with salad (£10.90) – but it is perfectly possible. The house wine is £10.50 a bottle. / 10.30 pm; closed Sun.

The Highgate NW5 £19* ★

79 Highgate Rd 7485 8442 8–2B

This large and loud gastropub – once a carpet showroom – has been a big hit, up Kentish Town way. There is a basement restaurant (too pricey for this guide), but for the real action you'd want to eat in the throbbing ground-floor bar anyway. Choose a tapas-type dish (from a weekly-changing list of five) for a fiver, followed perhaps by chicken escalope (£7.50), all washed down with house wine at £10.95 a bottle. / 10.30 pm; no Amex.

Hope & Sir Loin EC1 £ 20

94 Cowcross St 7253 8525 9–1A

The 'licensed breakfasts', served 7am-9.30am in the upstairs dining room of this Victorian pub near the Smithfield meat market, are so popular that it's advisable to book. Prices range from the £4.95 veggie breakfast, to a £12.95 steak extravaganza, and with beers at £3.20 a pint you can easily fill up within our budget.
At lunchtimes (noon-2pm), traditional English pub grub such as steak & kidney pie (£9) and spotted dick (£3.50) can be washed down with house wine at £12.95 a bottle. / breakfast & L only, closed Sat & Sun.

Hudson's SW15 £ 20 A

113 Lower Richmond Rd 8785 4522 10–1A

No one would claim that it's anything amazing on the food front, but this jolly Putney bistro is a consistent success-story. That's partially due to the reasonable prices of dishes such as Vietnamese summer rolls (£4.95) and shepherds pie (£9.95), and house wine at £9.95 a bottle. Breakfasts from around the world are something of a novelty feature (£5.95), and the 'happy hour' (4pm-7pm, Mon-Sat) – when house wine and many menu items come at reduced prices – offers particular budget-extending possibilities. / 10.30 pm.

Huong-Viet An Viet House N1 £ 14 ★★

12-14 Englefield Rd 7249 0877 1–1C

Ever-increasing renown has brought a greater sense of professionalism (and a drinks licence) to this large oriental refectory. It's part of a cultural centre on the outer fringes of Islington whose spacious and characterful premises were once De Beauvoir Town's public baths. The menu is vast, and – with most main courses around the £5 mark, and house wine at £7.45 a bottle – you really can stuff yourself and not worry about busting our budget. / 11 pm; closed Sun; no Amex.

The Ifield SW10 £ 20 A

59 Ifield Rd 7351 4900 5–3A

This Earl's Court gastropub is a relaxed and popular local destination. Starters cost around £5 for eggs Benedict, and the substantial main courses, which include fish & chips or bangers & mash, cost around a tenner. Puddings are of the comfort-food variety – chocolate fudge cake or bread & butter pudding (both £3.50) – and house wine costs £10 a bottle. / 11 pm; Mon-Thu D only, Fri-Sun open L & D.

Ikkyu W1 £ 18 ★

67a Tottenham Court Rd 7636 9280 2–1C

Great sushi and other tasty traditional Japanese dishes are the hallmarks of this top-value and extremely authentic-feeling basement near Goodge Street tube. You could have a large platter of sushi to share for about £12.50 at dinner, or ramen noodles with pork and vegetables (lunch only, £4.60) washed down with a glass of sake (£2.60) or a bottle of house wine (£11). / 10 pm; closed Sat & Sun L; no Switch; no smoking area.

Inaho W2 £15* ★★

4 Hereford Rd 7221 8495 6–1B

Japanese food may be becoming more available and affordable in London, but this tiny Bayswater café is still worth seeking out for its brilliant dishes at reasonable prices. The set lunch (£10) is the top-value choice – it might include salmon teriyaki, plus an appetiser, miso soup, rice and fruit. At other times, the teriyaki alone would cost £8.50 and a selection of assorted sushi is £14. The house wine is £8.50 a bottle. / 11 pm; closed Sat L & Sun; no Amex or Switch.

Incognico WC2 £20* ★★

117 Shaftesbury Ave 7836 8866 4–2B

This Gallic brasserie in Theatreland has established a reputation as a top 'value' destination, but only if you stick to the lunch and pre-theatre (5.30pm-7pm) menus, when there's a 3-course option for £12.50. Be warned, though – with house wine at £15 a bottle (£4 a glass), it does rather stretch our budget. / midnight; closed Sun.

India Club
Stand Continental Hotel WC2 **£ 13**
143 Strand 7836 0650 2–2D
Off the beaten track – up two flights of stairs in a nondescript hotel near Aldwych – this curious, Formica-clad institution has been going for some 50 years. It serves inexpensive curries at around a fiver a plate, with a good selection of vegetarian dishes and dhosas (fried pancakes, £3.60). You can bring your own wine (no corkage), or fetch a drink from the hotel bar. / 10.50 pm; closed Sun; no credit cards; need 6+ to book.

Indian Ocean SW17 **£ 15** ★
216 Trinity Rd 8672 7740 10–2C
It's nothing remarkable to look at, but this comfortable-enough Wandsworth subcontinental has long been a culinarily consistent performer. Curries are around the £6.25 mark, and the house wine £7.25 a bottle. / 11.45 pm; no smoking area.

Italian Kitchen WC1 **£15***
43 New Oxford St 7836 1011 2–1C
This unpretentious Italian, not far from the British Museum, used to be one of the best budget destinations in town. It's gone badly off the boil in recent times, but the 2-course set menu (at lunch and then between 4pm and 7pm) – perhaps buffalo mozzarella and tomato salad followed by spaghetti bolognaise for £7.95 – still makes it a worthwhile destination. The house wine is £12.95 a bottle. / www.italiankitchen.uk.com; 10.45 pm; no smoking area.

Itsu **£ 17** ★
103 Wardour St, W1 7479 4790 3–2D
118 Draycott Ave, SW3 7590 2400 5–2C
Level 2, Cabot Place East, E14 7512 5790 11–1C
These glossy Soho and Chelsea conveyor-sushi operations are as much about style as about substance, but they still make fun and elegant places for a light meal. You pay per plate (£2.50-£3.75) – which might contain anything from a conventional sushi dish to something rather more 'evolved' (and including puddings which are positively European). The house wine is £9.50 a bottle. / www.itsu.co.uk; 11 pm, W1 Fri & Sat midnight; E14 closed Sat & Sun; no smoking; no booking.

Jashan **£ 12** ★
1-2 Coronet Pde, Ealing Rd, HA0 8900 9800 1–1A
19 Turnpike Ln, N8 8340 9880 1–1C
If you haven't booked, expect to queue at these no-frills (but very professionally-run) cafés in Turnpike Lane and Wembley (veggie only). The menus offer an enormous choice, but all of good quality – at the former branch you might have the likes of sweetcorn & paneer pakoras (£3.75) followed by tandoori lamb (£5.75) and rice (£2.25). No alcohol. / www.jashanrestaurants.com; 10.45 pm; N8 D only; HA0, no smoking.

Jenny Lo's Tea House SW1 **£ 14** ★
14 Eccleston St 7259 0399 2–4B
Noodles, noodles and more noodles (£5-£7.50) are on offer at this small and welcoming parlour not far from Victoria Station, run by Jenny Lo, the daughter of Britain's most prolific Chinese cookery writer. Wash them down with house wine at £10.50 a bottle or with one of a range of therapeutic teas (crysanthemum tea, £2; 'long life tea' £1.85). / 10 pm; closed Sun; no credit cards; no booking.

Jin Kichi NW3 £ 20 ★★

73 Heath St 7794 6158 8–1A

There may not be much room for manoeuvre at this tiny Hampstead Japanese, but it's an authentic place with an excellent variety of dishes and extremely efficient staff. Starters are around £3.50 and main courses (perhaps prawn tempura) around £9.90, or you could opt for a 7-piece sushi set (£12.70). The house wine is £18 a bottle. / 11 pm; closed Mon, Tue-Fri D only, Sat & Sun open L & D.

Joy King Lau WC2 £ 16 ★

3 Leicester St 7437 1132 4–3A

This large Chinatown establishment is distinguished by very good cooking and (unusually for the area) a generally friendly welcome. Lunchtime is a good time to visit, for the notable dim sum – all dishes cost under £3, but the à la carte menu is also well realised – most main dishes cost about £6. House wine is £9.50, or drink tea (80p). / 11.30 pm.

Just Oriental SW1 £18*

19 King St 7976 2222 3–4D

A really handy destination to know about in swanky St James's, the basement bar of the imposing Just St James's restaurant is a comfortable place offering good-value oriental snacks (as well as nice, if not particularly inexpensive, cocktails). At lunchtime, there's a 3-course set menu for only £9.95. In the evenings, prices tend outside our limit, but you might still find this a handy place to share a satay selection (£15.50), say, as a prelude to a night on the town. The house wine is £12.50 a bottle.
/ www.juststjames.com/joabout.htm; midnight; closed Sat L & Sun.

K10 EC2 £ 19 ★★

20 Copthall Ave 7562 8510 9–2C

Polite, efficient service and a menu of creative dishes have made these modernistic Soho and City conveyor-belt sushi restaurants extremely popular. Dishes are relatively modestly priced (£1-£4), but go easy on the house wine, as it's £12.50 a bottle. / www.k10.net; 9.45pm; closed Sat & Sun; no smoking; no booking.

Kandoo W2 £ 14

458 Edgware Rd 7724 2428 8–4A

This Bayswater Lebanese is a useful stop-off on a grim stretch of the Edgware Road, offering competent cooking and welcoming service. Your menu choice might be chicken on the bone (£7.50) followed by Persian ice cream (£2.70). Bills are kept well under control by the fact that this is strictly a BYO place (no corkage).
/ 11.30 pm; no Amex.

Kaslik W1 £ 17

58 Greek St 7851 1585 4–2A

If they have Bohemians in Beirut – we've never been – we like to think that they might hang out in places like this low-lit and loungy (and quite tightly-packed) new Soho café. The food's not earth-shattering, but – with the likes of marinated chicken (£7.95) and houmous (£2.95), and French wine at £8.50 a bottle – this is quite a reasonably priced destination for the centre of town.
/ www.kaslikrestaurant.com; midnight.

Kastoori SW17 **£ 14** ★★

188 Upper Tooting Rd 8767 7027 10–2C

Mouthwatering Indian/East African vegetarian cooking at low low prices has for many years won a legendary reputation for this unassuming, family-run Tooting shop conversion. A la carte, most dishes are under £6. 'Thali' set lunch menus (around £8) are a particular bargain, and there's an unusually good range of wines, kicking off at £7.75 a bottle. / 10.30 pm; closed Mon L & Tue L; no Amex or Switch.

Kasturi EC3 **£ 16** ★

57 Aldgate High St 7480 7402 9–2D

On the eastern fringe of the City, this smart restaurant is establishing itself as a popular destination for quality subcontinental fare at reasonable prices; some dishes – such as tandoori nisha (£7.95) – are slightly unusual, too. The house wine is £10.95 a bottle. / www.kasturi-restaurant.co.uk; 11 pm; closed Sun; no smoking area.

Kazan SW1 **£ 19** A

93-94 Wilton Rd 7233 7100 2–4B

Pimlico, to a remarkable extent, remains something of a void for quality dining, so this low-lit new Turkish restaurant (related to the Sofra chain) has quickly established itself as a buzzy and popular local destination. You'd have to select with some care to stay within our price-limit – perhaps choosing a mixed salad with feta (£3.50), followed by a lamb kebab (£9.50) – but, with house wine at £12.50 a bottle, it's perfectly possible. / 11 pm.

Kennington Lane SE11 **£18*** ★

205-209 Kennington Ln 7793 8313 1–3C

This chic brasserie (somewhat out of place in grungy Kennington) has been a slightly inconsistent performer in recent times, but the 2-course set lunch and early evening menu (£11.50) offers the opportunity to check the place out at relatively low risk. Chicken and spinach terrine, followed by grilled tuna with ratatouille, would be typical choices, accompanied by a bottle of the house wine at £10.50. / www.kenningtonlanerestaurant.com; 10.30 pm; closed Sat L; smoking in bar only.

Khan's W2 **£ 10** ★

13-15 Westbourne Grove 7727 5420 6–1C

It must be some measure of the attractions of the cooking that this vast Bayswater subcontinental – often likened to an Indian railway station – seems to have survived its transition to being a 'dry' zone (you can't even BYO). Decent curries for around £3.95 are at the root of its appeal. / www.khansrestaurant.com; 11.45 pm; no smoking area.

Khan's of Kensington SW7 **£ 17** ★

3 Harrington Rd 7581 2900 5–2B

This more-than-serviceable South Kensington subcontinental offers a standard tandoori menu, plus a sprinkling of more unusual dishes, such as stuffed lotus leaves (£2.55). Main courses – often realised with quite a light touch – generally cost around £6.95, vegetable side dishes are £3.10 and kulfi is £2.95. The house wine is £9.95 a bottle. / 11.15 pm, Fri & Sat 11.45 pm; no smoking area.

Khew W1 £20*

43 South Molton St 7408 2236 3–2B

You wouldn't expect a Japanese 'raw bar' on the fringe of Mayfair to be a super-budget destination, and this stylish new establishment certainly isn't. Head for the set lunch (£12.95), though, and three interesting courses – perhaps miso soup, crispy prawn & coriander dumplings and chicken Penang served with steamed jasmine rice – are yours for less than the price of a hankie in many of the neighbouring boutiques. Wine, starting from £15.75 a bottle, is quite pricey, but the economical will drink green tea (£2.50). Dinner is not really an option. / www.khew.co.uk; closed Sun.

Khyber Pass SW7 £ 14

21 Bute St 7589 7311 5–2B

Despite some grumblings from old regulars about new ownership, the 'appeal' of this unpretentious – perhaps excessively so – South Kensington Indian seems little changed in years. For top value, share a 'Khyber Pass Special' (spring chicken in a mildly-spiced sauce, £12.50 for two), but even à la carte you can comfortably stay within our budget. The house wine is £9.25 a bottle. / 11.15 pm; need 4+ to book.

Konditor & Cook SE1 £ 16 ★★

66 The Cut 7620 2700 9–4A

Famous for its large selection of delicious handmade cakes and pastries, this café by the Young Vic is certainly not the place if you're on a diet! Breakfast is available from 8.30am-11.30am, and includes everything from muffins to a full traditional English breakfast. Lunch might include soup with a herb and cheese scone (£3.75), followed by chicken and avocado with bacon club sandwich (£6.95), washed down with house wine at £12.95 a bottle. / 8 pm; closed Sun; no Amex; no smoking area.

Krungtap SW5 £ 13

227 Old Brompton Rd 7259 2314 5–2A

It's by no means the 'destination' it once was, but this unpretentious Thai café maintains a regular following from Earl's Court locals, as it still offers good basic curries at reasonable cost (generally around £6.25). The house wine is £8 a bottle. / 10.30 pm.

Kulu Kulu £ 17 ★★

76 Brewer St, W1 7734 7316 3–2D
51-53 Shelton St, WC2 7240 5687 4–2C
39 Thurloe Pl, SW7 7589 2225 5–2C

Less gimmicky than many of their competitors, these genuine 'kaiten' (conveyor-belt sushi) bars concentrates on offering value in the food department. Prices are not high, with sushi sets ranging from £1.20 for 4 salmon rolls to £10 for a mixed 16-piece sashimi set, and noodle dishes around £3. Green tea is free, and house wine £12 a bottle. / 10 pm, SW7 10.30 pm; closed Sun; no Amex; no smoking area; no smoking, WC2; no booking.

Kwan Thai SE1 **£15***

Unit 1, Hay's Galleria 7403 7373 9–4D

This Thai restaurant has a pleasant riverside location – with outside tables on sunny days – that's just a brief stroll from the City. It offers a £7.95 quick lunch menu – you may choose corn cakes or spring rolls, followed by red chicken curry, chicken with ginger or pork with garlic & pepper, all served with rice. For an extra pound you could substitute your main course for a noodle dish, such as pad Thai. The house wine is £11.25 a bottle.
/ www.kwanthairestaurant.co.uk; 10 pm; closed Sat L & Sun; no smoking area.

Lahore Kebab House E1 **£ 13** ★★

2 Umberston St 7488 2551 11–1A

Every meat-eating lover of Indian food should make the trek to this famed East End Pakistani institution at least once. Start with spicy kebabs (75p) and roti (also 50p), or tikka (£2.50), before moving on to karahi gosht (lamb balti, £6) or the superb lamb chops (£6.50). Vegetable dishes such as sag aloo (spinach and potato) or tarka dhal (lentils) all cost £5. Finish with kheer (a sort of rice pudding with cardamom). BYO (no corkage). / 11.30 pm; no Amex; need 12+ to book.

Lan Na Thai SW11 **£20*** ★

2 Lombard Rd 7924 6090 10–1C

Given its odd but interesting Battersea location – on the other side of the river from Chelsea Harbour – you'd be unlikely to come across this grand riverside restaurant by accident, but it's still developed something of a name for the quality of its Thai cuisine. Sadly, the only time it comes within our budget is for lunch, when £12.50 buys you the likes of chicken and coconut soup, beef curry, aubergines in yellow bean sauce and jasmine rice, followed by mango sticky rice. Wine prices, starting at £18 a bottle, are rather exorbitant. / 10.30 pm.

Lansdowne NW1 **£20*** A

90 Gloucester Ave 7483 0409 8–3B

One of London's first wave of gastropubs, this riotously popular Primrose Hill spot now also boasts a calmer and more expensive dining room upstairs. Eat in the bar, from the blackboard menu, though, and you'll be well fed. Robust soups (£4), pâtés (£5.50-£7) and pizzas (from £6.50) are among the budget choice, but you can push the boat out quite a bit further if you wish. The house wine is £11.50 a bottle. / 10 pm; closed Mon L; no Amex; book only for upstairs.

La Lanterna SE1 **£20-**

6-8 Mill St 7252 2420 11–2A

Five minutes from Tower Bridge – an area not best known for budget dining opportunities – this bustling and unpretentious Italian is worth knowing about. While it's no bargain-basement destination, the food is good quality, and the service friendly. Pastas range from £7.50 to £12, followed perhaps by a tiramisu (£4). The house wine is £11.95 a bottle. / www.millsteetcafe.co.uk; 11 pm; closed Sun.

Latymers W6 £ 14 ★

157 Hammersmith Rd 8741 2507 7–2C

The area around the Hammersmith roundabout is hardly awash with foodie possibilities, which makes the Thai dining room of this grim-looking pub all the more notable. At lunch, one-plate dishes (for around a fiver) such as pad Thai or jungle curry with rice are the top-value choice. In the evening, there are starters, too, such as deep-fried stuffed chicken wings (£2.95). The house wine is £10.50 a bottle. / 10 pm; closed Sun D; no smoking; no booking at L.

Lemonia NW1 £ 19 Ⓐ

89 Regent's Park Rd 7586 7454 8–3B

You'll definitely need to book if you want to dine at this ever-popular, family-run taverna in Primrose Hill. You can probably just turn up on spec for lunch, though, which is a particularly good time for the bargain-hunter, whether you go for the 2-course menu (£7.25), or even the 3-course 'special' (£8.50). There's a range of Greek wines – house vino comes by the litre (£12.75). / 11.30 pm; closed Sat L & Sun D; no Amex.

Levant W1 £15* Ⓐ

Jason Court, 76 Wigmore St 7224 1111 3–1A

If your credit card is worn out by a morning in Selfridges, head round the corner to this funky North African restaurant bar. You can sample two courses for just £8.50 (served with complimentary mint tea, baklava and Turkish delight). You might have fried courgettes with mint and garlic salad followed by pomegranate marinated salmon. Go easy on the house vino, though, as it's £14 a bottle – indicative of the sort of prices you'd pay à la carte. / www.levantrestaurant.co.uk; 11.30 pm.

Lisboa Patisserie W10 £ 4 ★★

57 Golborne Rd 8968 5242 6–1A

This Portuguese pâtisserie, in North Kensington, has long been favoured by the area's trendy young things, so you'll have to fight for a seat on weekends and sunny days. The main attraction is the coffee and custard tarts (both under £1), but there's also a good selection of sandwiches (around £1.10). / 7.30 pm; L + early evening only; no Amex; no booking.

Little Basil NW3 £ 18

82 Hampstead High St 7794 6238 8–2A

A very handy destination, in the heart of Hampstead, this new Thai restaurant – which occupies charming premises whose occupants change surprisingly frequently – is a destination well worth knowing about. Though prices are reasonable (and can accommodate a full meal within our budget at any time), this is not really the sort of place where you'd spend an evening, but it's very handy for a break from shopping, ideally for the quick lunch menu (£8). The house wine is £10.50 a bottle. / 11 pm; no Amex; no smoking area.

Little Bay £ 14 A

228 Belsize Rd, NW6 7372 4699 1–2B
171 Farringdon Rd, EC1 7278 1234 9–1A
Rustic charm and amazingly low prices make for a busy atmosphere at this Kilburn bistro, where you'd be hard pushed to blow our budget however far out you pushed the boat. The set price menu (available lunch and dinner until 7.15) offers two courses for £5.95 and three for £7.45 – perhaps marinated baby octopus, breast of chicken stuffed with foie gras and mushrooms and white chocolate and pistachio parfait. The house wine is £9.35 a bottle. / 11.45 pm; NW6 no credit cards, EC1 no Amex; no smoking area; NW6 need 4+ to book.

LMNT E8 £ 18 A

316 Queensbridge Rd 7249 6727 1–2D
It's not only because Dalston is hardly over-blessed with quality eating-places that this former boozer has made quite a stir. It is in fact mainly due to the startling operatic-Egyptian décor, though the food – including dishes such as roast pigeon breast (£2.95) and rib-eye steak (£7.95) – is perfectly well done. The house wine is £10.90 a bottle. / www.lmnt.co.uk; 11 pm; no Amex.

Lobster Pot SE11 £18* A★

3 Kennington Ln 7582 5556 1–3C
This family-run seafood restaurant occupies a grungy location on a busy corner of Kennington Lane. Its bizarre 'sunken schooner' décor, therefore, comes as quite a shock. If you happen to be in the vicinity around lunchtime it's well worth remembering the excellent-value set meal – for £10 you might have New Zealand mussels followed by grilled sardines with Creole sauce (and for an extra £3.50 you could add a dessert such as a pancake with mango sauce), washed down with house wine at £11.50 a bottle. Don't event think of trying to dine here within our budget.
/ www.lobsterpotrestaurant.co.uk; 11 pm; closed Sun & Mon; booking: max 8.

Lomo SW10 £ 19 A

222-224 Fulham Rd 7349 8848 5–3B
This modern-style tapas bar has established itself as something of a fixture on Chelsea's 'Beach' (as this short stretch of the Fulham Road has, rather whimsically, become known in some quarters). It offers tasty snacks in a comfortable but unpretentious setting. Dishes, such as sizzling tiger prawns, rocket and manchego salad and spicy potatoes, are generally between £4 and £7, and the house vino is £10.50 a bottle. / www.lomo.co.uk; 11.30 pm; closed weekday L; no booking after 8.30 pm.

The Lord Palmerston NW5 £ 18 A★

33 Dartmouth Park Hill 7485 1578 8–1B
Otherwise a quintessential gastropub, this barely-converted boozer near Archway lacks any of the 'attitude' that sometimes comes with the breed. Quality is consistent, and prices – such as smoked salmon and baby tiger prawn salad with artichoke, asparagus & rocket (£9.50) and deep fried squid with new potato salad & aioli dressing (£10.50) – are reasonable. Starters, maybe soup or pasta, are under a fiver, and puds, such as banoffee pie, are £3.50. The house wine is £9.80 a bottle. / 10 pm; no Amex; no booking.

Lots Road SW10 £ 20 A
114 Lots Rd 7352 6645 5–4B
Plain and simple gastropub fare – burgers, salads and so forth, with few dishes more than £10 – are the stock in trade of this airy, elegant and comfortable gastropub, on the way in to Chelsea Harbour. The house wine is £11 a bottle. / 10 pm.

Lou Pescadou SW5 £19* ★
241 Old Brompton Rd 7370 1057 5–3A
Perhaps appropriately for a fish restaurant, standards at this long-established Earl's Court fish restaurant seems to continually ebbing and flowing, but at the moment seem to be at something of a high water mark. The 3-course set lunch menu (£10.90, £14.50 at weekends), however, has long been a reliable beacon of value – you might start with mussels with white wine and shallots, followed by shoulder of lamb, finishing with chocolate mousse. The house wine is £10.90 a bottle. / midnight.

Lowiczanka W6 £ 12
238-246 King St 8741 3225 7–2B
This cosy cafeteria, attached to the Polish Cultural Centre on the main drag in Hammersmith, is well known locally for its reasonable pricing. But while you could eat here at any time quite comfortably within our budget, why not eat lunch amongst the crowd of Polish emigrés who congregate for the £7.50 3-course set menu – you might have Polish sausages, minced pork balls in parsley sauce and homemade plum cake. House wine is £9.50, or you could choose from the wide variety of Polish beers and vodkas. / 10 pm.

Luigi's WC2 £ 20 A
15 Tavistock St 7240 1795 4–3D
This Covent Garden Italian is in a grand traditional style some might find a little passé nowadays, and it's generally rather pricey too. The 2-course pre-theatre set menu (£11, until 7.30pm), however, is well worth knowing about – you might have venison pâté or minestrone, followed by grilled salmon, with house wine at £13.50 a bottle. / 11.30 pm; closed Sun.

Lundum's SW7 £19* A★★
119 Old Brompton Rd 7373 7774 5–2B
This pretty, family-run Danish restaurant in South Kensington has attracted a devoted following, and it's the sort of place which would be ideal for a (slightly old-fashioned) date. It's out of our price-bracket in the evening, but makes an ideal venue for a relaxed lunch, when the 2-course menu (£12.75) – your selection might be salmon tartare with dill foam, followed by entrecote with tomatoes, spinach & roasted potatoes – can be accompanied by house wine at £13.25 a bottle. / 11 pm; closed Sun D.

Ma Cuisine TW1 £ 18 ★★
6 Whitton Rd 8607 9849 1–4A
If you've lived in London for a few years you may do a double take looking at the menu at this simple Twickenham bistro. The prices are such good value it looks like it's ten years out of date. Starters (say boundin blanc in pastry) – come in at about a fiver; main dishes (perhaps pork belly), come fully garnished for £8-£9 and puds are £3.50 (pot au chocolat, for instance). With top local chef John McClement in the kitchen – his main place two doors down charges £60 a head – it adds up to incredible value. Drink house wine at £3 a glass. / 11.30 pm; closed Sun.

Ma Goa SW15 **£ 19** ★

244 Upper Richmond Rd 8780 1767 10–2B

The atmosphere of this family-run Putney bistro is rather different from your typical London subcontinental, and the cuisine (Goan) is rather out of the ordinary too. Top value is to be had from the 2-course set menu (£7.95 at lunch, £9 in the early evening) from which you might choose shrimps 'balchao' cooked in tomato & pickling masala, followed by Goan pork vindaloo. There are also interesting specialities à la carte, including sausages with cinnamon & cloves (£4) and chicken cooked in 'amot-tik' (Goan hot & sour sauce, £8), though you'd need to exercise some care to stay within our price-limit. The house wine is £9.50 a bottle. / www.ma-goa.com; 11 pm; closed Mon, Tue–Sat D only, Sun open L & D.

Made in Italy SW3 **£ 20** ★

249 King's Rd 7352 1880 5–3C

Pizza and pasta dishes (around £9.50) are the specialities at this jolly and quite authentic – that's to say smoky and overcrowded – Chelsea spot. The house wine is £11.50 a bottle. / 11.30 pm; closed L Mon-Thurs; no credit cards.

Madhu's UB1 **£ 16** ★★

39 South Rd 8574 1897 1–3A

The Punjabi-influenced menu at this stellar Southall Indian spans the range from specialities such as boozi bafu (rich lamb stew, £7) to the more prosaic chicken tikka masala (£8). House wine is £8 a bottle, and there's also a good range of imported beers. / www.madhusonline.com; 11.30 pm; closed Tue, Sat L & Sun L.

Maggiore's WC2 **£18*** Ⓐ★

33 King St 7379 9696 4–3C

If one could only give the budget diner one piece of advice, it would be 'avoid Covent Garden'. This injunction is, fortunately, not applicable to this attractive and welcoming Continental (Italo-French) spot. It's particularly worth knowing about for the set lunch and pre-theatre menus (noon-3pm, 5pm-7pm) – for £10, you might have chilled cucumber soup followed by duck confit with cabbage and celeriac purée. Consistent with à la carte menu prices that are well outside our budget, the house wine is a weighty £14.50 a bottle. / www.maggiores.co.uk; 10.45 pm.

Maghreb N1 **£ 19**

189 Upper St 7226 2305 8–2D

Especially if you're looking for a group venue in Islington, it's well worth checking out this comfortable Moroccan bistro, where you can dine à la carte quite comfortably within our price-limit. Starters are the likes of merguez (spicy lamb) sausages (£4.65) and your main course might be aromatic duck tajine with apricots (£9.50). A bottle of the house wine is £10.95. / www.maghrebrestaurant.co.uk; 11.30 pm; D only.

Maison Bertaux W1 **£ 6** Ⓐ★

28 Greek St 7437 6007 4–2A

Gallic charm and idiosyncratic service still make Soho's oldest pâtisserie (est 1871) a destination of some note. It's a delightful place to breakfast on coffee (£1.50) and croissants (from £1.50), or to while away the afternoon scoffing mouth-watering cream cakes (£2.20-£4.50). / 8 pm; no credit cards; no smoking area; no booking.

Malabar W8 £ 18 A★

27 Uxbridge St 7727 8800 6–2B

A perennial local favourite, this civilised subcontinental, just off Notting Hill Gate, offers reliably good cooking at reasonable prices. Top value is the Sunday buffet lunch (£8.50), but even à la carte you can dine here quite comfortably within our price limit – most curries are under £7 (more for duck or seafood), veggie side dishes are £3.85, and rice and naans are around £2. House wine is £9.25 a bottle, or a Cobra beer is £2.80.

/ www.malabar-restaurant.co.uk; 11.15 pm; no Amex.

Malabar Junction WC1 £20* A★

107 Gt Russell St 7580 5230 2–1C

The bland façade of this smart Bloomsbury Indian belies the civilisation of its rear conservatory, and gives few clues as to the interesting Keralan cuisine on offer within. There's ample choice for vegetarians (spinach vadi, £3.50) and lots of fish (Cochin prawn curry, £9.50; fish curry £8), and the house wine is reasonably priced at £10 a bottle. Helpful staff encourage experimentation.

/ 11.30 pm; no smoking area.

The Mall Tavern W8 £ 9* ★

71-73 Palace Gardens Ter 7727 3805 6–2B

This plainly refurbished gastropub offers a stylish venue for a light weekday lunch, just off Notting Hill Gate – prices at other times somewhat exceed our budget. For £7.50, the midday menu offers a main course – such as fusilli with sweet tomatoes, courgettes & mascarpone, or sautéed mushroom bruschetta with shaved parmesan – accompanied by your choice of a glass of wine or a pint. / 10.30 pm.

Mandalay W2 £ 13 ★★

444 Edgware Rd 7258 3696 8–4A

Just around the corner from Lords, this friendly, family-run business dishes up some interesting and well-spiced Burmese cooking (which, as you'll know, combines Indian and oriental influences). The lunchtime special, at £5.90, buys you a selection of dishes (and coffee) – at other times, main dishes, such as crispy fried fish in spicy sauce, or noodles with chicken and coconut, will cost about the same amount. With starters around £3 and house wine at £7.90 a bottle, this is one of the few places were you really can dine without stinting yourself, and yet remain comfortably within our budget. / 10.30 pm; closed Sun; no smoking.

Mandarin Kitchen W2 £17* ★★

14-16 Queensway 7727 9012 6–2C

The bargain-hunter might be tempted to plump for the 3-course set menu here (£10.90), but sadly that doesn't usually include the seafood dishes which are the whole point of this famous (if basic) Bayswater Chinese – scallops (£2.20 each) and oysters with ginger and spring onions (£7.90) are typical of the sort of dishes which make a visit here a top culinary deal. (Tip: share a lobster between 2-3 people, for around £28.) The house wine is £10.50 a bottle.

/ 11.15 pm.

Mangal E8 £ 8 ★★

10 Arcola St 7275 8981 1–1C

This Dalston café doesn't have the loveliest of locations, but is worth a detour as one of the best cheap eats in town. There's no menu. You make your choice from the array of hearty kebabs at the glass-fronted chill counter which the chefs then prepare at the large grill dominating the front room. Dishes come served with rice, and you can also ask the waiter for salad and for what starters are 'on' that day. All-in-all, even with BYO wine, you won't get far into double digits per head. / midnight; no credit cards; need 10+ to book.

Mango Room NW1 £ 20 A★

10 Kentish Town Rd 7482 5065 8–3B

With its bright décor and imaginative British-Caribbean fusion cuisine, this Camden Town spot continues to please its fairly fickle local market. If, after a starter of, say, crab & potato balls (£4.50), you don't fancy the "famous" Camden curried goat, you could always opt for likes of jerk chicken – main dishes tend to be just under a tenner. The house wine will set you back £11.95 a bottle. / 10.45 pm; closed Mon L; no Amex.

Marine Ices NW3 £ 17

8 Haverstock Hill 7482 9003 8–2B

The Italian cooking at this long-in-the-tooth Chalk Farm institution – which is strongest in pizza and pasta dishes (around £7) – may not be art, but it isn't terribly pricey either. What's more – as any north London kid will tell you – the real point of a visit is the mouth-watering array of sorbets and ices (whose quality is such that they have in days gone by also supplied people like the Savoy). A sundae of vanilla ice cream with chocolate sauce and ginger is £4.50, or single scoops of sorbet are just £1.50. Grown-up children can drink wine at £8.90 per bottle. / 11 pm; no Amex; no smoking area.

Masala Zone W1 £ 14

9 Marshall St 7287 9966 3–2D

An ideal destination to recover from shopping in nearby Carnaby Street, this welcoming restaurant serves Indian street food in a comfortably modern canteen environment. For maximum budget-control go for a one-tray meal – perhaps a lamb thali (£8.50) – washed down with house wine at £9.75 a bottle, or an Indian beer at £3.10. / www.realindianfood.com; 11pm; no Amex; no smoking; no booking.

Mawar W2 £ 14 ★

175a Edgware Rd 7262 1663 6–1D

If you were going to run an award for glossiest restaurant in the capital, then this cellar down a shabby staircase on a busy stretch of road wouldn't be a strong contender. Once inside, it has a certain tacky charm, though, and the bargain, er basement prices for the hearty platters of enjoyable Malaysian grub should certainly bring a smile to your face. The place is unlicensed, but you can BYO (no corkage). / 10 pm; no smoking area.

Mediterraneo W11 £18* 🅐★

37 Kensington Park Rd 7792 3131 6–1A

Sibling to the ever-popular Osteria Basilico, this mock-rustic Italian has firmly established itself as a linchpin of the Notting Hill scene – so arrive early. It's quite pricey à la carte, but the 2-course set lunch (£11.50, including coffee), from which you might choose authentic Minestrone soup followed by salmon with sauteed spinach, offers a chance to eat here within our budget. House wine is £10.50 a bottle. / 11.30 pm; booking: max 8.

Mela WC2 £ 20 ★

152-156 Shaftesbury Ave 7836 8635 4–2B

'Country-style cooking' – that's Indian country-style cooking – has made a big name for this busy restaurant near Cambridge Circus. You can just about dine within our budget, but the real focus of interest for those counting the pennies is the lunchtime 'paratha' concept – select a bread or pancake with a choice of hot fillings to create a snack, such as chicken tikka naan (£3.95). The pre-theatre 3-course menu (5.30pm-7pm daily) is also of note – it's £10.95, the same as a bottle of the house wine.
/ www.melarestaurant.co.uk; 11.30 pm; no smoking area.

Melati W1 £ 17

21 Great Windmill St 7437 2745 3–2D

For a quick and interesting meal in the heart of the West End, you really won't do much better than this long-established (and rather basic) Indonesian bistro. It offers a long and comprehensive menu, from which a mixed satay platter (£6.25) and crispy banana fritters (£2.85) would be typical choices, or you might make a meal of starters – £9.95 buys a large selection. The house wine is £9.95 a bottle. / 11.30 pm, Fri & Sat 12.30 am.

Meridiana W8 £19*

59 Marloes Rd 7376 9550 5–1A

This long-established – and, in the nicest sense, rather tacky – Kensington trattoria is worth knowing about for an inexpensive meal in an otherwise pricey area. Every day, for lunch and dinner, you can have a 2-course meal for £10 (or 3 for £12.50) – perhaps asparagus & Parmesan gratinée, followed by chicken with cream & mushroom sauce, finishing with an Italian summer pudding. House wine is £10.50 a bottle. Add a £1.50 cover charge in the evenings. / 11 pm; closed Sun.

Meson don Felipe SE1 £ 15 🅐

53 The Cut 7928 3237 9–4A

It's the crowd and the authentically Spanish atmosphere which are the real attractions of this popular and long-established tapas bar, not far from Waterloo (great for a pre-Old Vic bite). That's not to detract from the quality of the tapas, however – all the usual dishes are available (£2-£5.50). The house wine is £10.75 a bottle, or drink sangria (£11.50 for a large jug). / 11 pm; closed Sun; no Amex; no booking after 8 pm.

Le Metro SW3 **£ 20**

28 Basil St 7591 1213 5–1D

In a quiet street by Harrods, in the basement of a discreet hotel, this wine bar/restaurant offers an ideal refuge from Knightsbridge consumerism. Starters (around £5.50) and main courses (around £9) are all quite well done – you might start with duck spring rolls, followed by chargrilled salmon nicoise. Wine is a big interest – le patron has his own cuvée – with the house selection priced at £10.95 a bottle. / www.capitalgrp.co.uk; 9.45 pm; closed Sun L & D, but open for breakfast; no smoking area.

Mildred's W1 **£ 18** ★

45 Lexington St 7494 1634 3–2D

This popular veggie café moved across Soho in recent times to the more spacious (and harder-to-find) premises once occupied by the Lexington. Panfried cherry tomatoes, halloumi and wilted spinach (£4.25), and 'masa harina' (£6.50) – cornflour and butternut squash balls served in a flour tortilla with sour cream, harissa sauce and chunky salsa – are typical dishes. Or try the 'burger' of the day (£6.20), washed down with organic house wine at £10.50 a bottle. / 11 pm; closed Sun; only Switch; no smoking; no booking.

Mirch Masala **£ 10** ★★

1416 London Road, SW16 8679 1828 10–2C

213 Upper Tooting Rd, SW17 8672 7500 10–2D

For top-quality Indian food at rock-bottom prices, you won't do much better than these plain but welcoming canteens in Norbury and, more recently, Tooting. For the best value get there between noon and 4pm for the buffet (£5.99), which offers three starters and five main courses, as well as rice and naan bread. BYO – no corkage charge. / midnight; no Amex; no smoking, SW17.

Mohsen W14 **£ 15** ★

152 Warwick Rd 7602 9888 7–1D

It may not have much of a view – the Olympia Homebase is not what even an estate agent would call a 'feature' – but this no-nonsense café packs 'em in with its generous and good-value Persian cooking. Starters, such as aubergine dip, are around the £2.50 mark, and main courses, principally lamb kebabs, are around the £8-£10 mark. BYO – no corkage. / 11.30 pm; no credit cards.

Mon Plaisir WC2 **£14*** A★

19-21 Monmouth St 7836 7243 4–2B

The pre-theatre menu (table must be vacated by 8pm) at this wonderfully old-fashioned Gallic bistro has long offered some of the very best value in the West End. Your 2-course menu (£13.95) might include chicken Caesar salad followed by roast marinated salmon, a glass of wine, coffee and service. Do note that prices at other times are well outside our limit. / www.monplaisir.co.uk; 11.15 pm; closed Sat L & Sun.

Moro EC1 **£18*** A★★

34-36 Exmouth Mkt 7833 8336 9–1A

This Moorish restaurant in Clerkenwell is that rarest of beasts – a continuing fashionable success. Though its prices are reasonable, it is therefore no great surprise that it's a little outside our budget à la carte. The bar, however, offers affordable tapas dishes – a selection might include Manchego cheese (£3.50) and houmous (£3) served with home-made bread – washed down with house wine at £11 a bottle. / www.moro.co.uk; 10.30 pm; closed Sat L & Sun.

Moshi Moshi £ 17

Canada Pl, E14 7512 9201 11–1C
Unit 24, Liverpool St Station, EC2 7247 3227 9–2D
7-8 Limeburner Ln, EC4 7248 1808 9–2A

Conveyor-belt sushi cafés – where you take your dishes off the belt as it passes in front of you, laden with goodies, and pay per plate (£1.20-£3.50) – may seem ten-a-penny nowadays. These City establishments, however, were the originals of the breed, and still offer good value and are extremely popular, especially at lunchtime. Sushi sets are also available from £11.40 upwards. The house wine is £11.50 a bottle, or Japanese beer at £2.90 a bottle.
/ www.moshimoshi.co.uk; 9.30 pm; closed Sat & Sun, EC4 L only; no Amex; no smoking; EC2 & E14 no booking.

Mr Kong WC2 £ 15 ★

21 Lisle St 7437 7341 4–3A

Sadly, there aren't actually that many places in Chinatown which one can positively recommend.The cooking at this one, however, is above-average and includes some interesting options, such as main courses of beef in chilli and black bean sauce (£5.90) and deep-fried baby squid (£6.50). Starters are around the £3.50 mark, and house wine is £7.80 a bottle. / 2.45 am.

Nautilus NW6 £ 16 ★

27-29 Fortune Green Rd 7435 2532 1–1B

A refurb a year or so ago swept away the former '60s style of this West Hampstead veteran chippy, but fortunately the change of style seems to have had little impact on the cooking. As ever, all the fish is coated in matzo-meal rather than batter before frying. Start with smoked salmon (£3) before tackling a plate of cod 'n' chips (£8.50), washed down with house wine at £8.50 a bottle.
/ 10 pm; closed Sun; no Amex; no booking.

Nayaab SW6 £ 17

309 New King's Rd 7731 6993 10–1B

The proud boast of this Parsons Green Indian is that its menu includes dishes that are unavailable elsewhere, such as nihari (slow-cooked lamb, £7.95) and twelve kadi murg (chicken in a unique sauce, £7.95). More conventional dishes are mostly under £6, with an impressive range of biryanis from just a pound more. A new range of special lunchtime dishes is also available, for under a fiver. The house wine is £10 a bottle. / midnight; D only.

New Mayflower W1 £ 18 ★

68-70 Shaftesbury Ave 7734 9207 4–3A

Don't be put off by the external appearance of this authentic Chinatown spot, where a clean and unfussy interior is disguised by odd, tinted windows. For the best chow, avoid the set menus, and try the more unusual dishes – even though the staff can be brusque don't be afraid to ask for advice. Most main dishes are about £8 and the house wine is £8.50 a bottle. / 3.45 am; D only.

New Tayyab E1 £ 10 A★

83 Fieldgate St 7247 9543 9–2D

Heaving from early evening onwards, this East End pub-conversion Pakistani offers good-quality, mainly meaty cooking to a wide-ranging crowd – even the odd Euro seems to stray into this unfamiliar territory! This is a BYO place, so you really can keep your budget strictly under control, especially when few dishes will set you back more than a fiver (and many are much less).
/ www.tayyabs.co.uk; 11.30 pm; no booking at L.

New World W1 £ 19

1 Gerrard Pl 7734 0677 4–3A

It's the lunchtime dim sum (from £1.80 per dish) – served from trolleys – which is the culinary highlight of this large and chaotic Chinatown landmark. Its gaudy red and gold façade may appear to more striking effect in the evening, but dinner is a less exciting affair (though the long menu offers ample choice within our budget). House wine is £11.50 a bottle. / 11.45 pm; xmas & Boxing Day; no smoking area; no booking, Sun L.

Nicolas Bar à Vins SW10 £ 16 ★

442 King's Rd 7352 9706 5–3B

The French, unlike the English, have no hang-up about offering good simple food in tacky (and sometimes rather tatty) surroundings. To that extent, this new World's End bistro (attached to a branch of the famous wine merchant) is one of the most authentic places to eat in London – it's nothing to look at, but realisation of such classics as vegetable terrine (£4.50) or smoked salmon with crème fraîche (£9.30) is always good. Best of all though, you can drink any bottle from the shelves without paying any corkage! / www.nicolas.com; 11 pm.

Noor Jahan £ 20

2a Bina Gdns, SW5 7373 6522 5–2B
26 Sussex Pl, W2 7402 2332 6–1D

The smart original branch of what is now a mini-curry-chain has offered pretty decent value to the burghers of South Kensington for nearly thirty years, and it has recently celebrated its longevity by launching a Bayswater sibling. Chicken tikka masala costs £7.95 (with pilau rice, £2.50) and lamb kebabs are £6. Wash it down with house wine at £9.95 a bottle. / 11 pm; no smoking area, W2.

North Sea Fish WC1 £ 18 ★

7-8 Leigh St 7387 5892 8–4C

This long-established chippy may be located in deepest Bloomsbury, but its dining room has something of the ambience of a seaside tea room. It's a more than usually comfortable institution of its type, and the fish 'n' chips (£8-£11) are pretty good too – early evenings are especially busy, so it's worth booking ahead. The house wine is £9.95 a bottle. / www.northseafishrestaurant.co.uk; 10.30 pm; closed Sun.

Noto EC2 £ 18 ★

2-3 Bassishaw Highwalk 7256 9433 9–2B

Filling fare without pretensions is the theme at this transport-café-style Japanese establishment in the Barbican, which offers a good range of sushi (£1.50-£3.20 per piece), noodles and curries (both around £7-£9). The house wine is £9.90 a bottle.
/ www.noto.co.uk; 9.45 pm; closed Sat & Sun; no Amex; no smoking at L.

O'Zon TW1 **£ 19**

33-35 London Rd 8891 3611 1–4A

If you're looking for a decent place to eat in the heart of downtown Twickenham, this Chinese restaurant is worth seeking out. An all-you-can-eat menu is available at any time for £14.50 – not very different from the amount you'd probably spend à la carte. The house wine is £9.80 a bottle. / 11 pm.

Old Parr's Head W14 **£ 14**

120 Blythe Rd 7371 4561 7–1C

This traditional Olympia pub provides the setting for some basic, tasty and cheap Thai cooking (which in summer can be enjoyed in a nice rear courtyard). A typical meal would be mixed starters (£7 for two people) followed by red Thai curry with rice (£6). House wine is £9.90 a bottle. / 10 pm; no Amex.

Opera NW3 **£16*** A★

68 Heath St 7794 6666 8–1A

This jolly oriental (also, slightly confusingly, known as China Dream) – conveniently located in a stylishly-converted boozer – has become a popular Hampstead destination for informal celebrations. It's a little beyond our budget à la carte, but you can always opt for dim sum (served all day every day, with dishes costing from £2.50 each). The house wine is £11 a bottle.

Ophim W1 **£19*** ★

139 Wardour St 7434 9899 3–2D

This richly-decorated new Soho Indian offers a treat for the budget diner – a buffet where £13.50 (£7.50 at lunch) literally buys you everything on the menu! All the dishes are delivered to your table, and re-filled when empty – the menu might include tomato & lemon soup, aubergine tandoori and tilapia fish in kaliwada batter. Only desserts (£3) and drinks (Cobra, £3) cost extra. / www.ophim.com; 11 pm, Fri & Sat 11.30 pm; no smoking area.

Orangery W8 **£ 19** A

Kensington Palace 7376 0239 5–1A

When enjoying a leisurely stroll in Kensington Gardens on a sunny day, there could be no better venue for a light bite. It was designed for Queen Anne in 1704 as a greenhouse in which to hold court summer entertainments. With starters under a fiver and main courses around £8, you could easily fit a 2-course meal inside our budget. But this really is the place for a traditional afternoon tea: splash out on 'The Royal Ascot' (£14.75), which includes a smoked salmon sandwich, a fruit scone with clotted cream and strawberries, Belgian chocolate cake and tea or coffee.

Oriental City Food Court NW9 **£ 12**

399 Edgware Rd 8200 6888 1–1A

If you want to sample exotic delights of the Orient for not that much more than the price of a tube fare (albeit to distant Colindale), it's well worth a trip to this Japanese shopping mall. It's not an especially comfortable experience, but you do get the opportunity to try a bewildering range of oriental dishes from various vendors, and you're unlikely to spend much more than a tenner in total. / 9 pm; no credit cards; no smoking area; no booking.

Osteria Antica Bologna SW11 £ 15 A★
23 Northcote Rd 7978 4771 10–2C
This long established Clapham osteria is as rustic and cosy a place as you'll find in London town. The food, which is both authentic and of high quality, is generally a little out of our price-bracket, but not if you visit for the £9.50 2-course lunch menu – you might choose fresh artichokes marinated in lemon & balsamic vinegar, followed by pheasant cooked in Barolo. By ordering the lunch menu you avoid the 90p cover charge, putting you in an even better position to enjoy the house wine, at £12.50 a bottle. / www.osteria.co.uk; 11 pm, Fri & Sat 11.30 pm.

Osteria Basilico W11 £20* A★
29 Kensington Park Rd 7727 9957 6–1A
The 'Tuscan farmhouse' setting is just part of the appeal which ensures that this Notting Hill spot is perennially packed with trendy local urbanites. To keep within our budget, you would have to choose carefully, but it's possible if you had something like green pea soup (£4.30) followed by one of the pizza or pasta main courses – spaghetti with seafood, or pizza 'Osteria', with Parma ham and rocket (all £6-£8). The house wine is £9.50 a bottle. / 11 pm; no booking, Sat L.

Ozer W1 £17* A★
4-5 Langham Pl 7323 0505 3–1C
Rather unusually, it's a fusion between Modern British and Turkish fare which is on the menu at this modernistic restaurant near Oxford Circus. It's a touch outside our budget à la carte, but there's always a 2-course set menu available at £8 before 7pm (and £11 afterwards), or a full mezze selection is £13.60 per person. The house wine is £12.50 a bottle. / midnight.

Il Pagliaccio SW6 £ 19 A
184 Wandsworth Bridge Rd 7371 5253 10–1B
This fun and friendly Fulham Italian is good value at any time of the week. With starters such as bruschetta starting from £2.65, and most pizzas and pastas under £7, you could easily stay within our budget à la carte as long as you avoid the slightly pricier meat and fish dishes (up to £12). For top value, though, seek out the weekday lunch menu (£7.50), which includes garlic bread, mixed salad or soup, with a good choice of pizzas, pastas and panini for main course, and a soft drink, beer or wine (otherwise £8.95 a bottle). / www.paggs.co.uk; midnight; no Amex.

Palms-on-the-Hill W8 £ 19
3-5 Campden Hill Rd 7938 1830 5–1A
The handy location of this long-standing pizza and pasta place makes it ideal for a lunch break from High Street Kensington shopping, and its appeal is heightened further by reasonable prices, especially by the standards of the area. With starters around £5.20 and most main courses under a tenner you could eat here a la carte within our budget, but even better value is the set 2-course menu for £9.25. The house wine is also reasonable at £9.95. / 11 pm; no Amex; no smoking area.

Pan-Asian Canteen Paxton's Head SW1 £ 17 ★

153 Knightsbridge 7589 6627 5–1D

A bit of a hidden gem, in the heart of Knightsbridge, this modernistic first-floor dining room of a grand traditional pub offers good Thai dishes – most priced around the £6 mark – at low-level communal tables. The house wine is £11.40 a bottle. / 10.30 pm; no smoking area.

The Papaya Tree W8 £ 19 ★

209 Kensington High St 7937 2260 7–1D

This family-run basement Thai restaurant seems a rather odd bedfellow of the big-name retailers which jostle along Kensington High Street. It's worth seeking out, though, either at lunchtime (when there are one-plate specials for a fiver), or to dine à la carte. Starters are around £4.95, main courses £7-£9, and house wine £11.95 a bottle. / 10.45 pm; no smoking area.

Pappa e Ciccia £ 17 A★

105-107 Munster Rd, SW6 7384 1884 10–1B
41 Fulham High St, SW6 7736 0900 10–1B
90 Lower Richmond Rd, SW15 8789 9040 10–1A

If you're going to check out these Fulham pizza and pasta stops, we'd especially recommend the original branch (first listed above). It offers quality Italian fare – perhaps tagliatelle carbonara (£7.50) or pizza (£8.50) – in cramped but characterful surroundings, and is popular for small parties. Best of all it's BYO – there's an off-licence practically next door. / 11 pm; Munster Rd, no credit cards; no Amex.

Paradise by Way of Kensal Green W10 £ 20 A

19 Kilburn Ln 8969 0098 1–2B

This ever-popular converted Kensal Green boozer is where the hip Notting Hill crowd goes when they're off duty from posing and being cutting-edge trendy. With its garden, it makes a particularly attractive sunny-day location. Good food – Italian pork sausages, mash and roasted red onion gravy (£9.50) followed by banoffee pie (£3.95) – can be washed down with a pint of bitter, or a bottle of the house vino (£10). / 10.45 pm; no Amex.

The Parsee N19 £ 20 ★★

34 Highgate Hill 7272 9091 8–1C

Like neighbouring Hampstead, Highgate has long been something of a mystery void when it comes to quality restaurants. Star chef, Cyrus Todiwala's new subcontinental – which specialises in the Parsee cuisine of India – offers unusual dishes such as 'akoori' (masala scrambled eggs, £3.50) all patiently explained by notably solicitous service. A typical main dish is £11 and house wine is £11.50 a bottle. / www.theparsee.com; 10.45 pm; D only, closed Sun; no smoking area.

Patio W12 **£19*** Ⓐ

5 Goldhawk Rd 8743 5194 7–1C

For a party night out on the cheap, you won't do much better than this characterful Polish spot in Shepherd's Bush. A 3-course set menu (£12.90) is always available – you might have blinis with smoked salmon, followed by rabbit in horseradish sauce, with Polish pancakes for pudding – and it even includes a warming free shot of vodka! Celebrations may be further fuelled by house wine at £10 a bottle, while live music regularly adds to the place's quirky party atmosphere. / 11.30 pm; closed Sat L.

Pâtisserie Valerie **£ 9**

17 Motcomb St, SW1 7245 6161 5–1D
105 Marylebone High St, W1 7935 6240 2–1A
44 Old Compton St, W1 7437 3466 4–2A
27 Kensington Church St, W8 7937 9574 5–1A

The array of tempting goodies in the window make this impressive chain of pâtisseries hard to resist. They are not just for the sweet-of-tooth, though – there's plenty in the savoury line, such as sandwiches (£2-£5), large salads (£7.95), mini-quiches (£2.75), and so on. The menu and style varies somewhat from branch to branch – our favourites are the Soho original and the big and bustly outlet near Harrods. / www.patisserie-valerie.co.uk; 7 pm, Sun 6 pm (Soho 7 pm); no smoking area; no booking.

Paul **£ 11**

115 Marylebone High St, W1 7224 5615 2–1A
29-30 Bedford St, WC2 7836 3304 4–3C

Covent Garden and Marylebone have recently joined company with almost all French cities of any note in having branches of that country's major bakery/café chain. They aren't the place for a blow-out, but very handy if you're looking for a light lunch – perhaps a quiche (£4.95) followed by one of the tempting pastries, maybe a tarte au citron (£2.50). No alcohol. / 8.30 pm; no smoking; no booking.

Pellicano SW3 **£19*** ★

19-21 Elystan St 7589 3718 5–2C

This backstreet trattoria is a useful Chelsea stand-by, and especially handily located for Brompton Cross shoppers. It offers good value if you go for the 2-course set lunch (£12.50), when your selection might be tuna, red onion and butter bean salad followed by asparagus and prawn risotto, washed down by house wine at £13 a bottle. You couldn't dine here within our price range. / 11 pm.

The Pepper Tree **£ 12** Ⓐ

537-539 Garratt Ln, SW18 8879 3599 10–2B
19 Clapham Common S'side, SW4 7622 1758 10–2D

Even if you pushed the boat right out, you would find it difficult to spend over our price limit at this ever-popular Thai refectory in Clapham (which has now spawned an Earlsfield offshoot) – the most expensive starter and main course together come to less than £15. Thai fishcakes followed by red prawn curry with coconut rice would be a typical selection, washed down with house wine at £9.50 a bottle. You may have to queue, but it's unlikely to be for long. / 11 pm, Mon & Sun 10.30 pm; no Amex; no smoking area; no booking at D.

Père Michel W2 **£ 19**

11 Bathurst St 7723 5431 6–2D

This Gallic bistro near Lancaster Gate is an old-fashioned, quite 'authentic' kind of place. You would tend to exceed our price-limit à la carte, but the set 2-course lunch for £12 is well worth seeking out. For this you might choose prawns with garlic mayonnaise or artichoke vinaigrette, followed by halibut mornay or chicken with mustard sauce. House wine is a reasonable £11 a bottle. / 11 pm; closed Sat L & Sun.

Petit Auberge N1 **£ 17**

283 Upper St 7359 1046 8–2D

This is emphatically not a foodie choice, but if you're looking for a 'something for all the family' destination in Islington, this bistro makes a good choice. It offers a long menu of simple Gallic-inspired dishes – snails (£4.50) and rabbit casserole (£8.95), for example – at quite reasonable prices. There is also a 2-course set lunch menu for just £5.50 (or 3 for £6.95) – perhaps deep fried whitebait followed by grilled chicken with mushroom sauce. The house wine is £9.50 a bottle. / 11 pm; no Amex.

Le Petit Prince NW5 **£ 17**

5 Holmes Rd 7267 3789 8–2B

Rather tackily themed around the illustrations of St Exupery's children's fable, this budget Kentish Town bistro, in business since 1977, is one of the London's few really genuine little Gallic places. The food has no great aspirations, but prices are so modest that you can have a 3-course splurge within our price-limit – perhaps onion soup (£2.80), followed by the speciality, couscous (£7.50), and then chocolate mousse (£2.90). House wine is £8.90 a bottle. / 10.30 pm; closed Mon, Sat L & Sun L.

Phoenicia W8 **£18*** ★

11-13 Abingdon Rd 7937 0120 5–1A

You couldn't dine here within our budget, but it's the 2- and 3-course set lunch and early dinner menus (£9.95 and £11.95) which are top tips for budget diners at this long-established, family-run Kensington Lebanese. Typical dishes include a choice of kebabs, grilled aubergines and so on, washed down with house wine at £13.90 a bottle. / www.phoeniciarestaurant.co.uk; 11.45 pm; no smoking area.

The Phoenix SW3 **£ 19** A

23 Smith St 7730 9182 5–2D

The King's Road has always been a surprisingly poor culinary destination, so it's worth knowing about this stylish and comfortable new gastropub, 100 yards off the main drag. The food's nothing remarkable, but realisation of dishes such as eggs benedict (£5.95) and Toulouse sausage with mash (£8.95) is perfectly competent, and wines (from £11) not exorbitant for this part of town. / www.geronimo-inns.co.uk; 9.45 pm; no Amex; need 6+ to book.

Phoenix Bar & Grill SW15 £20* A★

162-164 Lower Richmond Rd 8780 3131 10–1A

Notwithstanding a bit of PR hype in recent times about a star Italian chef advising the kitchen, this white-painted fixture on the outskirts of Putney remains the epitome of a good quality, neighbourhood spot. It's packed with families and couples at the weekend, but for lunch (except Sunday) and early evenings (Sun-Thu) there's a good 2-course set deal (£13.50) – representative menu would be asparagus & tarragon soup followed by suckling pig. House wine is £10.95 a bottle. / 11 pm; no smoking area.

The Pilot W4 £ 19

56 Wellesley Rd 8994 0828 7–2A

Nice places to eat are thin on the ground in the vicinity of Gunnersbury tube, so it's well worth bearing in mind this trendified boozer (which benefits from a pleasant garden). The food doesn't aim to set the world on fire, but realisation of dishes such as chicken liver parfait (£5.50) and sausages & mash (£8.50) is very competent. The house wine is £10 a bottle. / 10 pm.

La Piragua N1 £ 15

176 Upper St 7354 2843 8–2D

For a cheap and cheerful night out – especially for a party – you won't do much better than this vibrant, tightly-packed Latino spot in Islington. Most starters, perhaps grilled sardines, are £2.50, and most main courses (which come garnished) are under a tenner – although Argentinian steak, the house speciality, is £11.95. The South American house wine is £9.50 a bottle. / www.lapiragua.co.uk; midnight; no Amex.

Pizza on the Park SW1 £ 19 A

11 Knightsbridge 7235 5273 5–1D

This airier and grander than usual PizzaExpress offers all the usual pizzas (£7- £10) as well as more substantial dishes, such as chilli con carne, at similar prices. It makes quite an elegant place to kick the day off – they do a wide-ranging breakfast menu – and there's also a major cabaret venue in the basement (significant charge). The house wine is £12.50 a bottle. / midnight; no smoking area.

PizzaExpress £ 17

Branches throughout London

Ever since they made the great dash for growth – there seems to be a PE on every corner nowadays – satisfaction with London's great middle class stand-by chain has been on the wane. Sheer consistency of 'offer' is both a strength and weakness – in some ways, it's nice to feel that one knows the mainly-pizza (£4.95-£7.75) menu pretty much by heart, but on the downside the whole experience can seem stuck in a bit of a time warp. No visitor, however, should miss what remains a definitive London experience. The house wine is £10.95 a bottle. / www.pizzaexpress.co.uk; 11 pm-midnight; most City branches closed all or part of weekend; most branches don't take bookings.

Pizzeria Castello SE1 £ 16 ★

20 Walworth Rd 7703 2556 1–3C

This popular pizzeria has long thrived by offering very good value for money, and reliably good pizzas and pastas (£4.70-£6). The menu offers quite a lot besides, with starters such as baked aubergine with Parmesan & tomato (£3.30), and main courses including chicken stuffed with crab meat (£7.90). House wine is £8.90 a bottle. Look out for a change of location in 2004.
/ 11 pm, Fri & Sat 11.30 pm; closed Sat L & Sun.

Pizzeria Oregano N1 £ 18 ★

19 St Albans Pl 7288 1123 8–3D

In a side street a few yards away from the chain-extravaganza which is Islington's Upper Street lurks an unpretentious, individually-owned pizzeria whose pizzas (£4.95-£8.95) are generally above the norm. The house wine is £9.95 a bottle. / 10.45 pm; closed Mon; no Amex; no smoking area.

The Place Below EC2 £ 13 A★

St Mary-le-Bow, Cheapside 7329 0789 9–2C

The position has improved somewhat in recent years, but the heart of the City still doesn't offer much in the way of reasonably priced lunching of any interest – expect a midday crush at this unusual veggie, interestingly housed in the crypt of the impressive St Mary-le-Bow. You might start with fennel, red lentil and tomato soup (£2.70) followed by a salad (£7.50) or the quiche of the day, such as spinach, roast potato & Mozzarella (£6.50). You may want to leave space for the likes of apple & blueberry crumble (£2.80). Unlicensed – coffee and juices are under £2.
/ www.theplacebelow.co.uk; L only, closed Sat & Sun; no Amex; no smoking; need 15+ to book.

(Ognisko Polskie) The Polish Club SW7 £16* A

55 Prince's Gate, Exhibition Rd 7589 4635 5–1C

It may be run and mainly patronised by members of London's extensive Polish community, but this grand, traditional club dining room in South Kensington is very welcoming to all comers. In summer, a lovely terrace is a further attraction. The food is nourishing and hearty more than it is subtle. A simple 3-course menu (£11) is available all day – you might have tomato soup, followed by fried haddock, with grapes to finish, washed down with house wine at £11.20 a bottle. / 11 pm; jacket & tie.

Polygon Bar & Grill SW4 £20* A

4 The Polygon 7622 1199 10–2D

This rather trendy modern British brasserie/grill is quite a find in the backstreets of Clapham (especially for those who would prefer to avoid the High Street 'passagiata'). To stay within our budget you'll have to go for the lunch menu (noon-2.30pm) or early-bird evening special (6pm-7.30pm), when you get two courses for £12.50. They might be pumpkin & mushroom cannelloni followed by warm Asian duck breast salad, washed down with house wine at £12 a bottle. / www.thepolygon.co.uk; 10.45 pm; closed Sun D.

Poons WC2 £ 14

4 Leicester St 7437 1528 4–3A

Good, basic Chinese cooking served in reasonably smart surroundings has long helped to make this convenient spot, just off Leicester Square, a useful West End rendezvous. It still is, though standards have been somewhat erratic of late. Set meals are available from £7.50 a head, or you could easily dine à la carte within our price limit, especially with house wine at a reasonable £7.70 a bottle. / 11.30 pm; no smoking area.

Poons, Lisle Street WC2 £ 13

27 Lisle St 7437 4549 4–3B

This Chinatown café, the original of the Poons empire, is pretty basic but it does the job, and at budget prices too. Starters are about £3.50 and main courses around £6, and portions are large – your choice might be deep-fried soft shell crab followed by crispy duck. The house wine is £7.90 a bottle. / 11.30 pm; no Amex; no smoking area.

Popeseye £ 20 ★

108 Blythe Rd, W14 7610 4578 7–1C

277 Upper Richmond Rd, SW15 8788 7733 10–2A

These excellent, no-frills bistros in Brook Green and Putney are among the very best places in London for a decent Scottish steak. An 8oz popeseye (rump) with chips will set you back £12.45, so you'd burst our budget if you had a pud (£4.75). Treat a salad (£3.45) as a starter, and – with house wine at £11.50 a bottle – you can just about squeak within it. / 10.30 pm; D only, closed Sun; no credit cards.

Porchetta Pizzeria £ 12 ★

33 Boswell St, WC1 7242 2434 2–1D

141-142 Upper St, N1 7288 2488 8–3D

147 Stroud Green Rd, N4 7281 2892 8–1D

Sheer value has won a huge following (as evidenced by big queues, especially at the Finsbury Park original) for these lively, brightly-lit north London pizzerias. They really are very inexpensive, with starters under £5, pizzas around £6 and the house wine at £9 a litre. If you're looking for a blow-out at a truly budget level, you won't do much better. / midnight, WC1 10.30 pm; WC1 closed Sat L & Sun, N1 & N4 D only Mon-Thurs; no Amex; need 5+ to book.

Pret A Manger £ 6

Branches throughout London

Unlike the American burger-chain which is a one-third shareholder, this designer-metallic take-away chain goes from strength to strength, Extremely reliable sandwiches (£1.15-£3.05) are at the heart of its 'offer', but you will also find wraps, baguettes, salads and sushi (£1.99-£5). You might want to finish with a particularly good fruit salad (£1.69) or a slice of cake (£1.15) and a coffee (£1.25). Prices are a little higher if you eat in. / www.pret.com; 3 pm-6 pm, Leicester Sq & St. Martin's Ln 11 pm; closed Sun (except some West End branches), City branches closed weekends; no credit cards; no smoking; no booking.

The Prince Bonaparte W2 £ 19

80 Chepstow Rd 7313 9491 6–1B

This was once a very grotty Bayswater boozer, but it has been tarted up (a bit) in recent years, and nowadays attracts a sizeable and devoted younger following thanks in large part to the quality of its satisfying grub. You might have the soup of the day (£4.50), followed by sausages & mash (£9), and washed down with a bottle of the house vino (£12.40). / 10 pm; no booking.

(Tapa Room)
The Providores W1 £19* A★

109 Marylebone High St 7935 6175 2–1A

Especially if you're looking for somewhere for an interesting breakfast or brunch, this odd-but-interesting Marylebone newcomer – the latest project from the man who established the famous Sugar Club – is well worth seeking out. During the week, English breakfasts (£7.60) are served (9am-11.30am), or at weekends, brunch (highly recommended) is available from 10am-3pm. At other times, the likes of mixed antipasti will set you back £9, accompanied by house wine at £12.50 a bottle.
/ www.theprovidores.co.uk; 10.30 pm.

Pucci Pizza SW3 £19* A

205 King's Rd 7352 2134 5–3C

Many competitors have come (and many of those gone) over the years, but this classic hang-out for Chelsea's young and beautiful just goes on and on. Like at so many Italians, you'll have to stick to the pizzas, pastas and salads at this rustic-looking pizzeria if you don't want to blow your budget, but these are all perfectly well done. The house wine is £11.50 a bottle. / 12.30 am; closed Sun L; no Amex.

The Quality Chop House EC1 £18* ★

94 Farringdon Rd 7837 5093 9–1A

If you are willing to bear the famously uncomfortable wooden benches, the lunch menu is a bargain at this 'progressive working class caterer' (as it says on the window), much of whose décor is still as it was a century ago. For £9.75, you might have tomato and basil soup followed by Shepherd's Pie, washed down with house wine at £11 a bottle. A la carte, you'd tend to stray beyond our budget. / 11.30 pm; closed Sat L; no smoking area.

Queen's Pub & Dining Rm NW1 £ 19

49 Regents Park Rd 7586 0408 8–3B

It's something of a Primrose Hill landmark, and this imposing-looking tarted-up boozer makes a useful destination if you're looking for reliable gastropub staples. A typical meal might be seared peppered tuna (£9) followed by rhubarb crumble (£4.45), and washed down with house wine at £10.30 a bottle.
/ www.geronimo-inns.co.uk; 9.45 pm; no Amex.

Ragam W1 £ 14 ★

57 Cleveland St 7636 9098 2–1B

This Fitzrovia south Indian vegetarian is neither smart nor spacious, but, for many years, it has secured a following by offering good quality cooking at reasonable prices. There aren't many dishes over £5, so you really can splurge and stay safely within our budget. The house wine is surprisingly expensive at £9.90 a bottle. / 10.30 pm.

Raks W1 £12* ★

4 Heddon St 7439 2929 3–2C

A top destination for a shopping lunch, this bare but trendy Turkish establishment has a handy location just a few yards off Regent Street. At lunchtime, there's a good-value 2-course menu (£6.95), from which you might choose houmous followed by a chicken shish kebab. The house wine is £11.50 a bottle. / www.raksgroups.com; midnight.

Rani N3 £16 ★

7 Long Ln 8349 4386 1–1B

This Finchley Indian has a number of interesting and fresh-tasting vegetarian dishes on its menu. One good-value option is the 2-course dinner (£14), though the à la carte dishes (many Gujerati) are also within our budget, with starters costing about £3.30 and mains around £5. House wine is £9.70 a bottle. / www.raniuk.com; 10 pm; D only; no smoking.

Ranoush £14 ★

338 Kings Rd, SW3 7352 0044 5–3C
131-135 Earls Court Rd, SW5 7352 0044 5–2A
43 Edgware Rd, W2 7723 5929 6–1D

There are plenty of things you can't do at this late-night Lebanese diner in Bayswater – there's no alcohol for starters, and don't think of paying by cheque or credit card. For a fresh mango & melon juice (£1.90) in the early hours, however – or a snack such as houmous (£3.50) or Lebanese pizza (£1.25), or a shawarma (£3) – there is no better place. It now also has branches in the King's Road and Earl's Court.

Raoul's Café W9 £20

13 Clifton Rd 7289 7313 8–4A

Why are there not more informal bistro/pâtisseries like this useful Maida Vale fixture? It's considered the height of fashion in these parts to start the day with a croissant and a cappuccino here – and as the breakfast menu is available until 6pm, you don't even have to get up early! Later on in the day, when the menu changes, you might opt for the likes of soup of the day (£4.25) followed by stuffed cornfed chicken breast (£10.25). The house wine is £9.95 a bottle. / 10.15 pm; no smoking area; no booking at L.

Rasa £19* ★★

6 Dering St, W1 7629 1346 3–2B
55 Stoke Newington Church St, N16 7249 0344 1–1C

It's no great surprise that, for top value, you have to seek out the Stoke Newington original of this dynamic southern Indian duo in preference to its glossier Mayfair offshoot. The subtle veggie fare at both locations, though, is dynamite. At the former, starters are £2.50, main dishes are around a fiver, and the house wine £8.95 a bottle. At the latter, you'd need to exercise a lot of care to remain comfortably within our price-limit. / 10.30 pm; N16 closed Mon L-Thu L, W1 closed Sun L; no smoking.

Rasa Travancore N16 **£ 17** ★

56 Stoke Newington Church St 7249 1340 1–1C

The Rasa chain is something of a byword for quality and good-value Indian cooking – see above. What singles this (cramped but welcoming) Stoke Newington branch out is that carnivores are fully catered-for, too. As ever, prices are reasonable – starters (perhaps seafood soup or lamb rice balls) are under a fiver, and curries (for example, Keralan chicken curry with paratha and lemon rice) are around £7 – with veggie options particularly inexpensive. The house wine is £9.95 a bottle. / www.rasarestaurants.com; 10.45 pm; D only; no smoking.

The Real Greek N1 **£19*** A★

15 Hoxton Market 7739 8212 9–1D

Theodore Kyriakou is London's leading exponent of modern Greek cuisine, and his restaurant is considerably beyond the budget of this guide. However, there are two possibilities for Hellenophiles wanting to try the place – the set lunch (and pre-theatre) menu is a mere £10 for two courses (3 for £13.50), and the large and atmospheric 'Mezedopolio' meze bar attached to the restaurant has dishes ranging from £1.90-£6. Wine, from an all-Greek list, is £11.75 a bottle, and Greek Mythos beer is £2.95. / www.therealgreek.co.uk; 10.30 pm; closed Sun; no Amex.

Real Greek Souvlaki & Bar EC1 **£ 18** A★★

140-142 St John St 7253 7234 9–1A

This stylish, airy new Clerkenwell bar/restaurant shows all the originality that's made such a success of Hoxton's renowned Real Greek. The specialities here are inspired by Greek street food – there's an intriguing mezedes menu (£2.25-£6) and a variety of souvlakis (from £3.75 to £9.25 for a double). These can be washed down with your choice from the large and unusual selection of Greek beers and Ouzos, or the house wine costing £11 for a bottle. / www.therealgreek.co.uk; 10.45 pm; no Amex.

Rebato's SW8 **£ 17** A

169 South Lambeth Rd 7735 6388 10–1D

'Vauxhall' and 'festive' are not words which come together especially naturally, so it's all the more worth seeking out this jolly Spanish bar/restaurant. The highlight is the tapas bar at the front, which sells tasty and very affordable dishes (£2.95-£4.50). To the rear, the restaurant isn't quite such good value, but has its own tacky charm. The house wine is £9.75 a bottle. / www.rebatos.com; 10.45 pm; closed Sat L & Sun.

The Red Pepper W9 **£ 20** ★

8 Formosa St 7266 2708 8–4A

You wouldn't guess to look at it, but this Maida Vale pizzeria has a big reputation for the quality of its cooking and, as a result, is always packed. Pizzas from the wood-burning oven (£6-£9) are the speciality (and also the only real budget choice), but, with house wine at £12 a bottle, our price limit should just about allow slack for a tiramisu (£5). / www.theredpeppergroup.com; 11 pm; closed weekday L; no Amex.

Red Veg W1 £ 8 ★

95 Dean St 7437 3109 3–1D

Even dedicated carnivores should drop by this tiny veggie café/take-away, just south of Oxford Street. The amazingly authentic-tasting burgers are juicy and delicious – they've just never had anything to do with cows – and there's an interesting array of other snacks including felafel and plantain chips. There's no booze, but you could easily eat and run for a fiver, and stuff yourself silly for a tenner.
/ www.redveg.com; 10 pm; closed Sun; no credit cards; no smoking; no booking.

Riccardo's SW3 £ 20 A

126 Fulham Rd 7370 6656 5–3B

In pricey Chelsea, this Italian tapas restaurant is a popular choice with locals and visitors alike. Everything on the menu comes in starter-size portions, and most dishes cost £5-£11, however, so this would not be a sensible choice for a blow-out. Choose between a selection of salads (such as spinach, prosciutto & Parmesan), pasta dishes (including linguine with clams), meaty dishes (Tuscan antipasti or beef carpaccio) and pizzas. The house wine is £12.95 a bottle. / 11.30 pm.

Rick's Café SW17 £ 19

122 Mitcham Rd 8767 5219 10–2C

They certainly haven't wasted too much money on the décor, but this cramped and friendly bistro has established quite a following, down Tooting way. And with dishes such as Parmesan salad (£4.50) and roast mackerel (£8.95), and house wine at £10 a bottle, you can just about dine here within our budget at any time. / 11 pm; no Amex.

Rocket £ 17 A

4-6 Lancashire Ct, W1 7629 2889 3–2B
Brewhouse St, SW15 8789 7875 10–2B

Sometimes budget destinations are a bit on the tacky side, but that accusation could certainly not be levelled at these chic bar/restaurants (one handily located off Bond Street, the other occupying an impressive new Putney riverside site). The notionally Mediterranean menu is in fact mainly Italian, with pizza the speciality – wood-fired pizzas cost around £8. Kick off with the likes of buffalo Mozzarella salad (£5.50). House wine costs £12 a bottle.
/ www.freedombrewery.com; SW15 10.30 pm, W1 11.30 pm; W1 closed Sun.

The Rôtisserie £18* ★★

56 Uxbridge Rd, W12 8743 3028 7–1C
134 Upper St, N1 7226 0122 8–3D

The 2-course set menus almost always available (restrictions very between restaurants) make these pleasantly unpretentious rôtisserie-bistros really top-value destinations. A mere £12.50 (£10.95 at the Islington branch) buys you the sort of protein-intensive fare that often can't be found within our price range – perhaps chargrilled spare ribs followed by a rib-eye steak 'n' chips, washed down with house wine at £9.75 a bottle.
/ www.therotisserie.co.uk; 10.30 pm; Fri-Sun D only, except Sun L & D, HA5 closed Mon.

Rôtisserie Jules £ 15

6-8 Bute St, SW7 7584 0600 5–2B
133 Notting Hill Gate, W11 7221 3331 6–2B

The fast-food style surroundings aren't pretty to look at, nor particularly comfortable, but these simple Gallic rotisseries do offer quality protein very cheaply. The choice is generally chicken, chicken or chicken (a quarter-bird is £4.95, half is £6.75) accompanied by fries (£2) or a salad (£2.50). For a party – if you give them advance notice – they will roast a leg of lamb for you (£28, serves 5-6 people). A bottle of the house wine is £7.50 (the SW7 branch is unlicensed, BYO). / 11 pm.

Royal China £20* ★★

40 Baker St, W1 7487 4688 2–1A
13 Queensway, W2 7221 2535 6–2C
68 Queen's Grove, NW8 7586 4280 8–3A
30 Westferry Circus, E14 7719 0888 11–1C

Large in scale, and decorated in a (mercifully quite singular) '70s disco style, these are the capital's quality benchmark for Chinese restaurants. You can just about keep within our budget at any time, but it's the great-value dim sum (from £2.20 a dish during the day) which are the special attraction. A la carte dishes kick off at about £5.50, and the house wine is £12 a bottle. / 10.45 pm, Fri & Sat 11.15 pm; E14 no bookings Sat & Sun L.

Royal Court Bar
Royal Court Theatre SW1 £17*

Sloane Sq 7565 5061 5–2D

It's for sheer handiness that we include this 'zoo' of a bar, beneath Sloane Square. Though it's notionally attached to the famous theatre, it has a life quite of its own (though it's obviously best to avoid the hectic pre-curtain-up hour if you can). Snacks such as spinach and parmesan tart (£5.95) or soup (£4.25) are a forte, washed down with house wine at £12.50 a bottle. Lunchtime shoppers can take advantage of a 2-course menu for £10. / 10.30 pm; closed Sun; no smoking area.

La Rueda £20* A

102 Wigmore St, W1 7486 1718 3–1A
642 King's Rd, SW6 7384 2684 5–4A
66-68 Clapham High St, SW4 7627 2173 10–2D

Give the restaurant at this famous, bottle-lined Clapham tapas bar a miss – the point of this place is the vibrant atmosphere in the bar, especially at weekends. The buzz is fuelled by house wine at £10 a bottle, and sustenance comes in the form of all the usual tapas dishes (mostly a fiver). It also has OK branches in Chelsea and near Selfridges. / 11.30 pm.

Running Horse W1 £ 17

50 Davies St 7493 1275 3–2A

Shopping on Oxford Street and batteries running low? – seek out this trendy but welcoming gastropub, which offers simple fare at reasonable prices. Very good sausages & mash – a satisfying meal in themselves for around £7.95 – are a house speciality. The house wine is £10.95 a bottle. NB: the management proposes to take this establishment slightly upmarket during the currency of this guide, so check prices. / www.therunninghorselondon.co.uk; 10 pm; need 8+ to book.

Rusticana W1 £ 19

27 Frith St 7439 8900 4–3A

Still not as well known as it should be, this friendly, family-run Italian restaurant in Soho is a handy destination for a (quick and) satisfying meal in the centre of town. It's the sort of place you could spend a little beyond our budget à la carte, but there's no embarrassment about having a bowl of pasta (£6) and some cheesecake (£3.50). Wines start at £10.50 a bottle. / www.rusticanasoho.co.uk; 11.30 pm; no smoking area.

Sabai Sabai W6 £16*

270-272 King St 8748 7363 7–2B

It may be something of an atmosphere-free zone, but this airy Hammersmith Thai has a steady following thanks to the quality of its cooking. Starters, such as spring rolls and chicken satay, are around the £4 mark, and most curries are about £6. The house wine is £8.75 a bottle. / www.come.to/sabai; 11.30 pm; closed Sun L; no smoking area.

Sabras NW10 £ 16 ★★

263 High Rd 8459 0340 1–1A

Despite recent improvements, Willesden Green is hardly oversupplied with good eating venues, making this venerable veggie Indian café all the more worth knowing about. Its extensive menu incorporates southern specialities such as bhel poori (£3.50) and dhosas (£6.50-£7.50). The house wine is £10 a bottle. / 10.30 pm; D only, closed Mon; no Amex; no smoking area.

Le Sacré-Coeur N1 £10* A

18 Theberton St 7354 2618 8–3D

You could probably just squeeze a meal at this jolly bistro off Upper Street into our budget at any time. But why scrimp when you can visit on any weekday lunchtime and take advantage of the set lunch at a mere £5.50 for two courses, or £6.95 for three? You might have carrot & celeriac soup, followed by lamb stew with a raspberry pancake to finish. At these prices, you can allow for a bottle of house wine (£9.50) a head, and still stay within our price-limit! / 11 pm, Fri & Sat 11.30 pm.

Sagar W6 £ 13 ★★

157 King St 8741 8563 7–2C

Don't be put off by the indifferent popadoms and boring chutneys that kick of a meal at this unpromising-looking shop conversion on Hammersmith's main drag. The top quality vegetarian Indian food which follows is some of the best in London, and prices are unbelievably low. Start with vegetable samosas (£2.75) or potato puria (£2.95), and perhaps follow with a curry – the most expensive is saag paneer at £3.95. Alternatively choose a set thali – a big and satisfying meal for £7.95. With house wine at £8.95 a bottle, this is the kind of value that you rarely find. / 10.45 pm; no smoking area.

St John EC1 £19* ★

26 St John St 7251 0848 9–1B

If a snack such as roast bone marrow salad (£6.20) or deep-fried tripe (£5.25) is your idea of a treat, the bar of this intriguing all-white Smithfield restaurant – in a former smokehouse – is just the place for you. The house wine is £13.50 a bottle. (The neighbouring restaurant is famous for its offal-heavy menu, but a meal here would take you beyond our price-limit.) / www.stjohnrestaurant.co.uk; 11 pm; closed Sat L & Sun.

Sakonis HA0 £ 13 ★★

129 Ealing Rd 8903 9601 1–1A

For brilliant and cheap Indian cooking, it's difficult to match this large Wembley canteen, which offers an all-veggie menu. The varied menu – which includes some Chinese dishes – can seem rather daunting at first, but nothing is very expensive, and most of it is utterly delicious. You might have spring rolls followed by mushroom biryani, with coconut shell kulfi to finish, and still spend less than £15 – it helps that they don't allow alcohol! / 9.30 pm; no Amex; no smoking.

The Salusbury NW6 £ 20

50-52 Salusbury Rd 7328 3286 1–2B

The functions of pub and dining room are divided between two parallel rooms at this cosy old Queen's Park boozer, which has been revitalised in recent times. Superior snacks and a hot dish of the day are dispensed from the bar, while the restaurant serves simple Mediterranean food, such as risotto and pastas (£7 small; £9.50 large), plus a few heartier dishes such as roast rabbit (£10) and some classic desserts. The house wine is £10 a bottle. / 10.15 pm; closed Mon L; no Amex.

Sapori WC2 £19-

43 Drury Ln 7836 8296 4–2D

It's perhaps no coincidence that this buzzy Italian rendezvous is, by the standards of touristy Covent Garden, a little off the beaten track. Perhaps that's why, unlike many places hereabouts, it consistently offers tasty and enjoyable food at reasonable prices – most pizza and pasta dishes are around the £8 mark, and the house wine is £10.50 a bottle. / 11.30 pm; closed Sun; no Amex.

Sarastro WC2 £17* A

126 Drury Ln 7836 0101 2–2D

It's technically possible to stay within price-limit at this madcap Theatreland institution – but only if you opt for the set lunch or pre-theatre menus (available noon-6.30pm) which offer two courses for £10. The (notionally Turkish) cooking, however, is really not the point of the place – people come for the wildly Baroque décor and theatrical atmosphere, which make it ideal for a boisterous group visit (when you'd probably blow our budget big time). The house wine is £11.75 a bottle. / www.sarastro-restaurant.com; 11.30 pm.

Sarkhel's SW18 £ 18 ★★

199 Replingham Rd 8870 1483 10–2B

Udit Sarkhel quit the kitchen of one of London's leading Indian restaurants to set up on his own in Southfields, and the place is really making a name for itself. The set lunch and early evening menu (until 8pm) offers three courses for £9.95. A la carte, a fairly standard list is supplemented by unusual regional specials from £6.50. House wine is £10.90 a bottle. / www.sarkhels.com; 10.30 pm, Fri & Sat 11 pm; closed Mon; no Amex; no smoking area.

Satsuma W1 **£ 18**

56 Wardour St 7437 8338 3–2D

This stylish Japanese diner in Soho serves up healthy food at refectory tables – it's a popular place, and there's often a queue. Apart from noodles (yasai ramen, £5.70), there are good sushi and sashimi, which may tempt you over budget. Bento boxes (complete with rice, miso soup and pickles) range from £9.90 for tofu steak to £15.90 for the Satsuma bento. Kirin beer is £3.90 for a large bottle. / www.osatsuma.com; 11 pm, Wed & Thu 11.30 pm, Fri & Sat 11.45pm; no smoking; no booking.

Seashell NW1 **£ 18** ★

49 Lisson Grove 7224 9000 8–4A

This famous chippy near Marylebone Station has become a firm fixture on the tourist map, so it's more often than not crammed with coach parties eating our National Dish (£8.50) with an equally traditional pud such as treacle sponge (£3) for 'afters'. This goes on until 7pm, after which the atmosphere mellows and the prices rise. House wine is £10.95 a bottle. / www.seashellrestaurant.co.uk; 10.30 pm; closed Sun; no smoking area.

Sedir N1 **£ 16**

4 Theberton St 7226 5489 8–3D

This no-nonsense Turkish bistro, just off the glitzier part of Islington's Upper Street, offers inexpensive fare in unpretentious surroundings. Mixed mezze (£5.75) will easily feed two people, followed by the 'chef's special' selection of cooked meats, with salad and rice (£8.50). Wash it down with a bottle of house wine at £9.95. / 11.30 pm, Fri & Sat midnight.

Segafredo Zanetti W1 **£ 13** ★

72 Baker St 7486 2229 2–1A

The first London outpost of the famous Italian coffee brand is a Marylebone café that's useful for a tasty snack at any time of day. Our top selection would be a small plate of antipasti (£5.95), perhaps with a cake (around £3) for pudding. As you'd hope, the coffee is pretty good, but wine is also available, with choices starting off at £9.25 a bottle.

Shampers W1 **£19*** A

4 Kingly St 7437 1692 3–2D

There are not many places in town where dinner is cheaper than lunch – this wine bar, only five minutes' walk from Piccadilly Circus, is one such, and well worth bearing in mind if you're spending a night in the West End. With its haphazardly arranged paintings interspersed with wine racks, it looks rather dated – in the nicest way – and the fare tends to be fairly traditional. You might have squid with chilli, ginger & garlic (£5.75) followed by homecooked Denhay ham with egg 'n' chips (£8.75), washed down with house wine at £11.50 a bottle. / 11 pm; closed Sun (& Sat in Aug).

Shanghai E8 £ 18 𝔸

41 Kingsland High St 7254 2878 1–1C

Sited in the tastefully restored, tiled premises of a once-famous pie 'n' eel shop, this friendly Dalston Chinese makes a pleasant change from all those faceless Chinatown behemoths. Set menus are available (3-courses, £12.50) at any time, or go for the extensive lunchtime dim sum menu. A la carte, you might choose barbecue spare ribs (£3.20), followed by king prawns (£7.20) with special fried rice (£4.20), washed down by house wine at £9.10 a bottle. Get a seat in the boothed front section if you can.

/ www.wengwahgroup.com; 11 pm; no Amex.

J Sheekey WC2 £20* 𝔸★★

28-32 St Martin's Ct 7240 2565 4–3B

This one's a bit of a cheat – you'd need to skip coffee to stay within our price-limit – but we feel we've got to include the most talked-about restaurant in town (at least as judged by our most recent survey). It's a discreet, clubby little place, in the heart of Theatreland. The trick is to eat in the bar, thus avoiding the restaurant's £1.50 cover charge, and to visit for the weekend set lunch, which offers two courses for £14.25 – in keeping with the place's fishy emphasis, you might have smoked haddock hash followed by Sheekey's fish pie, accompanied by house wine at £12.75 a bottle. / midnight.

Sherlock's Grill
Sherlock Holmes Hotel W1 £20* ★

108 Baker St 7958 5210 2–1A

In the recent revamp, any vague attempt to retain a link between this newly modern Marylebone dining room and the famous, fictional, local supersleuth have been entirely abandoned. The cooking, however, exceeds hotel restaurant expectations, and some good-quality dishes emerge from the mesquite wood burning oven which is one of its features. A la carte prices are somewhat outside our budget, but lunchers can enjoy the likes of celeriac soup followed by calves liver with a stuffed jacket potato for a reasonable £12.50. Beware house wine, though, at £16.50 a bottle.

/ www.sherlockholmeshotel.com; 10.30 pm; no smoking.

Shish £ 16

2-6 Station Pde, NW2 8208 9292 1–1A
313 Old St, EC1 7749 0990 9–1D

This buzzing Willesden Green destination brings a revolutionary level of style to the kebab experience, and it has been a deserved success (especially given its out-of-the-way location). Downstairs, you can consume the likes of cold mezze (£1.95) and chicken shish kebab (£4.95), washed down with house wine at £9.90 a bottle, or beers from £1.50. Upstairs, there's a popular bar. A branch has recently opened in more-obviously-trendy Clerkenwell. / 10.30 pm.

Le Shop SW3 £ 18

329 King's Rd 7352 3891 5–3B

There are remarkably few crêperies worth recommending, and this Chelsea fixture, complete with booming classical 'background' music, is one of the front-runners. It offers a wide range of pancake-based temptations both sweet and savoury – you might have a chicken & ratatouille crêpe (£7), followed by one filled with bananas & rum (£5). The house wine is £11.95 a bottle.

/ www.leshop-chelsea.co.uk; midnight.

Simpson's Tavern EC3 £ 16 A

38 1/2 Cornhill 7626 9985 9–2C

This timeless chophouse, in a City back-alley, offers an experience as close as you'll find to how it must have been to eat in London two centuries ago. It's very popular with younger bankers and stockbrokers, happy to queue for such delights as steak & kidney pie, or a chop from the grill (all around the £6 mark) and steamed syrup pudding (£2.60), washed down with house wine at £11.50 a bottle. / 3 pm; L only, closed Sat & Sun.

Singapore Garden NW6 £17* ★

83-83a Fairfax Rd 7328 5314 8–2A

You'd have to scrimp a bit to dine comfortably within our price range at this long-established Swiss Cottage pan-oriental, but the lunch menu offers top value. For £8.50, you might have the likes of satay, followed by Malay chicken curry, with toffee banana to finish, washed down with house wine at a not inconsiderable £13.50 a bottle. / 10.45 pm, Fri & Sat 11.15 pm.

(Ground Floor) Smiths of Smithfield EC1 £16* A★

67-77 Charterhouse St 7251 7997 9–1A

There are three floors of dining possibilities at this impressively-converted warehouse, overlooking Smithfield meat market. Prices rise with altitude, so the budget diner is best sticking to the bar area on the ground floor, where breakfast-type dishes such as the 'Full English' (£6.50) are served all day – weekends are especially busy. There are also daily lunchtime 'market specials', such as bangers & mash, pies and quiches (£4-£6). If you have room, a Portuguese custard tart would make a fine dessert for £1. The house wine is £11.75 a bottle. / www.smithsofsmithfield.co.uk; 10.30 pm; L only; no booking.

Smithy's WC1 £ 18

15-17 Leeke St 7278 5949 8–3D

Up-and-coming King's Cross still has quite a way to up-and-come, so there's still not a huge variety of places for a tasty and civilised meal anywhere near the railway station. This makes it all the more worth seeking out this strikingly housed wine bar, which, in addition to a wide range of wines (from £10.50 a bottle) and beers, offers perfectly competent cooking – a typical meal might be grilled asparagus (£4.25) followed by a home-made beefburger (£6.95). / 9 pm; closed Sat & Sun.

So.uk £ 19 A

93-107 Shaftesbury Ave, W1 7494 3040 4–3A
165 Clapham High St, SW4 7622 4004 10–2D

Given that the food is far from being the main point of this loungey Moroccan joints in Clapham – and now also in the heart of Theatreland – it's surprisingly good. But this is really an 'atmosphere' recommendation – if you're looking for a place to hang out with a bottle of house vino (£13) and a few tapas-type dishes (£3.95-£4.95, or a platter for two costs £12.50), you really won't find many places with a better vibe.

Solly's Exclusive NW11 £20*

148 Golders Green Rd 8455 0004 1–1B

There's a more expensive (but superbly kitsch) upstairs restaurant, but for top value seek out the downstairs, diner-style section of this kosher institution in Golders Green. Houmous or tabouleh (both £3.50) and lamb shawarma (£9.50), washed down with house wine at £14 a bottle, are typical of the Middle Eastern fare on offer. / 10.45 pm; closed Fri D & Sat; no Amex; no smoking area.

Sosho EC2 £ 20 A

2a Tabernacle St 7920 0701 9–1C

Originally called Soshomatch, this large bar/restaurant remains one of the hippest hang-outs SOuth of SHOreditch. Its prime attraction is as a bar, but there's a raised seating area for eating which feels more than just incidental. The food is a cut above bar snacks – you might have a chicken Caesar or burger for about £7.50. You can drink beer or wine, but it's hard not to be tempted by a cocktail: Match spring punch (£6) anyone? / www.matchbar.com; Mon 10 pm, Tues-Sat midnight to 3 am; closed Sun.

Souk WC2 £ 19 A

27 Litchfield St 7240 1796 4–3B

It's as a central party venue that this cosy, low-lit and atmospheric Moroccan really scores. The food is rather incidental, but it's also within our budget, even à la carte – couscous with lamb sausage, for example, is £8.95. For top value, however, visit at lunch time, when there's a 3-course set menu for £12.50 including mint tea and baklava, washed down with house wine at £12 a bottle. / www.souk.net; 11.30 pm; no smoking area.

Soup Opera £ 8

6 Market Pl, W1 7637 7882 3–1C
17 Kingsway, WC2 7379 1333 2–2D
Warwick Rd, SW5 7370 8331 5–3A
Concourse Level, Cabot Pl East, E14 7513 0880 11–1C
18 Bloomfield St, EC2 7588 9188 9–2C
56-57 Cornhill, EC3 7621 0065 9–2C

The name says it all about this makes-a-change-from-sandwiches chain. To blow away the blues on a cold winter's day, it's difficult to beat the delights of a quick cup of, perhaps, Tuscan bean with Italian sausage, complete with bread and a piece of fruit, for £4.20 (or a seriously large portion for £6.50). Puddings (fruit salad and the like) are around £1.75, and a coffee will set you back £95p. / www.soupopera.co.uk; 4 pm-6 pm; closed Sat & Sun; no credit cards; no smoking; no booking.

Southeast W9 W9 £ 18 ★

239 Elgin Ave 7328 8883 1–2B

This inexpensive Maida Vale café serves a pan-Asian menu encompassing such starters as chicken satay and prawn & sweetcorn cakes (both under a fiver). Main courses include a selection of curries or dishes such as pad Thai (£6-£7). House wine is £10.75 a bottle, and Tiger beer £2.75. / 11 pm; no smoking area.

Spago SW7 £ 17

6 Glendower Pl 7225 2407 5–2B

Conveniently-located only a couple of minutes' walk from the tube station in pricey South Kensington, this well-established pit stop is a perennially popular destination for the local 'Euros'. Hearty portions of pizza and pasta are the culinary attraction – starters cost around £5 and most main dishes are £7. The house wine is £9.80 a bottle. / 11.30 pm; no credit cards.

Spread Eagle SE10 £20* A★

1-2 Stockwell St 8853 2333 1–3D

This ancient heart-of-Greenwich pub-conversion gives the impression of trading on Olde Englishness, but it in fact offers surprisingly good cooking in contemporary Gallic style. It only falls within our budget (just) for the £13.50, 2-course set lunch (Mon-Thu), which might comprise the likes of caremelised onion tart, followed by cornfed chicken with thyme and garlic, washed down with house wine at £15.50 a bottle. / www.spreadeagle.org; 10.30 pm; closed Mon L & Sun D.

Sree Krishna SW17 £ 13 ★

192-194 Tooting High St 8672 4250 10–2C

This unprepossessing, long-established Tooting subcontinental claims to have introduced southern Indian cuisine to the UK. The long menu includes Keralan pancakes and rice cakes (listed as Ever Popular Specialities), dhosas (£1.95), poori masala (£2.45) and plenty of exotic curries at reasonable prices. House wine is £8.50 a bottle. / 10.45 pm, Fri & Sat midnight.

Standard Tandoori W2 £ 12

21-23 Westbourne Grove 7229 0600 6–1B

Even in 1968, there wasn't much revolutionary about this then-new Bayswater curry-house. Little, apart from the prices, has changed since, but the formula has stood the test of time. Starters are generally less than £4, curries under £6 and the house wine £7.95 a bottle. / 11.45 pm; no smoking area.

Star Café W1 £ 13

22 Gt Chapel St 7437 8778 3–1D

Soho may be London's trendy 24-hour centre, but it's remarkably thinly provided with places for a decent cooked breakfast. It is therefore worth seeking out this rather hidden-away café, where a fiver buys you the full works (with coffee) or, later in the day, an omelette or pasta dish. There are also daily specials, such as seared tuna, from £6. The house wine is £9.50 a bottle. / www.thestarcafesoho.co.uk; 3.30 pm; closed Sat & Sun; no credit cards; no smoking area.

The Station W10 £ 18 ★

41 Bramley Rd 7229 1111 6–2A

Even by West Kensington's often gritty standards, this large, newly converted pub occupies a decidedly 'urban' location, with large picture windows looking on to the arches of Latimer Road tube. Bizarrely, though, it's also the possessor of a huge and beautifully-tended garden out back, making it a great summer destination. It's a great place to go if you've got a real appetite, as dishes such as organic Hereford beefburger with mature cheddar & smoked bacon (£7.95) and sticky toffee pudding with bourbon bean vanilla ice-cream (£3.75) come in ample portions. The house wine is a reasonable £10.50 a bottle. / www.priorybars.com; 10 pm.

The Stepping Stone SW8 £20* 𝔸★★

123 Queenstown Rd 7622 0555 10–1C

It's one of the best 'local' restaurants in town, so it's no great surprise that this Battersea spot is outside our budget in the evenings. At lunchtime, though, you might choose the likes of mackerel escabeche with grilled olive bread (£4.75) followed by fresh tagliatelle with wild mushrooms (£9.25), accompanied by house wine at £11.75 a bottle. / www.thesteppingstone.com; 11 pm, Mon 10.30 pm; closed Sat L & Sun; no Amex; no smoking area.

Stick & Bowl W8 £ 10 ★

31 Kensington High St 7937 2778 5–1A

The suitably basic name speaks volumes about this quick, absolutely no-frills oriental diner. At prices like these though – hot & sour soup is £2, special fried noodles at £4.60 and house wine at £7.90 a bottle – it's difficult to beat its attractions as a pit stop, or a respite from Kensington shopping. It's certainly always crowded. / 10.45 pm; no credit cards; no booking.

Stone Mason's Arms W6 £ 18 𝔸

54 Cambridge Grove 8748 1397 7–2C

It's not got the best of locations – on a busy Hammersmith highway – but that does nothing to discourage a strong following from trendy locals for this popular gastropub. Your choice from the blackboard menu might be roast sweet potato with aubergine, peppers & ricotta (£7.75) or chicken breast on black olives & cashew nuts (£9.50), followed by a sticky toffee pudding or raspberry tiramisu (both £3.75). The house wine is £10 a bottle. / 9.45 pm.

Strada £ 19

15-16 New Burlington St, W1 7287 5967 3–2C
9-10 Market Pl, W1 7580 4644 3–1C
6 Great Queen St, WC2 7405 6295 4–1D
237 Earl's Court Rd, SW5 7835 1180 5–2A
175 New King's Rd, SW6 7731 6404 10–1B
105-106 Upper St, N1 7276 9742 8–3D
11-13 Battersea Rise, SW11 7801 0794 10–2C
375 Lonsdale Rd, SW13 8392 9216 10–1A
102-104 Clapham High St, SW4 7627 4847 10–2D
8-10 Exmouth Mkt, EC1 7278 0800 9–1A

More stylish than average, for a chain, this group of Italian restaurants has generally managed to maintain its standards, despite its heady growth. Starters are around £5-£7 and pizza or pasta dishes shouldn't set you back more than about £9 (with meat and fish dishes rather more expensive). The house wine is £6.90 for half a litre. / www.strada.co.uk; 11 pm; no smoking area; some booking restrictions apply.

Stratford's W8 £20* ★

7 Stratford Rd 7937 6388 5–2A

You certainly won't spend a penny less than our price-limit, but if you like fish it's worth seeking out this Gallic restaurant in a sleepy Kensington backwater. The set menu is served all evening, and two courses – perhaps fried prawns followed by sautéed chicken – will set you back £13.50, accompanied by house wine at £10.80 a bottle. A la carte, of course, you would spend quite a lot more than our budget. / 11.30 pm.

The Sun & Doves SE5 £ 18 A

61 Coldharbour Ln 7733 1525 1–4C

This bright, breezy and Bohemian Denmark Hill gastropub is a perennially popular local hang-out (especially in summer, when the large garden comes into its own). The modish, Mediterranean-influenced food sustains interest, too, with such items as rocket salad with Parmesan & pine nuts (£4.25), or snapper fillet with herbed noodles (£8.95). House wine is £11.25 a bottle.
/ www.sunanddoves.co.uk; 10.30 pm; no smoking area; no booking.

Sushi-Say NW2 £ 18 ★

33b Walm Ln 8459 7512 1–1A

The friendly welcome and accomplished fare make it worth the expedition to the depths of north London (well, Willesden Green) to find this estimable Japanese. Prices are not bargain-basement, but you could start with seafood dumplings (£4.65), then go for the assorted sushi – 8 pieces for £11.80. House wine is £9.80 a bottle, or drink tea for 60p. / 10.30 pm; closed Mon, Tue-Fri D only, Sat & Sun open L & D; no smoking.

The Swan W4 £ 18 A★

119 Acton Ln 8994 8262 7–1A

This slightly unlikely find – in a tranquil backwater between Chiswick and Acton – is a charming old watering hole with a lovely garden. Best of all the place has managed to retain its pubby character while the food has undergone a trendy makeover. The cooking is superior and reasonably priced, and the twice-daily changing menu offers the likes of three inventive salads (£6), followed by sautéed mushroom bruschetta with sage, garlic, cream & shaved Parmesan (£7). The wine selection starts at £10.50 a bottle. / 10.30 pm; closed weekday L; no Amex; no booking, Fri & Sat.

Sweetings EC4 £14* A

39 Queen Victoria St 7248 3062 9–3B

This one's a bit of cheat – you couldn't accommodate the good-but-simple fish cooking at this City-institution seafood bar within our budget. But if you're prepared to slum it standing at the bar with a generously-filled sandwich (£3.95-£5.50) and a bottle of the house wine (£14.50), you won't find a more characterful place for a convivial lunch. And don't forget to wear your pinstripes. / L only, closed Sat & Sun; no booking.

Tajine W1 £ 20 ★

7a Dorset St 7935 1545 2–1A

Just a good-all-round inexpensive place – this friendly Marylebone Moroccan café offers such delights as aubergine Zaalouk (£3.95) and lamb tajine with pears (£10.75), washed down with house wine at £10.50 a bottle. / www.originaltajines.com; 10.30 pm; closed Sat L & Sun; no Amex.

Talad Thai SW15 £ 14 ★★

320 Upper Richmond Rd 8789 8084 10–2A

The queues at this popular Putney-fringe Thai restaurant say it all – the food's great and so are the prices. Eating is communal and there are few frills on the ambience front, but with the BYO option you're guaranteed a great meal that won't cost the earth. Standard dishes like spring rolls and green curry cost around a fiver. Wine is available – the house selection is £10.95 a bottle – but you can BYO to keeps costs down. / 10 pm; no Amex; no smoking.

Tandoori Lane SW6 £ 18 ★

131a Munster Rd 7371 0440 10–1B

The menu at Fulham's most reliable curry house is hardly innovative and isn't notably cheap (with main courses costing around £7 and side dishes about £3), but exceptional service and relatively smart décor ensure consistent popularity. House wine is somewhat steep at £12.50 a bottle, so stick to bottled beers at £4.90 for a large bottle of Kingfisher. / 11.30 pm; no Amex.

Tandoori of Chelsea SW3 £ 17 ★

153 Fulham Rd 7589 7749 5–2C

If you're shopping down Brompton Cross way, it is worth remembering the set lunch menu (served daily) at this long-established, and very comfortable, basement subcontinental. For £9.95 you could choose between chicken korma and bhuna ghosh; both are accompanied by fresh mixed vegetables and pilau rice. With house wine at £12.50 a bottle, this is not the sort of place that falls within our budget à la carte. / midnight.

Taro £ 14

10 Old Compton St, W1 7439 2275 4–2B
61 Brewer St, W1 7734 5826 3–2D

The jovial Mr Taro presides over this duo of simple Japanese canteens in Soho. The Old Compton Street original is cosier and has more of a following than his newer one, near Cambridge Circus, but both deliver a wide selection of dishes at bargain prices. Sushi sets start from three pieces for £1.50, and bowls of ramen or main dishes like chicken teriyaki are £5-6. / 10.30 pm; no Amex; no smoking; no booking.

Tartuf N1 £ 15 ★

88 Upper St 7288 0954 8–3D

Pizza-like 'tartes flambées' with savoury and sweet toppings are the speciality (from Alsace) of this small and friendly Islington spot. You can eat as much as you like for £11.90, while a 2-course weekend lunch is only £6.90. House wine is £10.95 a bottle. / midnight; no Amex.

Tas £ 16 A

33 The Cut, SE1 7928 2111 9–4A
72 Borough High St, SE1 7403 7200 9–4C

These Turkish eateries have made a big name for themselves by offering a rare combination of quality and value. They make ideal venues for inexpensive group gatherings, thanks to menus (always available) whose prices go as low at £6.95 – for that, you might have houmous followed by kofte with couscous, served with bread and white cheese pate, washed down by house wine at £10.50 a bottle. / 11.30 pm.

Tas Pide SE1 **£ 16** Ⓐ

20-22 New Globe Walk 7928 3300 9–3B

The speciality of this Anatolian offshoot of the famously cheap Tas chain is the eponymous 'pide' (pea-day) – a crisp boat-shaped dough dish baked in the restaurant's wood-fired oven. As well as serving traditional fillings such as minced lamb, parsley and mint, the restaurant has introduced some European-influenced varieties, such as oak-smoked cured beef. Prices really are very reasonable (£5.45-£7.25), and you could add a starter such as houmous with diced lamb & pine nuts (£3.45) as well as a pudding (such as baklava, £2.95), and remain comfortably within our budget. The Anatolian house wine is £10.50 a bottle. / www.tasrestaurant.com; 11.30 pm.

(Café 7)
Tate Modern SE1 **£ 20** Ⓐ

Bankside 7401 5020 9–3B

It's the impressive view of the City which gives Tate Modern's stark 7th-floor café what might be called 'destination' status. The unremarkable food – perhaps pea soup with minted creme fraiche (£4.95) followed by haddock & chips with mushy peas and tartare sauce (£8.95) – is at least reasonably priced, though house wine (£13 a bottle) is less so. Recent 'tweaks' to its layout – including the fact that they now take bookings – may just improve matters. / www.tate.org.uk; 5.30 pm, Fri & Sat 9.30 pm; L only, except Fri & Sat open L & D; no smoking.

Tawana W2 **£ 18** ★

3 Westbourne Grove 7229 3785 6–1C

It's the good-value cooking, rather than any special charm of setting or service, which is the attraction of this busy and popular Thai, just off Queensway. Starters and main courses are generally around the £5-£7 mark, so, with house wine at £9.50 a bottle, it's really not too difficult to keep within our budget. / 11 pm.

Tendido Cero SW5 **£ 19** ★

174 Old Brompton Rd 7370 3685 5–2B

Cambio de Tercio, arguably London's most consistently successful Spanish restaurant, now boasts an offshoot tapas bar, just across the road. This being South Kensington, prices are not bargain-basement – most dishes are around the £4-£6 mark – but costs are kept under control by the fact that (unusually for this part of town), this is a BYO establishment. / 11 pm; closed Sun D; no credit cards.

Thai Bistro W4 **£ 18** ★

99 Chiswick High Rd 8995 5774 7–2B

Good quality Thai grub is unceremoniously served at this popular Chiswick refectory, where customers sit at shared tables to enjoy regional specialities, including a plethora of veggie options. Starters, including spring rolls and fishcakes, are all priced around £4.50, with curries at £5.95 and rice at £1.50. House wine is £10.50 a bottle, or swig Thai beers from £2.75. / 11 pm; closed Tue L & Thu L; no Amex; no smoking.

Thai Café SW1 £ 16
22 Charlwood St 7592 9584 2–4C
They don't stand much on ceremony at this Pimlico corner café, but – the area hardly being awash with tolerable places to eat, at any price level – it attracts a steady following with its menu of oriental staples at reasonable prices. Most starters are around the £4 mark, and most main courses around £5-£7. The house wine is £9.65 a bottle. / 10.30 pm; closed Sat L & Sun L; no smoking area.

Thai Canteen W6 £ 12
206 King St 8742 6661 7–2B
This simple newcomer a short walk from the UCI Hammersmith inherits long thin premises that have been through numerous former incarnations. As the name hints, the selection here is of curries and noodle dishes which fall short of being art but which are tasty and affordable. You might have duck spring rolls (£3.50) followed by chilli fish curry (£5), washed down with strong Thai beer (£1.90 per bottle). That is the only alcohol available for purchase, but you can BYO for very modest corkage. / 10 pm, Fri & Sat 10.30 pm; closed Mon D & Sun; no credit cards.

Thai Corner Café SE22 £ 13 ★
44 North Cross Rd 8299 4041 1–4D
A bit of a local 'fave' down East Dulwich way, this unpretentious Thai spot offers all the standard Thai dishes at prices made all the more reasonable by the fact that this is a BYO place. Most main courses are around £5.50, with starters and desserts both around £4. / 10.30 pm; no credit cards.

Thai Garden SW11 £ 17
58 Battersea Rise 7738 0380 10–2C
Although it's been here for a number of years, this airy Battersea Thai has attracted a bit more attention since it presented a fresher new face to the world. Service is friendly, too, so it's well worth checking out the long menu which offers extensive permutations of the standard repertoire – most curries are around the £7 mark, and the house wine £10.50 a bottle. / www.thaigarden.co.uk; 11 pm, Fri & Sat 11.30 pm; D only.

Thai Noodle Bar SW10 £ 17 A
7 Park Walk 7352 7222 5–3B
Useful for a satisfying meal in an area that can be pretty pricey – just off Chelsea's so-called 'Beach' – this smartly-furnished oriental does just what its name suggests. With main-course dishes such as duck with jasmine rice (£7.95) or tiger prawn curry (£8.95), it's within our budget at any time, but the 2-course set lunch (£8.50, including coffee) is the top deal. The house wine is £10.80 a bottle. / 11 pm.

Thai on the River SW10 £17* A★
15 Lots Rd 7351 1151 5–4B
This is decidedly not the venue for a budget dinner date, but go to this swanky Chelsea Thai for lunch on a sunny day, and you may get a fabulous river view thrown in with your bargain 2-course set lunch (Tue-Fri, £7.95). You might choose crispy spring rolls followed by green chicken curry or roast duck in sweet tamarind sauce. The house wine is a hefty £14.95 a bottle, so beer at £3.50 a bottle may be the better bet. / www.thaiontheriver.co.uk; 11 pm, Fri & Sat 11.30 pm; closed Mon L & Sat L.

Thailand SE14 £ 9* ★★

15 Lewisham Way 8691 4040 1–3D

Probably still the best Thai cooking in town – certainly in traditional style – is to be found at this rather unprepossessing Lewisham spot. A la carte, you'd scrimp to stay within our price range, but if you want to check out the quality of the cooking it's worth making a bit of a detour for the 2-course set lunch, especially as it's an amazingly reasonable £3.95. House wine is £10.95 a bottle (and there's also an incredible array of malt whiskies). / 11.30 pm; closed Mon, Sat L & Sun L; no Amex; no smoking.

The Thatched House W6 £ 19 A

115 Dalling Rd 8748 6174 7–1B

This smartened-up Hammersmith boozer is rather more comfortable than your typical West London gastropub. The cooking may not be at the cutting edge, but realisation of dishes such as crab cakes with mango & pineapple salsa (£5.50) and baked cod with tomato, basil & olives (£10.50) is pretty consistent. With house wine at £10.95 a bottle, you'll have to take some care to stay within our price-limit. / www.establishment.ltd.uk; 10 pm; closed Mon, Tue & Sun D; no Amex.

Toff's N10 £ 14

38 Muswell Hill Broadway 8883 8656 1–1B

This Muswell Hill chippy was once perhaps the most famous in north London, and rightly so. It's been through some ups and downs following a change of ownership, but now seems to be re-establishing itself as a destination of real note. Cod 'n' chips, complete with coffee and bread & butter, will set you back only £7.50 before 5.30pm – thereafter, it's £8.95, the same price as a bottle of the house vino. / 10 pm; closed Sun; no smoking area; no booking, Sat.

Tokyo City EC2 £ 19 ★

46 Gresham St 7726 0308 9–2B

Handily-located for a light City lunch – not far from the Bank of England – this Japanese snackery offers such budget possibilities as bento boxes (£6.50-£13.50), in addition to sushi (at £1.50-£2.85 a piece), with house wine at £10.80 a bottle. As is the way with Japanese places, you could spend a lot more if you wanted to. / www.tokyocity.co.uk; 9.45 pm; closed Sat & Sun.

Tokyo Diner WC2 £ 14

2 Newport Pl 7287 8777 4–3B

This Japanese diner – situated, oddly, in the heart of Chinatown – is worth knowing about for an inexpensive and central light meal. The sushi and noodles on offer are fairly standard but well done, with main dishes generally under £8. The house wine is a reasonable £8.95. / 11.30 pm; no Amex; no smoking area; no booking, Fri & Sat.

Tom's W11 £17*

226 Westbourne Grove 7221 8818 6–1B

There's often a queue for breakfast in the dining room of this fashionable deli/café, which stays open all day. Eggs Benedict (£6.45) and Tom's toastie (ham & cheese baguette, £4.95) are the sort of fare on offer, but the real attraction is hanging out with the beautiful people of Notting Hill. It's not really an alcoholic sort of place, but you can BYO if you want to (£1.50 corkage), or buy wines from the deli downstairs. / 8 pm; closed Sat D & Sun D; no Amex; no smoking; no booking.

The Trafalgar Tavern SE10 **£ 20** A
Park Row 8858 2437 1–3D
This large and historic Greenwich inn occupies a superb Thames-side location and is blessed with some magnificent views. Combined with its menu of old-fashioned pub grub (with fish specialities), it's a good venue for wiling away a lazy afternoon, either in the bar or the restaurant. You could start with Greenwich whitebait with paprika mayonnaise (£5.95) followed by fish 'n' chips in beer batter (£8.90). House wine is £12.50 a bottle, or drink lager from £2.50 a pint.
/ www.trafalgartavern.co.uk; 9 pm; closed Mon D & Sun D; no Amex; no booking at weekends.

Troika NW1 **£ 17**
101 Regent's Park Rd 7483 3765 8–2B
This cosy all-day Russian tea room – and there are not many of those in town – is situated minutes from Chalk Farm tube. It offers a variety of unusual dishes at competitive prices, such as blinis with Danish caviar (£3.90) or herrings (£3.20), followed by mushroom pieroj (£5.50) or pelmeni (pork dumplings, £6.50). Many visitors, however, are pleased to plump for the less adventurous English breakfast (£3.95). House wine is £8.95 a bottle, or a shot of vodka will set you back £1.80. / 10.30 pm; no smoking area.

Troubadour SW5 **£ 17** A
265 Old Brompton Rd 7370 1434 5–3A
It's been much expanded in recent times, but this rare example of a notable London coffee shop has retained most of its Bohemian charm. Its Earl's Court premises remain particularly popular as a breakfast destination – a full English is £5.95 – and it's also fine for a light lunch. We would recommend the place less strongly for dinner (when it's really more of interest as a buzzy bar, often with live music or poetry readings). / www.troubadour.co.uk; 11 pm; no Amex.

Tsunami SW4 **£20*** ★★
Unit 3, 5-7 Voltaire Rd 7978 1610 10–1D
Good-quality Japanese cooking at reasonable prices is carving an ever-bigger name for this Clapham yearling (located just off the main drag, by the High Street railway station). Main dishes range from £7.95-£16.50, so you'll need to exercise a little caution to eat a full meal here within our price-limit. However, you could take friends and share plates of sushi (from £1.80 per piece), tempura (from £1) and skewers (£3.50-£5.95). Miso soup and rice are both £1.75, and a bottle of house wine is £12. / 10.45 pm, Fri & Sat 11.15 pm; no Amex; no smoking area.

Two Brothers N3 **£ 19** ★
297-303 Regent's Park Rd 8346 0469 1–1B
The Manzi brothers' airy North Finchley chippy is not especially characterful, but it retains a big following. It's not especially cheap either – cod 'n' chips with bread, butter & tartare sauce is £8.15 (£9.55 in the evenings) and house wine £10.05 a bottle – so it must have something to do with the quality of the cooking.
/ www.twobrothers.co.uk; 10.15 pm; closed Mon & Sun; no smoking area; no booking at D.

Uli W11 £ 17 ★★

16 All Saints Rd 7727 7511 6–1B

For a combination of charm, interesting cooking and economy at any time of day, it's hard to beat this south east Asian café in one of Notting Hill's hippest restaurant streets. For the summer, there's even a pleasant courtyard at the rear. On the menu you might find the likes of five-spice pork rolls (£5), vegetable tempura (£4) and shredded chilli beef (£7), washed down with house wine at £10 a bottle. / www.uli-oriental.co.uk; 11 pm; D only, ex Sun open L & D; no Amex.

Uno SW1 £18*

1 Denbigh St 7834 1001 2–4B

If you're looking for a 'modern' restaurant in Pimlico, this percussive Italian is one of still-too-few choices hereabouts. You could easily spend beyond our budget – especially if you went for a 'proper' proteinaceous main course – but this is a useful enough venue for a pizza or a plate of pasta (all in the £5 to £9 range). The house wine is £8.30 a bottle. / 11.30 pm.

The Vale W9 £18* ★

99 Chippenham Rd 7266 0990 1–2B

This local restaurant in Maida Hill has made a great success in an area that might seem unpromising. If you stick to the set menus, you can eat well here within our price range at any time of day. Two courses will set you back £9.50 at lunch or £12 at dinner – you might have gazpacho or roast peppers stuffed with feta, tomatoes olives & mint, followed by purple potato ravioli with artichokes, poached egg & truffle oil or salmon fishcake with buerre blanc. The house wine is £10.50 a bottle. / 11 pm; closed Mon L, Sat L & Sun D; no Amex; no smoking area.

Vama SW10 £16* A★★

438 King's Rd 7351 4118 5–3B

Lunchtimes offer the budget Chelsea diner the opportunity to check out the stylish and romantic surroundings of one of the best Indians in town. On Mon-Sat, £7.50 will buy you a set thali, which consists of rice, naan bread, lentils, chicken tikka masala and cumin potatoes. On Sundays, there's a varied buffet (£12.95). Don't hit the bottle too hard, though – a bottle of the house vino will set you back £13. / www.vama.co.uk; 11 pm.

Veeraswamy W1 £20* A★

Victory Hs, 99 Regent St 7734 1401 3–3D

You'll have to choose from the useful range of set menus – including a 2-course lunch and pre-theatre (5.30pm-6.30pm) menu for £12.50 – to stay within budget at this innovative subcontinental, conveniently close to Piccadilly Circus. It's on the site of London's longest-running Indian (est 1927), although you'd never know it from the jazzy, contemporary décor. Beware house wine at a hefty £15 a bottle. / www.realindianfood.com; 11.30 pm.

Vegia Zena NW1 — £14* ★

17 Princess Rd 7483 0192 8–3B

On a good day you can still find Italian cooking of more than usual interest at this unpretentious Primrose Hill restaurant. Your selection from the 2-course weekday lunch menu (£8.95, the same price as a bottle of the house wine) might comprise the likes of linguine with tomato & chilli followed by lamb chops with sautéed potatoes. You'd have to scrimp a little to dine here within our price limit. / www.vegiazena.com; 11 pm.

El Vergel SE1 — £ 10 ★★

8 Lant St 7357 0057 9–4B

The name means "The Orchard", and this homely café in a hidden corner of Borough certainly provides a fertile haven of good cheer and fantastically affordable grub, with no stinting on the portions of robust Spanish and South American fare. Aside from the daily specials board, regular items include home-made corn chips (70p) with salsa (£1.30), large salad bowls (at around £2.50), steak & cheese sandwiches ('churrasco', £3.50), and, to finish, cheesecake (£1.50). There's a small wine list starting at £8 a bottle, or drink San Miguel at £2.30 a bottle. / www.elvergel.co.uk; breakfast & L only, closed Sat & Sun; no credit cards; no smoking; no booking after 12.45 pm.

Viet Hoa E2 — £ 12

70-72 Kingsland Rd 7729 8293 9–1D

This basic but good-quality café, on the Hackney-Shoreditch border, has made a big name with its good, cheap Vietnamese cooking. With starters from 90p, mains about £5 and puddings costing around £2, you can eat well and stay within budget. House wine is a cheap £7.99 a bottle. / 11.30 pm; no Amex.

Viet-Anh NW1 — £ 11

41 Parkway 7284 4082 8–3B

It's nothing special to look at, but this Vietnamese café in the heart of Camden Town has won many fans for the quality of its cooking and the friendliness of its service. You'd be hard put to break through our price-limit, too – most of the main courses are around £5, and the house wine is £9 a bottle. / 11 pm; no Amex; no smoking area.

Vijay NW6 — £ 14 ★★

49 Willesden Ln 7328 1087 1–1B

This weather-beaten Kilburn Indian has consistently produced good standards over many years. Southern Indian vegetarian dishes, such as dhosas (potato and lentil pancakes, £3.50) are something of a speciality, but more standard meaty curries (£6-£8) are also available. The house wine is £7.85 a bottle. / www.vijayindia.com; 10.45 pm, Fri & Sat 11.45 pm.

Vingt-Quatre SW10 — £ 20

325 Fulham Rd 7376 7224 5–3B

Twenty-four hour opening is still less common than you might think, so this pleasant diner – on the trendy strip of road known as the 'Chelsea Beach' – is worth remembering. The cooking is fairly simple, but standards are consistent – you might have Cumberland sausages with onion rings (£9.50), followed by strawberry cheesecake (£5.25), washed down with the house wine at £11 a bottle. The 'night menu' (10.30pm-midday) offers breakfast and brunch staples. / open 24 hours; no booking.

Vrisaki N22 £ 20 ★

73 Myddleton Rd 8889 8760 1–1C

If you have a boundless appetite, this large Bounds Green Greek is the place for you. Experience suggests that you are unlikely to be able to finish the enormous set mezze – which will set you back £32 for two people, washed down with house wine at £8.50 a bottle. / midnight; closed Sun; no Amex.

Wagamama £ 17

109-125 Knightsbridge, SW1 7201 8000 5–1D
8 Norris St, SW1 7321 2755 4–4A
101a Wigmore St, W1 7409 0111 3–1A
10a Lexington St, W1 7292 0990 3–2D
4a Streatham St, WC1 7323 9223 2–1C
1 Tavistock St, WC2 7836 3330 4–3D
14a Irving St, WC2 7839 2323 4–4B
26a, Kensington High St, W8 7376 1717 5–1A
11 Jamestown Rd, NW1 7428 0800 8–3B
45 Bank St, E14 7516 9009 11–1C
1a Ropemaker St, EC2 7588 2688 9–1C
22 Old Broad St, EC2 7256 9992 9–2C
109 Fleet St, EC4 7583 7889 9–2A

The originators of the no-frills, oriental noodle canteen concept now seem to have sights all over London (as have their imitators), but they continue to provide good-value ramen dishes (soupy, noodly things) and stir-fries (£5-£8). There are also set meals, of which the top-of-the-range offering, the 'Absolute Wagamama', gives you chicken ramen, dumplings and a Kirin beer for just under a tenner. You'll probably have to queue at peak times. / www.wagamama.com; 10 pm-midnight; EC4 & EC2 closed Sat & Sun; no smoking; no booking.

The Walmer Castle W11 £ 17 A

58 Ledbury Rd 7229 4620 6–1B

If you want to hang out with the younger Notting Hill trust fund babies – without spending too much on the association – this first-floor Thai dining room above a trendy pub is the place for you. Prices are reasonable, with starters and desserts around the £4 mark and main courses about £6. A typical two-course meal might be sweetcorn fritters followed by green Thai curry, accompanied by a bottle of house wine at £9.95. / 10.30 pm; closed weekday L; no booking after 7.30 pm.

White Cross TW9 £ 15 A

Water Ln 8940 6844 1–4A

Richmond is such an attractive town that it's a shame it still offers relatively few places for a pleasant and inexpensive lunch. This large Young's pub near Richmond Bridge, with its charming riverside garden, is therefore all the more worth bearing in mind. The food is nothing remarkable, but dishes such as soup of the day (£2.95) and chicken & mushroom pie (£6.25, or £7 on weekends) are perfectly well done. The house wine is £10.45 a bottle, and a pint of bitter will set you back £2.30. / www.youngs.co.uk; L only; no Amex; no booking.

White Horse SW6 £ 19

1 Parsons Grn 7736 2115 10–1B

Fulham's 'Sloaney Pony' (as this large pub is affectionately known throughout south west London) is an ever-popular destination with a wide range of eating options (including, in summer, a barbecue). Realisation of such dishes as goat's cheese, hazelnut & pear salad (£6.25) followed, perhaps, by salmon fishcakes with a poached egg (£8.25), is pretty reliable. There's an impressive selection of wines (house is £11.25 a bottle) and also a good number of real ales.
/ www.whitehorsesw6.com; 10.30pm; no smoking in dining room.

William IV NW10 £20* A★

786 Harrow Rd 8969 5944 1–2B

The one-plate set lunch, which includes a main course plus a glass of wine or beer for £7.50, and the two course Sunday lunch (£14) are the special attractions for the budget diner at this relaxed and friendly Kensal Green gastropub (whose special feature is a charming rear terrace). A la carte, with most main courses around the £11 mark, you'd struggle a bit to stay within our budget. The house wine is £10.90 a bottle, and a pint of London Pride is £2.70.
/ www.william-iv.co.uk; 10.30 pm, Fri & Sat 11 pm.

Willie Gunn SW18 £ 20 A

422 Garratt Ln 8946 7773 10–2B

Paris has the Café de la Paix, and Earlsfield has Willie Gunn – a jolly and extremely popular brasserie through which 'le tout Earlsfield' will pass… if you wait long enough. Thanks to the reasonable prices – for example soup of the day with soda bread (£4) and Thai green chicken curry with rice (£9.50), and house wine at £11 a bottle – you can dine here within our budget at any time. / 11 pm.

The Windsor Castle W8 £ 18 A

114 Campden Hill Rd 7243 9551 6–2B

Few London pubs can match the charm of this quaint Georgian tavern near Notting Hill Gate, whose walled garden is a particular attraction. The enjoyable pub grub isn't that cheap, but offers ample choice within our price range, with dishes like sausages & mash (£9) or fish 'n' chips costing £7.95. Skip starters and go for the homely puds at around £3.45. House wine is £11 a bottle, but pints of Adnams are a popular alternative at £2.60.
/ www.windsor-castle-pub.co.uk; 9.30 pm; no smoking area at L; no booking.

Wine & Kebab SW10 £19* ★

343 Fulham Rd 7352 0967 5–3B

This friendly taverna has long been a late-night haven for the local Chelsea youth – possibly due to the fact that it's one of the few places in the area with a late licence. The top-value tip is to share the generous mezze (£29 for two people), and wash it down with the house wine at £8 a bottle. / 1.30 am; D only.

Wine Factory W11 £ 18

294 Westbourne Grove 7229 1877 6–1B

As the name might lead one to suppose, the real attraction at this rather sparse Notting Hill eaterie is the excellent-value wine list. The food is rather less of an excitement, but priced reasonably enough for this trendy part of town – Mozzarella, tomato & avocado salad (£4.50) followed by one of a good selection of pizzas (£7.50) would make a typical meal. This could be accompanied by a bottle (or two) of house wine at the astonishing price of £7 a go. / 11 pm; closed Sun D; no Amex.

The Wine Library EC3 £ 20 𝔸

43 Trinity Sq 7481 0415 9–3D

There's a set charge (£14.95) for the buffet – cheeses, pâtés, quiche, bread, salad, cold meats, fruit and coffee – served in these atmospheric City cellars (now open until 8pm). The point of the place, though, is not the food, but the selection of wines (£8-£400), upon which corkage of only £4.50 is charged. So get your pinstripes on – and don't forget to book! / 8 pm; L & early evening only, closed Sat & Sun.

Wódka W8 £18* 𝔸★

12 St Alban's Grove 7937 6513 5–1B

It's a little out of our price bracket à la carte, but this Kensington fixture's hidden-away location makes it a very suitable destination for a decadent lunch. The 2-course menu (£10.90) offers such Eastern European delights as krupnik (barley soup with bacon) and bozbash (lamb with saffron, pomegranate & coriander), washed down with house wine at £11.50 a bottle. / www.wodka.co.uk; 11.15 pm; closed Sat L & Sun L.

Wong Kei W1 £ 14

41-43 Wardour St 7437 8408 4–3A

It has long been the supposed rudeness of the staff which has been the principal selling-point of this popular Chinatown destination, but sadly they seem to have mellowed a bit of late. The value of the cooking, however, is such that the place remains as busy as ever, and there are some interesting choices for the adventurous. Most main courses are around the £6.50 mark – just a pound less than a bottle of house wine. 'Cash only' means what it says. / 11.15 pm; no credit cards; no booking.

Woodlands £12* ★

37 Panton St, SW1 7839 7258 4–4A
77 Marylebone Ln, W1 7486 3862 3–1A
12-14 Chiswick High Rd, W4 8994 9333 7–2B

It's rather pricey à la carte, but the lunchtime and pre-theatre buffet (£5.99) at the very central West End branch of this international chain of veggie Indians (with other branches in India and Singapore) offers good value. At other times, you might try the house speciality, dhosas (lentil & rice pancakes), with a variety of fillings and coconut chutney, from £4.95. The house wine is £9.95 a bottle. / www.woodlandsrestaurant.co.uk; 10.45 pm.

World Food Café WC2 £ 16

First Floor, 14 Neal's Yd 7379 0298 4–2C

Open only at lunch (when it is very popular), this Covent Garden café, overlooking Neal's Yard, has a justified reputation for the quality of its global veggie fare. Choices range from falafel or Mexican tortillas (around £6.75) to Indian thali or Turkish meze (£7.95). Puddings, such as chocolate cake, are £3.45. Sadly, BYO is no longer an option, so drink fresh juices from £1.95. / L only, closed Sun; no Amex; no smoking; no booking.

Yas W14 £ 17

7 Hammersmith Rd 7603 9148 7–1D

Those who claim London as a 24-hour city still have the slight problem that finding decent nosh after midnight is still all but impossible in many parts of town. Not at this popular Persian by Olympia, however, where your meal might consist of 'kuku-ye sabzi' (a Persian-style quiche of herbs, walnuts & cranberries, £3.95) and stewed lamb with celery & saffron rice (£8.50), washed down with house wine (during licensed hours) at £10.50 a bottle. */ www.yasrestaurant.com; 5 am.*

Yelo N1 £ 17

8-9 Hoxton Sq 7729 4626 9–1D

If you want to be at the heart of the Hoxton action, the outside terrace of this noodle parlour on the square puts you in poll position. The food – with dishes such as Thai dim sum (£3.95) and fish with tamarind sauce (£4.95) – is well-priced and competently done, and house wine is reasonable at £8.95 a bottle. */ www.yelothai.co.uk; 11 pm; no booking.*

Yming W1 £16* A★★

35-36 Greek St 7734 2721 4–2A

If you're looking for a really good-quality Chinese meal within our budget, avoid the tourist-traps of Chinatown and skip over Shaftesbury Avenue to seek out this still under-appreciated Soho fixture. You'd need quite a lot of self-control to stay within our price limit à la carte, but it's certainly possible if you visit from noon-6pm, when you can have three courses – perhaps prawn toast, a meat dish, and lychees, plus coffee or tea – for only £10 (the same price as a bottle of the house wine). */ www.yming.com; 11.45 pm; closed Sun; no smoking area.*

Yoshino W1 £18* ★★

3 Piccadilly Pl 7287 6622 3–3D

It used to be so authentic that they only did the lunch menu in Japanese, but the attractions of this handily-located café (just by Piccadilly Circus) are now a touch more accessible to those who speak only English. A la carte prices are a little outside our range, but if you stick to one of the wide range of bento boxes (£5.80-£19) – for example, the £9.80 box contains sashimi, tofu, grilled fish and sweet omelette, accompanied by rice, vegetables, pickles and miso soup – you can stay happily within our limit. It's best to stick to drinking complimentary tea, though, as the house wine is £13.50 a bottle. */ www.yoshino.net; 10 pm; closed Sun; no smoking.*

Yum Yum N16 £ 18 A★

30 Stoke Newington Church St 7254 6751 1–1C

The Stoke Newington restaurant scene continues to get ever more competitive, but this ornately decorated Thai restaurant maintains its eminent position. Top value is the 2-course set lunch menu (£6.95, including coffee), which might include deep-fried vegetables with plum sauce followed by 'prize-winning' lamb & peanut butter curry. Even à la carte, though, and with house wine (from a decent list) at £9.50 a bottle, you can eat within our budget at any time. Note that, at dinner, there is a minimum charge of £10 per person. */ www.yumyum.co.uk; 10.45 pm, Fri & Sat 11.15 pm.*

Zamoyski NW3 £ 18

85 Fleet Rd 7794 4792 8–2A

With care, you could sample the traditional Polish cuisine on offer at this atmospheric Hampstead restaurant at any time of the week and still remain comfortably within our budget. Starters such as placki losos (herrings with sour cream, apples & onions) and main courses like ruski pierog (wild mushroom & saurkraut pie) will undoubtedly leave you feeling satisfied. Drink house wine at £10.95, or go Polish and have a shot of vodka for £2. / 11 pm; closed Mon, Tue–Sat D only, Sun open L & D; no smoking area.

Zamzama NW1 £ 14 A

161-163 Drummond St 7387 6699 8–4C

If you're looking for Indian food in whizzy modern surroundings, look no further than this futuristic newcomer, not far from Euston station. The setting rather eclipses the food, but the realisation of such dishes as cheese-stuffed chicken with mango sauce (£6.75) or, more prosaically, lamb curry (£5.50) is perfectly competent. The house wine is £7.50 a bottle. / www.zamzama.co.uk; 11.30 pm; closed Sat L & Sun.

ZeNW3 NW3 £20* ★

83 Hampstead High St 7794 7863 8–2A

Situated in the heart of historic Hampstead, this impressively-minimalist '80s Chinese makes a pleasant venue for its good-quality set lunch (£13.80), which includes two starters and a main course with rice and vegetables – you might have spring rolls, soup and crispy aromatic duck. A la carte, the place is well beyond our budget. The house wine is £12.50 a bottle. / www.zenw3.com; 11 pm; no Amex.

Zero Degrees SE3 £ 15 A

29-31 Montpelier Vale 8852 5619 1–4D

There's quite an 'industrial' feel to the impressive modern décor of this Blackheath microbrewery. On the food front, you might go for a wood-fired pizza (around £8), or a sustaining snack such as bruschetta (£2.95), and the excellent house beers start from £2.30 a pint. / www.zerodegrees-microbrewery.co.uk; 11.30 pm.

Zimzun SW6 £ 17 A★

Fulham Broadway Centre 7385 4555 5–4A

If you've not been down to Fulham Broadway for a while, you might be surprised to find that you no longer leave the tube through a Victorian arcade, but via a shiny new shopping centre. Up on the first floor, this (presumably chain-prototype) Thai restaurant is trying very hard offering, at least in these early days, tasty food in an unusually stylish setting. You could eat here comfortably within our budget at any time, but lunchtimes see a simple all-in menu for just £5.95. Wines are pricey (starting at £14.50 a bottle), so beer (from £2.95) may be a better bet. / www.zimzun.co.uk; 11 pm; no Amex; smoking in bar only.

INDEXES & CUISINES

BREAKFAST
(WITH OPENING TIMES)

Central
Balans: *all branches (8)*
Bank Aldwych *(7 Mon-Fri, Sat 8)*
Bar Italia *(7)*
Bistro 1: *Beak St W1 (11, Sun)*
Carluccio's Caffè: *Market Pl W1 (10); Barrett St W1 (8)*
Eagle Bar Diner *(8 am Mon-Fri)*
Exotika *(8)*
Food for Thought *(9.30)*
Fortnum's Fountain *(8.30)*
La Galette *(8.30 Mon-Fri, 10 Sat & Sun)*
Giraffe: *W1 (8, Sat & Sun 9)*
Maison Bertaux *(8.30)*
Pâtisserie Valerie: *Old Compton St W1 (7.30, Sun 9); Marylebone High St W1 (8, Sun 9)*
Paul: *WC2 (7.30)*
Pizza on the Park *(8.15)*
Tapa Room (Providores) *(9, Sat & Sun 10)*
Sherlock's Grill *(6.30)*
Soup Opera: *all central branches (7.30)*
Star Café *(7)*

West
Adams Café *(7.30, Sat 8.30)*
Balans West: *all branches (8)*
Beirut Express *(7.30)*
Café 206 *(8)*
Café Crêperie de Hampstead *(Mon-Fri 9)*
Café Laville *(10)*
Chelsea Bun Diner: *all branches (7)*
La Delizia *(10)*
Fileric *(8)*
Lisboa Patisserie *(7.45)*
Le Metro *(7.30, Sun 8.00)*
Pâtisserie Valerie: *W8 (7.30, Sun 9)*
Ranoush: *W2 (9)*
Raoul's Café *(8.30, Sun 9)*
Le Shop *(10.30)*
Soup Opera: *SW5 (7.30)*
The Station *(Sat & Sun 11 am)*
Tom's *(8, Sun 10)*
Troubadour *(9)*
Vingt-Quatre *(24 hrs)*
White Horse *(11 (Sat & Sun))*

North
Banners on the Hill: *N19 (9); N8 (9, Sat & Sun 10)*
Café Mozart *(9)*
Chamomile *(7)*
Dartmouth Arms *(11, Sat & Sun 10)*
Gallipoli: *all branches (10.30)*
Giraffe: *all north branches (8, Sat & Sun 9)*
Shish: *NW2 (Sat & Sun 10)*
Troika *(8.30)*

South
Balham Kitchen & Bar *(8)*
Bar Estrela *(9 am)*
Boiled Egg *(9, Sun 10)*
Chelsea Bun Diner: *all branches (7)*
Chez Lindsay *(daily before 12:30 pm)*
Eco Brixton: *SW9 (8.30)*
Film Café *(9.30)*
Gastro *(8)*
Giraffe: *SW11 (8, Sat & Sun 9)*
Hudson's *(10 Sat & Sun)*
Konditor & Cook *(8.30)*
La Lanterna *(8, Mon-Sat)*
Tate Modern (Café 7) *(10)*
El Vergel *(8.30)*

East
Bar Capitale: *EC4 (6 (coffee only))*
Brick Lane Beigel Bake *(24 hrs)*
Carluccio's Caffè: *E14 (10); EC1 (8)*
Fox & Anchor *(7)*
Futures *(7.30 Mon-Fri)*
Hope & Sir Loin *(7 Mon-Fri)*
The Place Below *(7.30)*
The Real Greek Souvlaki *(10)*
Smiths (Ground Floor) *(7am, Sat & Sun 9am)*
Soup Opera: *all east branches (6.30)*

BYO
(BRING YOUR OWN WINE)

Central
Exotika
Food for Thought
India Club
Ragam
World Food Café

West
Alounak: all branches
Blah! Blah! Blah!
Café 209
Chelsea Bun Diner: SW10
Kandoo
Mawar
Mohsen
Pappa e Ciccia: Munster Rd SW6
Rôtisserie Jules: SW7
Tendido Cero
Thai Canteen
Tom's

North
Ali Baba
Diwana B-P House
Geeta
Huong-Viet
Seashell

South
Amaranth

Eco Brixton: SW9
Mirch Masala: all branches
Thai Corner Café

East
Lahore Kebab House
Mangal
New Tayyab
The Place Below

CHILDREN

(H – HIGH OR SPECIAL CHAIRS
M – CHILDREN'S MENU
P – CHILDREN'S PORTIONS
E – WEEKEND ENTERTAINMENTS
O – OTHER FACILITIES)

Central
Abeno *(hp)*
Ask!: *SW1, Grafton Way W1, Park St W1 (hp)*
Balans: *all branches (hp)*
Bank Aldwych *(hmo)*
Bank Westminster *(hm)*
Bar Italia *(h)*
Benihana: *W1 (h)*
Brahms *(p)*
La Brasserie Townhouse *(hm)*
Café du Jardin *(p)*
Carluccio's Caffè: *Market Pl W1, Barrett St W1 (h)*
Chowki *(h)*
Chuen Cheng Ku *(h)*
Cristini *(p)*
Eagle Bar Diner *(hpm)*
Ebury Street Wine Bar *(p)*
Efes Kebab House: *all branches (h)*
Food for Thought *(p)*
Fortnum's Fountain *(hmpe)*
Gaby's *(hp)*
La Galette *(h)*
Giraffe: *all branches (hm)*
Golden Dragon *(h)*
Gourmet Pizza Co.: *all branches (h)*
Govinda's *(h)*
Grenadier *(p)*
Harbour City *(h)*
Hard Rock Café *(hmo)*
Incognico *(p)*
Italian Kitchen *(m)*
Joy King Lau *(h)*
Khew *(h)*
Levant *(m)*
Maggiore's *(p)*
Malabar Junction *(h)*
Masala Zone *(hp)*
Mela *(h)*
Mr Kong *(hp)*
New Mayflower *(h)*
New World *(h)*
Ophim *(h)*
Ozer *(h)*
Paul: *WC2 (h)*
Pizza on the Park *(he)*
Poons *(h)*
La Porchetta Pizzeria: *WC1 (h)*
Tapa Room (Providores) *(h)*
Raks *(h)*
Rocket: *W1 (p)*
Royal China: *all branches (h)*
La Rueda: *all branches (hp)*
Rusticana *(h)*
Sapori *(hp)*
Satsuma *(h)*
Shampers *(p)*
J Sheekey *(hp)*
Sherlock's Grill *(hm)*
Souk *(h)*
Star Café *(h)*
Strada: *all central branches (h)*
Tajine *(h)*
Uno *(hm)*
Veeraswamy *(h)*
Wagamama: *all branches (h)*
World Food Café *(h)*
Yoshino *(h)*

West
The Abingdon *(hp)*
Abu Zaad *(h)*
Aglio e Olio *(h)*
Alounak: *W14 (h)*
The Anglesea Arms *(hp)*
Ask!: *SW3, SW6, SW7, W11, Whiteley's, 151 Queensway W2, Spring St W2, W4, W8 (hp)*
Aziz *(h)*
Balans West: *all branches (hp)*
Bar Japan *(h)*
Ben's Thai *(p)*
Benihana: *SW3 (h)*
Bersagliera *(hm)*
Blue Elephant *(he)*
Blue Lagoon *(h)*
Brilliant *(hp)*
Bush Bar & Grill *(hm)*
Café 206 *(p)*
Café 209 *(p)*
Café Crêperie de Hampstead *(h)*
Calzone *(hp)*
Carpaccio's *(hp)*
Chelsea Bun Diner: *all branches (hp)*
Chula *(hp)*
Le Colombier *(hp)*
Coopers Arms *(p)*
The Crown & Sceptre *(hp)*
Dakota *(hm)*
Daquise *(p)*
La Delizia *(h)*
Formosa Dining Room *(h)*
Frantoio *(hp)*
Galicia *(p)*
The Gate: *all branches (h)*
Giá *(h)*
Giraffe: *all branches (hm)*

Gourmet Burger Kitchen: *all branches (hp)*
The Havelock Tavern *(hp)*
Kandoo *(h)*
Khan's *(h)*
Khan's of Kensington *(p)*
Latymers *(h)*
Lots Road *(p)*
Lou Pescadou *(hm)*
Lowiczanka *(hm)*
Lundum's *(p)*
Made in Italy *(h)*
Madhu's *(h)*
Malabar *(hp)*
The Mall Tavern *(hp)*
Mandalay *(hp)*
Mandarin Kitchen *(h)*
Mawar *(h)*
Mediterraneo *(h)*
Meridiana *(h)*
Mohsen *(h)*
Nayaab *(h)*
Noor Jahan: *W2 (p)*
Osteria Basilico *(h)*
Il Pagliaccio *(hmo)*
Palms-on-the-Hill *(hme)*
The Papaya Tree *(h)*
Pappa e Ciccia: *all west branches (hm)*
Paradise by Way of Kensal Green *(hm)*
Pellicano *(hp)*
Phoenicia *(h)*
The Phoenix *(p)*
Ognisko Polskie *(hp)*
Pucci Pizza *(p)*
Raoul's Café *(h)*
Riccardo's *(hmo)*
Rôtisserie: *all branches (h)*
Rôtisserie Jules: *all branches (hm)*
Royal China: *all branches (h)*
La Rueda: *all branches (hp)*
Sabai Sabai *(h)*
Sagar *(p)*
Le Shop *(hp)*
Spago *(h)*
The Station *(m)*
Strada: *all west branches (h)*
The Swan *(p)*
Tendido Cero *(hp)*
Thai Noodle Bar *(p)*
Thai on the River *(h)*
Tom's *(h)*
Troubadour *(h)*
The Vale *(hp)*
Vama *(hp)*
Wagamama: *all branches (h)*
The Walmer Castle *(hp)*
White Horse *(hm)*
William IV *(h)*
Yas *(hp)*
Zimzun *(p)*

North
Afghan Kitchen *(h)*
Ali Baba *(h)*
Anglo Asian Tandoori *(h)*
Ask!: *N1, Hawley Cr NW1, NW3 (hp)*
Banners on the Hill: *N19 (hm); N8 (hmo)*
Bar Mezé: *all branches (h)*
Benihana: *NW3 (he)*
La Brocca *(p)*
Bu San *(h)*
Café de Maya *(hp)*
Café Mozart *(hpe)*
Chamomile *(h)*
Chez Liline *(p)*
Daphne *(hp)*
Dartmouth Arms *(p)*
Don Pepe *(hp)*
Frederick's *(hm)*
Furnace *(p)*
Gallipoli: *all branches (h)*
The Gate: *all branches (h)*
Geeta *(h)*
Giraffe: *all branches (hm)*
Gourmet Burger Kitchen: *all branches (hp)*
Great Nepalese *(p)*
The Green *(hp)*
Huong-Viet *(h)*
Jashan: *all branches (hp)*
Lansdowne *(h)*
Lemonia *(p)*
The Little Bay: *NW6 (p)*
The Lord Palmerston *(p)*
Maghreb *(p)*
Mango Room *(h)*
Marine Ices *(hmp)*
Nautilus *(hp)*
Petit Auberge *(m)*
Le Petit Prince *(p)*
La Piragua *(h)*
Pizzeria Oregano *(hm)*
La Porchetta Pizzeria: *all north branches (hp)*
Rani *(hm)*
The Real Greek *(p)*
Rôtisserie: *all branches (h)*
Royal China: *all branches (h)*
Sabras *(p)*
Le Sacré-Coeur *(h)*
Sakonis *(h)*
The Salusbury *(hm)*
Seashell *(hp)*
Sedir *(hp)*
Shish: *NW2 (hm)*
Singapore Garden *(h)*
Solly's Exclusive *(h)*
Strada: *N1 (h)*
Tartuf *(h)*
Toff's *(hm)*
Troika *(hp)*
Two Brothers *(hm)*
Vegia Zena *(hp)*

Wagamama: *all branches (h)*
Yum Yum *(h)*
Zamoyski *(p)*
ZeNW3 *(h)*

South
A Cena *(hp)*
The Abbeville *(hp)*
Alma *(hp)*
Antipasto & Pasta *(h)*
Antipasto e Pasta *(hp)*
Arancia *(h)*
Ask!: *all south branches (hp)*
Babur Brasserie *(hp)*
Balham Kitchen & Bar *(hp)*
Baltic *(hm)*
Bankside *(h)*
Bar Estrela *(hp)*
Bar Mezé: *all branches (h)*
Bengal Clipper *(h)*
Boiled Egg *(hme)*
Bread & Roses *(ho)*
Buona Sera: *SW11 (h)*
Butlers Wharf Chop-house *(h)*
Café Portugal *(hp)*
Cantinetta Venegazzú *(hp)*
The Castle *(hm)*
Chelsea Bun Diner: *all branches (hp)*
Chez Lindsay *(h)*
Cinnamon Cay *(hm)*
Coromandel *(p)*
The Depot *(hm)*
don Fernando's *(hp)*
Eco: *SW4 (hp)*
Film Café *(hp)*
Fish in a Tie *(h)*
Fujiyama *(h)*
Gastro *(p)*
Giraffe: *all branches (hm)*
Gourmet Burger Kitchen: *all branches (hp)*
Gourmet Pizza Co.: *all branches (h)*
Indian Ocean *(h)*
Kastoori *(p)*
Kennington Lane *(m)*
Kwan Thai *(h)*
Lan Na Thai *(h)*
La Lanterna *(h)*
Lobster Pot *(hp)*
Ma Cuisine *(hp)*
Ma Goa *(hm)*
Mirch Masala: *all branches (h)*
O'Zon *(hm)*
Ost. Antica Bologna *(p)*
Pappa e Ciccia: *SW15 (h)*
The Pepper Tree: *all branches (h)*
Phoenix *(h)*
Pizzeria Castello *(h)*
Polygon Bar & Grill *(hp)*
Rick's Café *(hp)*
La Rueda: *all branches (hp)*
Sarkhel's *(hm)*
Spread Eagle *(hp)*
Sree Krishna *(h)*
The Stepping Stone *(hmo)*
Strada: *SW11, SW4 (h)*
The Sun & Doves *(hp)*
Tas: *all branches (h)*
Tas Pide *(hp)*
Tate Modern (Café 7) *(hmo)*
Thai Corner Café *(p)*
The Trafalgar Tavern *(hm)*
Tsunami *(h)*
El Vergel *(o)*
Willie Gunn *(h)*
Zero Degrees *(h)*

East
Alba *(hp)*
Ask!: *EC1 (h)*
Carluccio's Caffè: *all east branches (h)*
Carnevale *(p)*
Faulkner's *(hm)*
The Fox *(p)*
Frocks *(hp)*
Gourmet Pizza Co.: *all branches (h)*
Haz *(h)*
Kasturi *(m)*
Lahore Kebab House *(h)*
LMNT *(p)*
Moro *(hp)*
The Quality Chop House *(p)*
The Real Greek Souvlaki *(h)*
Royal China: *all branches (h)*
St John *(h)*
Shanghai *(hp)*
Simpson's Tavern *(p)*
Strada: *EC1 (h)*
Viet Hoa *(h)*
Wagamama: *all branches (h)*

ENTERTAINMENT
(CHECK TIMES BEFORE YOU GO)

Central
Bank Aldwych *(jazz, Sun)*
Bank Westminster *(DJ, Wed-Sat)*
Cabanon *(jazz, Fri)*
Café du Jardin *(jazz pianist, Wed-Sat)*
Eagle Bar Diner *(DJ, Tue-Sat)*
The Easton *(DJ, Fri & Sat)*
Efes Kebab House: *Gt Portland St W1 (belly dancer, nightly)*
Hakkasan *(DJ, nightly)*

Levant
(live music, Mon-Wed; DJ & bellydancer Thu-Sun)
Pizza on the Park
(jazz, nightly)
Raks
(jazz Thu; DJ, Fri-Sun)
La Rueda: *W1*
(Spanish music & dancing, Fri & Sat)
Sarastro
(opera, Sun & Mon)
Souk
(belly dancer, live music & DJ, Thu-Sat)

West
Lowiczanka
(Gypsy music, Fri & Sat)
Patio
(Gypsy band, Fri & Sat)
The Prince Bonaparte
(DJ, Fri & Sat)
Spago
(band, Fri; singer, Sat)
The Station
(DJ, Thu-Sat; jazz, Sun)
Vama
(jazz, Sun)
William IV
(DJ, Fri & Sat)

North
La Brocca
(jazz, Thu)
Don Pepe
(singer & organist, Thu-Sat)
The Green
(magician, Thu)
The Highgate
(DJ, Sat & Sun)
Troika
(Russian music, Fri & Sat)
Zamoyski
(Russian music, Sat)

South
Baltic
(jazz, Sun & Mon)
Bengal Clipper
(pianist, nightly)
Film Café
(film theatre)
La Lanterna
(live music, Fri)
Meson don Felipe
(flamenco & guitarist, nightly)
Rick's Café
(saxophonist, Sun (winter only))
La Rueda: *SW4*
(disco, Fri & Sat)
So.uk: *SW4*
(DJ, Wed-Sun)
Talad Thai
(karaoke)
Tas: *Borough High St SE1 (guitarist, nightly); The Cut SE1 (live music, nightly)*
Tas Pide
(guitarist, nightly)
The Trafalgar Tavern
(band, Sat & Sun)
Zero Degrees
(jazz & blues, Mon)

East
Cantaloupe
(DJ, Fri & Sat)
Elephant Royale
(live music, Wed-Sat)
LMNT
(opera, Sun)
Sosho
(DJ, Thu-Sat)
Tokyo City
(karaoke)

LATE

(OPEN TILL MIDNIGHT OR LATER AS SHOWN; MAY BE EARLIER SUNDAY)

Central
Balans: *W1 (5 am, Sun 1 am)*
Bar Italia *(4 am, Fri & Sat open 24 hours)*
Benihana: *all branches (Fri & Sat only)*
Boulevard *(1)*
Café du Jardin *(1)*
Café Emm *(Fri & Sat only, 12.30 am)*
Efes Kebab House: *Gt Portland St W1 (Fri & Sat only, 3 am)*
Hard Rock Café *(12.30 am, Fri & Sat 1 am)*
Incognico
Itsu: *W1 (midnight, Fri & Sat)*
Melati *(Fri & Sat only, 12.30 am)*
Mr Kong *(2.45 am)*
New Mayflower *(3.45 am)*
Ozer
Pizza on the Park *(1)*
La Porchetta Pizzeria: *all branches (midnight)*
Rasa: *all branches (Fri & Sat only)*
J Sheekey

West
Alounak: *all branches*
Anarkali
Balans: *W8 (1 am); SW5 (1 am)*
Beirut Express *(1.45 am)*
Benihana: *all branches (Fri & Sat only)*
Blue Elephant
Calzone *(midnight, Fri & Sat 12.30 am)*
Chelsea Bun Diner: *SW10 (midnight)*
La Delizia
Lou Pescadou
Nayaab
Il Pagliaccio
Patio
Pucci Pizza *(12.30 am)*
Ranoush: *W2 (3 am)*
Riccardo's
Le Shop
Spago
Tandoori of Chelsea
Vingt-Quatre *(24 hours)*
Wine & Kebab *(2 am)*
Yas *(5 am)*

North
Ali Baba
Banners: *N8 (Fri & Sat only)*
Benihana: *all branches (Fri & Sat only)*
Don Pepe
The Little Bay: *all branches*
La Piragua
La Porchetta Pizzeria: *all branches (midnight)*
Rasa: *all branches (Fri & Sat only)*
Tartuf *(midnight)*
Vrisaki

South
Buona Sera: *SW11*
Gastro

East
Brick Lane Beigel Bake *(24 hours)*
Lahore Kebab House
The Little Bay: *all branches*

NO-SMOKING AREAS
(* COMPLETELY NO SMOKING)

Central
Bistro 1: *James St W1, WC2*
Boulevard
La Brasserie Townhouse
Busaba Eathai: *all branches**
Chada: *all branches*
Chiang Mai
Chowki
Chuen Cheng Ku
Food for Thought*
Fortnum's Fountain
Gaby's
La Galette*
Giraffe: *all branches**
Govinda's*
Hakkasan
Hard Rock Café
Ikkyu
Italian Kitchen
Itsu: *all branches**
Kulu Kulu: *WC2*; W1*
Maison Bertaux
Malabar Junction
Masala Zone*
Mela
Mildred's*
New World
Ophim
Pan-Asian Canteen
Pâtisserie Valerie: *all branches*
Paul: *all branches**
Pizza on the Park
Poons
Poons, Lisle Street
Rasa: *all branches**
Red Veg*
Royal Court Bar
Rusticana
Satsuma*
Sherlock's Grill*
Souk
Soup Opera: *all branches**
Star Café
Strada: *all branches*
Taro: *all branches**
Thai Café
Tokyo Diner
Wagamama: *all branches**
World Food Café*
Yming
Yoshino*

West
Abu Zaad
Ben's Thai
Blue Lagoon
Brilliant
Café Crêperie de Hampstead*
Café Laville
Churchill Arms
The Crown & Sceptre
Daquise
Fish Hoek
Giraffe: *all branches**
Gourmet Burger Kitchen: *all branches**
Itsu: *all branches**
Khan's
Khan's of Kensington
Kulu Kulu: *SW7*
Latymers*
Mandalay*
Mawar
Le Metro
Noor Jahan: *W2*
Palms-on-the-Hill
The Papaya Tree
Pâtisserie Valerie: *all branches*
Phoenicia
Raoul's Café
Sabai Sabai
Sagar
Soup Opera: *all branches**
Southeast W9
Standard Tandoori
Strada: *all branches*
Thai Bistro*
Tom's*
The Vale
Wagamama: *all branches**
White Horse*
The Windsor Castle
Zimzun*

North
Anglo Asian Tandoori
Bar Mezé: *all branches*
Café de Maya
Café Japan
Café Mozart*
Cantina Italia

Chamomile
Chutneys*
Diwana B-P House
Frederick's
The Gate: *NW3*
Giraffe: *all branches**
Gourmet Burger Kitchen: *all branches**
Jashan: *HA0**
Little Basil
The Little Bay: *all branches*
Marine Ices
Oriental City
The Parsee
Pizzeria Oregano
Rani*
Rasa: *all branches**
Rasa Travancore*
Sabras
Sakonis*
Seashell
Shish: *all branches**
Solly's Exclusive
Strada: *all branches*
Sushi-Say*
Toff's
Troika
Two Brothers
Viet-Anh
Wagamama: *all branches**
Zamoyski

South

Amaranth
Babur Brasserie
Bankside
Bar Mezé: *all branches*
Bread & Roses
Café Portugal
Chada: *all branches*
Coromandel
The Depot
don Fernando's
Eco: *SW4*
Film Café
Fujiyama
Gastro
Giraffe: *all branches**
Gourmet Burger Kitchen: *all branches**
Indian Ocean
Kennington Lane*
Konditor & Cook
Kwan Thai
Mirch Masala: *SW17**
The Pepper Tree: *all branches*
Phoenix
Sarkhel's
The Stepping Stone
Strada: *all branches*
The Sun & Doves
Talad Thai*
Tate Modern (Café 7)*
Thailand*
Tsunami
El Vergel*

East

Apium*
Arkansas Café*
Brick Lane Beigel Bake*
Don Pedro
Elephant Royale
Faulkner's
Gourmet Pizza Co.: *E14*
Haz
Itsu: *all branches**
K10*
Kasturi
The Little Bay: *all branches*
Moshi Moshi: *all branches**
Noto*
The Place Below*
The Quality Chop House
Shish: *all branches**
Soup Opera: *all branches**
Strada: *all branches*
Wagamama: *all branches**

OUTSIDE TABLES
(* PARTICULARLY RECOMMENDED)

Central

Ask!: *Grafton Way W1*
Aurora*
Balans: *all branches*
Bank Westminster
Bar Italia
Boulevard
Brahms*
Café du Jardin
Carluccio's Caffè: *Market Pl W1, Barrett St W1**
Chada: *W1*
The Easton
Efes Kebab House: *Gt Titchfield St W1*
The Endurance
Giraffe: *W1*
Gordon's Wine Bar*
Hard Rock Café
Hellenik
Khew
Mela
Ozer
Pizza on the Park
Tapa Room (Providores)
Rocket: *all branches*
La Rueda: *all branches*
Running Horse
Sapori
Sarastro
Soup Opera: *W1*
Strada: *Market Pl W1*; New Burlington St W1*
Tajine

Uno

West
The Abingdon*
The Anglesea Arms
Ask!: *SW6, Spring St W2, W4*
The Atlas*
Balans West: *all branches*
The Brackenbury*
The Builder's Arms
Bush Bar & Grill*
Café 206
Café Crêperie de Hampstead
Café Laville*
Calzone
The Chelsea Ram
Le Colombier*
The Crown & Sceptre*
Dakota*
La Delizia
Il Falconiere
The Gate: *W6**
Giá
Giraffe: *all west branches*
Golborne House
The Havelock Tavern
Kandoo
Latymers
Lisboa Patisserie
Lou Pescadou
Lundum's
Made in Italy
The Mall Tavern
Mediterraneo
Meridiana
Mohsen
Nicolas Bar à Vins
Old Parr's Head
Osteria Basilico
Il Pagliaccio
Pappa e Ciccia: *all branches*
Paradise by Way of Kensal Green
Pellicano
Père Michel
The Phoenix
The Pilot*
Ognisko Polskie*
The Prince Bonaparte
Raoul's Café
The Red Pepper
Riccardo's
Rôtisserie Jules: *SW7*
La Rueda: *all branches*
The Station*
Stone Mason's Arms
The Swan*
Thai on the River*
The Thatched House*
Tom's*
Troubadour
Uli*
Vama
White Horse*
William IV*
The Windsor Castle*
Wine Factory

North
Ask!: *N1, NW3*
Banners on the Hill: *N19*
Benihana: *NW3*
La Brocca
Café Mozart*
Chamomile
The Chapel*
Daphne*
Dartmouth Arms
Frederick's*
Gallipoli: *all branches*
The Gate: *NW3*
Giraffe: *N1*
Gourmet Burger Kitchen: *NW6*
The Green
The Highgate
Lansdowne
Lemonia
Little Basil
The Little Bay: *all branches*
The Lord Palmerston
North Sea Fish
Petit Auberge
Queen's Pub & Dining Rm
The Real Greek
Rôtisserie: *N1*
Le Sacré-Coeur
The Salusbury
Sedir
Singapore Garden
Solly's Exclusive
Strada: *N1*
Tartuf
Troika
Vegia Zena*
Yelo

South
The Abbeville
Antipasto & Pasta
Antipasto e Pasta
Arancia
Ask!: *SE1*
Babur Brasserie
Balham Kitchen & Bar
Baltic
Bar Estrela*
Bar Mezé: *all south branches*
Boiled Egg*
Bread & Roses*
Buona Sera: *SW11*
Butlers Wharf Chop-house*
Cantinetta Venegazzú*
The Castle*
Chelsea Bun Diner: *SW11*
Cinnamon Cay

The Depot*
don Fernando's
Film Café
Gastro
Giraffe: *SW11*
Gourmet Burger Kitchen: *SW11*
Gourmet Pizza Co.: *SE1**
Hudson's
Kennington Lane*
Kwan Thai*
Lan Na Thai
La Lanterna
Ma Cuisine
Ost. Antica Bologna
Pappa e Ciccia: *all branches*
The Pepper Tree: *all branches*
Phoenix
Popeseye: *SW15*
Rocket Riverside: *all branches*
La Rueda: *all branches*
Spread Eagle
Strada: *SW11*
The Sun & Doves*
White Cross*

East
Arkansas Café
Ask!: *EC1*
Bar Capitale: *all branches*
Carluccio's Caffè: *all east branches*
Carnevale*
The Eagle
Elephant Royale*
The Fox
Frocks*
Gourmet Pizza Co.: *E14*
The Little Bay: *all branches*
LMNT
Moro
New Tayyab
The Place Below*
Royal China: *E14*

PRE/POST THEATRE

(EVENING OPENINGS TIMES ARE GIVEN; * OPEN ALL DAY)

Central
Boulevard
Café du Jardin
Chiang Mai
Chuen Cheng Ku
Deca
Le Deuxième
Gaby's
Gopal's of Soho
Gordon's Wine Bar
Harbour City
Incognico
Italian Kitchen
Luigi's
Melati
Mon Plaisir
Mr Kong
New World
Poons
Poons, Lisle Street
Satsuma
Shampers
J Sheekey
Tokyo Diner
Wagamama: *WC1*
Wong Kei

North
Frederick's

East
Alba

PRIVATE ROOMS

(FOR THE MOST COMPREHENSIVE LISTING OF VENUES FOR FUNCTIONS – FROM PALACES TO PUBS – SEE HARDEN'S LONDON PARTY GUIDE, AVAILABLE IN ALL GOOD BOOKSHOPS)
*** PARTICULARLY RECOMMENDED**

Central
Aperitivo *(30)*
Aurora *(20)*
Bam-Bou *(14, 20)**
Bank Aldwych *(30)*
Bank Westminster *(20,20)**
Benihana: *W1 (10)*
Bistro 1: *Beak St W1 (20); James St W1 (25); WC2 (30)*
Boulevard *(80)*
La Brasserie Townhouse *(40)*
Cabanon *(12)*
Café du Jardin *(60)*
Chiang Mai *(30)*
Chuen Cheng Ku *(56)*
Deca *(16)*
Efes Kebab House: *Gt Titchfield St W1 (45)*
Fortnum's Fountain *(56)*
Gaby's *(20)*
Golden Dragon *(40)*
Grumbles *(12)*
Hakkasan *(80)*
Harbour City *(80,60,40)*
Ikkyu *(10)*
Italian Kitchen *(10)*
Jenny Lo's *(20)*
Joy King Lau *(60)*
Khew *(14)*
Levant *(10,12)*
Luigi's *(14,20,35)*
Maggiore's *(25-30)*
Mela *(40)*
Melati *(35)*
Mon Plaisir *(28)*
Mr Kong *(40)*
New World *(200)*

Pan-Asian Canteen *(41)*
Pizza on the Park *(100)*
Poons, Lisle Street *(15,35)*
Raks *(75)*
Rasa: *W1 (85)*
Rocket: *W1 (10,25)*
Royal China: *W1 (12)*
Royal Court Bar *(20)*
Sarastro *(6-28)*
Shampers *(45)*
Sherlock's Grill *(7)*
Smithy's *(70)*
Souk *(20,15,55,45)*
Star Café *(35)*
Thai Café *(22)*
Veeraswamy *(36)*
Yming *(13,19)*

West

Abu Zaad *(25)*
Adams Café *(24)*
Anarkali *(40)*
The Atlas *(40)*
Bar Japan *(6)*
Ben's Thai *(20)*
Benihana: *SW3 (12)*
Blah! Blah! Blah! *(35)*
Blue Lagoon *(30)*
The Brackenbury *(30)*
Brilliant *(125)*
Bush Bar & Grill *(50)*
Carpaccio's *(45)*
Chelsea Bun Diner: *SW10 (35)*
The Chelsea Ram *(18)*
Le Colombier *(28)*
Coopers Arms *(25)*
Dakota *(30)**
Daquise *(25,50)*
Il Falconiere *(35)*
Giá *(20)*
Golborne House *(35)*
Good Earth *(40)*
The Ifield *(25)*
Kandoo *(25,25)*
Khan's *(200)*
Khan's of Kensington *(30)*
Krungtap *(30)*
Kulu Kulu: *SW7 (15)*
Lomo *(20)*
Lou Pescadou *(45)*
Lowiczanka *(60)*
Made in Italy *(20)*
Madhu's *(50)*
Malabar *(40)*
The Mall Tavern *(20)*
Meridiana *(50)*
Nayaab *(45)*
Nicolas Bar à Vins *(30)*
Noor Jahan: *W2 (16)*
Il Pagliaccio *(60)*
Paradise by Way of Kensal Green *(20)*
Patio *(50)*
Pellicano *(25)*
Père Michel *(25)*
Phoenicia *(36)*
Ognisko Polskie *(20,50)*
Pucci Pizza *(50)*
Raoul's Café *(18)*
Riccardo's *(8)*
Rôtisserie Jules: *W11 (56)*
Royal China: *W2 (15,20)*
Le Shop *(35)*
Southeast W9 *(30)*
Spago *(40)*
Standard Tandoori *(55)*
The Station *(100)*
Stick & Bowl *(20)*
Stratford's *(30)*
Tandoori Lane *(16)*
Tawana *(50)*
Thai Noodle Bar *(25)*
Thai on the River *(90)*
The Thatched House *(30)*
Troubadour *(34)*
Uli *(32)*
The Vale *(14,30,40)*
Vama *(30)*
White Horse *(45)*
William IV *(35)*
Wine Factory *(45)*
Wódka *(30)*
Yas *(34)*

North

Afghan Kitchen *(25)*
Anglo Asian Tandoori *(30-40)*
Bradley's *(65)*
Cantina Italia *(30)*
The Chapel *(30)*
Chutneys *(60,35)*
Daphne *(50)*
Diwana B-P House *(35)*
Frederick's *(18,32)*
Furnace *(40)*
Geeta *(36)*
The Green *(12)*
Gung-Ho *(24)*
Huong-Viet *(28)*
Lemonia *(40)*
Little Basil *(30)*
The Lord Palmerston *(30)*
Mango Room *(30)*
North Sea Fish *(80)*
The Parsee *(18)*
Petit Auberge *(45)*
La Piragua *(70)*
Rasa: *N16 (45)*
The Real Greek *(8,20)*
Royal China: *NW8 (15,20)*
Seashell *(30)*
Sedir *(42)*
Singapore Garden *(6)*
Solly's Exclusive *(100)*
Sushi-Say *(6)*
Tartuf *(40)*

Vegia Zena *(20)*
Vrisaki *(14)*
Yum Yum *(30)*
Zamoyski *(40)*
Zamzama *(40)*
ZeNW3 *(24)*

South

Alma *(70)*
Amaranth *(30)*
Antipasto & Pasta *(30)*
Arancia *(8)*
Balham Kitchen & Bar *(20,25)*
Baltic *(35)*
Bankside *(70)*
Bar Estrela *(40)*
Bar Mezé*: EC1 (12)*
Bread & Roses *(65)*
The Castle *(30)*
Chez Lindsay *(36)*
Coromandel *(30)*
don Fernando's *(100)*
Fish in a Tie *(40,20,60)*
Fujiyama *(35,10,25)*
Hudson's *(12)*
Kennington Lane *(40)*
Kwan Thai *(50)*
La Lanterna *(85,50)*
Lobster Pot *(14)*
Ma Goa *(35)*
Pizzeria Castello *(80)*
Spread Eagle *(35)*
Sree Krishna *(50,60)*
Talad Thai *(40)*
Tas*: Borough High St SE1 (140); The Cut SE1 (35)*
Thailand *(28)*
The Trafalgar Tavern *(200)**
White Cross *(30)*

East

Alba *(30)*
Arkansas Café *(50)*
Cantaloupe *(20)*
The Evangelist *(50)*
Fox & Anchor *(24)*
Frocks *(30)*
Hope & Sir Loin *(20)*
Moro *(12)*
Moshi Moshi*: EC4 (60)*
The Real Greek Souvlaki *(25)*
Royal China*: E14 (15,20)*
St John *(18)*
Shanghai *(40,40)*
Sosho *(100)*

ALSATIAN

★
Tartuf *(N1)*

AMERICAN

-
Arkansas Café *(E1)*
Dakota *(W11)*

AUSTRALIAN

A★
Cinnamon Cay *(SW11)*

BRITISH, MODERN

A★★
Frederick's *(N1)*
The Stepping Stone *(SW8)*

★★
Konditor & Cook *(SE1)*

A★
Bank Aldwych *(WC2)*
Bank Westminster *(SW1)*
The Brackenbury *(W6)*
Café du Jardin *(WC2)*
The Depot *(SW14)*
Formosa Dining Room *(W9)*
The Fox *(EC2)*
The Havelock Tavern *(W14)*
The Lord Palmerston *(NW5)*
Mango Room *(NW1)*
Phoenix *(SW15)*
William IV *(NW10)*

★
The Abbeville *(SW4)*
The Anglesea Arms *(W6)*
Bradley's *(NW3)*
La Brasserie Townhouse *(WC1)*
Le Deuxième *(WC2)*
The Highgate *(NW5)*
Kennington Lane *(SE11)*
The Mall Tavern *(W8)*
The Quality Chop House *(EC1)*
St John *(EC1)*
Sherlock's Grill *(W1)*
The Station *(W10)*
The Vale *(W9)*

A-
The Abingdon *(W8)*
Aurora *(W1)*
The Builder's Arms *(SW3)*
Bush Bar & Grill *(W12)*
Coopers Arms *(SW3)*
Dartmouth Arms *(NW5)*
The Evangelist *(EC4)*
Fortnum's Fountain *(W1)*
Frocks *(E9)*
Golborne House *(W10)*
The Green *(NW2)*
The Ifield *(SW10)*
Lansdowne *(NW1)*
LMNT *(E8)*
Lots Road *(SW10)*
Paradise by Way of Kensal Green *(W10)*
The Phoenix *(SW3)*
Sosho *(EC2)*
Stone Mason's Arms *(W6)*
The Sun & Doves *(SE5)*
The Thatched House *(W6)*
Willie Gunn *(SW18)*

-
Balham Kitchen & Bar *(SW12)*
Bankside *(SE1)*
The Castle *(SW11)*
The Chapel *(NW1)*
The Chelsea Ram *(SW10)*
The Crown & Sceptre *(W12)*
The Easton *(WC1)*
Ebury Street Wine Bar *(SW1)*
Le Metro *(SW3)*
The Pilot *(W4)*
The Prince Bonaparte *(W2)*
Queen's Pub & Dining Rm *(NW1)*
Raoul's Café *(W9)*
Rick's Café *(SW17)*
Smithy's *(WC1)*
Vingt-Quatre *(SW10)*
White Horse *(SW6)*

BRITISH, TRADITIONAL

A★
Butlers Wharf Chop-house *(SE1)*

★
The Endurance *(W1)*
The Quality Chop House *(EC1)*

A-
Grenadier *(SW1)*
Simpson's Tavern *(EC3)*
The Trafalgar Tavern *(SE10)*
The Windsor Castle *(W8)*
The Wine Library *(EC3)*

-
Ffiona's *(W8)*
Fox & Anchor *(EC1)*

Hope & Sir Loin *(EC1)*

DANISH

A★★

Lundum's *(SW7)*

EAST & CENT. EUROPEAN

A-

Café Mozart *(N6)*

-

Troika *(NW1)*

FISH & SEAFOOD

A★★

J Sheekey *(WC2)*

★★

Chez Liline *(N4)*
Mandarin Kitchen *(W2)*

A★

Lobster Pot *(SE11)*

★

Bradley's *(NW3)*
Lou Pescadou *(SW5)*
Stratford's *(W8)*

A-

The Cow *(W2)*
The Evangelist *(EC4)*
Gastro *(SW4)*
Polygon Bar & Grill *(SW4)*
Sweetings *(EC4)*

-

Balham Kitchen & Bar *(SW12)*
Rick's Café *(SW17)*

FRENCH

★★

Incognico *(WC2)*
Ma Cuisine *(TW1)*

A★

Chez Lindsay *(TW10)*
Deca *(W1)*
Maggiore's *(WC2)*
Mon Plaisir *(WC2)*
Spread Eagle *(SE10)*

★

Cabanon *(W1)*
Lou Pescadou *(SW5)*
Nicolas Bar à Vins *(SW10)*

A-

La Bouchée *(SW7)*
Le Colombier *(SW3)*
Gastro *(SW4)*
Le Sacré-Coeur *(N1)*

-

Café Crêperie de Hampstead *(SW7)*
La Galette *(W1)*
Père Michel *(W2)*
Petit Auberge *(N1)*
Le Petit Prince *(NW5)*

FUSION

★★

Tsunami *(SW4)*

A★

Bam-Bou *(W1)*
Cinnamon Cay *(SW11)*
Tapa Room (Providores) *(W1)*

GREEK

A★★

The Real Greek Souvlaki *(EC1)*

A★

Hellenik *(W1)*
The Real Greek *(N1)*

★

Vrisaki *(N22)*
Wine & Kebab *(SW10)*

A-

Lemonia *(NW1)*

-

Bar Mezé *(EC1, N10, SW11)*
Daphne *(NW1)*

INTERNATIONAL

★

Govinda's *(W1)*

A-

Alma *(SW18)*
Bread & Roses *(SW4)*
Café Emm *(W1)*
Café Laville *(W2)*
Coopers Arms *(SW3)*
Gordon's Wine Bar *(WC2)*
Hudson's *(SW15)*
Sarastro *(WC2)*
Shampers *(W1)*
Tate Modern (Café 7) *(SE1)*
White Cross *(TW9)*
The Windsor Castle *(W8)*

-
Balans West (SW5, W1, W8)
Banners (N8)
Banners on the Hill (N19)
Boulevard (WC2)
Brahms (SW1)
Chelsea Bun Diner (SW10, SW11)
Exotika (WC2)
Film Café (SE1)
Giraffe (N1, NW3, SW11, W1, W4, W8)
Grumbles (SW1)
Palms-on-the-Hill (W8)
Royal Court Bar (SW1)
Running Horse (W1)
Star Café (W1)

ITALIAN

A★
A Cena (TW1)
Frantoio (SW10)
Giá (SW3)
Maggiore's (WC2)
Ost. Antica Bologna (SW11)
Osteria Basilico (W11)
Pappa e Ciccia (SW15, SW6)

★
Aglio e Olio (SW10)
Alba (EC1)
Antipasto e Pasta (SW4)
Cantinetta Venegazzú (SW11)
Cristini (W1)
La Delizia (SW3)
Made in Italy (SW3)
Pellicano (SW3)
Pizzeria Castello (SE1)
Pizzeria Oregano (N1)
La Porchetta Pizzeria (N1, N4, WC1)
The Red Pepper (W9)
Vegia Zena (NW1)

A-
Aperitivo (W1)
Arancia (SE16)
Bersagliera (SW3)
La Brocca (NW6)
Buona Sera (SW11, SW3)
Café 206 (W11)
Carpaccio's (SW3)
Luigi's (WC2)
Il Pagliaccio (SW6)
Pizza on the Park (SW1)
Riccardo's (SW3)

-
Antipasto & Pasta (SW11)
Cantina Italia (N1)
Carluccio's Caffè (E14, EC1, N1, W1, W5)
Il Falconiere (SW7)
Italian Kitchen (WC1)
La Lanterna (SE1)
Marine Ices (NW3)
Meridiana (W8)
Rusticana (W1)
The Salusbury (NW6)
Sapori (WC2)
Spago (SW7)
Strada (EC1, N1, SW11, SW13, SW4, SW5, SW6, W1, WC2)
Uno (SW1)
Wine Factory (W11)

MEDITERRANEAN

★★
El Vergel (SE1)

A★
The Eagle (EC1)
Mediterraneo (W11)
The Swan (W4)

★
Made in Italy (SW3)
Raks (W1)

A-
The Atlas (SW6)
Fish in a Tie (SW11)
The Little Bay (EC1, NW6)
Rocket (W1)
Rocket Riverside (SW15)
Troubadour (SW5)

-
Bistro 1 (W1, WC2)
Cantaloupe (EC2)
The Chapel (NW1)
Raoul's Café (W9)
Tom's (W11)

POLISH

A-
Wódka (W8)

A-
Baltic (SE1)
Patio (W12)
Ognisko Polskie (SW7)

-
Daquise (SW7)
Lowiczanka (W6)
Zamoyski (NW3)

PORTUGUESE

★★
Lisboa Patisserie *(W10)*

★
Bar Estrela *(SW8)*

Ⓐ-
Café Portugal *(SW8)*

RUSSIAN

-
Troika *(NW1)*

SPANISH

Ⓐ★★
Moro *(EC1)*

★
Bar Estrela *(SW8)*
Tendido Cero *(SW5)*

Ⓐ-
don Fernando's *(TW9)*
Don Pedro *(EC1)*
Don Pepe *(NW8)*
Lomo *(SW10)*
Meson don Felipe *(SE1)*
Rebato's *(SW8)*
La Rueda *(SW4, SW6, W1)*

-
Galicia *(W10)*

STEAKS & GRILLS

★★
Rôtisserie *(N1, W12)*

★
Popeseye *(SW15, W14)*

Ⓐ-
Polygon Bar & Grill *(SW4)*
Simpson's Tavern *(EC3)*

-
Arkansas Café *(E1)*
Fox & Anchor *(EC1)*
Hope & Sir Loin *(EC1)*
Rôtisserie Jules *(SW7, W11)*

VEGETARIAN

★★
Blah! Blah! Blah! *(W12)*
Chiang Mai *(W1)*
The Gate *(NW3, W6)*
Geeta *(NW6)*
Kastoori *(SW17)*
Rasa *(N16, W1)*
Sabras *(NW10)*
Sakonis *(HA0)*
Vijay *(NW6)*

Ⓐ★
Blue Elephant *(SW6)*
Malabar Junction *(WC1)*
The Place Below *(EC2)*

★
Carnevale *(EC1)*
Chutneys *(NW1)*
Diwana B-P House *(NW1)*
Food for Thought *(WC2)*
Futures *(EC3)*
Govinda's *(W1)*
Jashan *(HA0, N8)*
Mildred's *(W1)*
Rani *(N3)*
Red Veg *(W1)*
Sree Krishna *(SW17)*
Woodlands *(SW1, W1, W4)*

-
Blue Lagoon *(W14)*
India Club *(WC2)*
Masala Zone *(W1)*
Sedir *(N1)*
World Food Café *(WC2)*

AFTERNOON TEA

Ⓐ-
Aurora *(W1)*

-
Daquise *(SW7)*
Pâtisserie Valerie *(SW1, W1, W8)*

BURGERS, ETC

Ⓐ★
Smiths (Ground Floor) *(EC1)*

★
Gourmet Burger
Kitchen *(NW6, SW11, SW15, SW6)*
Red Veg *(W1)*

Ⓐ-
Eagle Bar Diner *(W1)*
Hard Rock Café *(W1)*

-
Arkansas Café *(E1)*

CREPES

Ⓐ★
Chez Lindsay *(TW10)*

-
Café Crêperie de
Hampstead *(SW7)*

La Galette *(W1)*
Le Shop *(SW3)*

FISH & CHIPS

★★
Faulkner's *(E8)*

★
Brady's *(SW18)*
Nautilus *(NW6)*
North Sea Fish *(WC1)*
Seashell *(NW1)*
Two Brothers *(N3)*

-
Fryer's Delight *(WC1)*
Toff's *(N10)*

ICE CREAM

-
Marine Ices *(NW3)*

PIZZA

★★
Basilico *(NW3, SW11, SW14, SW6)*

A★
Osteria Basilico *(W11)*

★
Bar Capitale *(EC2, EC4)*
La Delizia *(SW3)*
Eco *(SW4)*
Eco Brixton *(SW9)*
Furnace *(N1)*
Made in Italy *(SW3)*
Pizzeria Castello *(SE1)*
Pizzeria Oregano *(N1)*
La Porchetta Pizzeria *(N1, N4, WC1)*
The Red Pepper *(W9)*

A-
Bersagliera *(SW3)*
La Brocca *(NW6)*
Buona Sera *(SW11, SW3)*
Pizza on the Park *(SW1)*
Pucci Pizza *(SW3)*
Rocket *(W1)*
Rocket Riverside *(SW15)*
Zero Degrees *(SE3)*

-
Ask! *(EC1, N1, NW1, NW3, SE1, SW1, SW13, SW3, SW6, SW7, W1, W11, W2, W4, W8)*
Calzone *(SW10)*
Cantina Italia *(N1)*
Gourmet Pizza Co. *(E14, SE1, W1)*
La Lanterna *(SE1)*
Marine Ices *(NW3)*
Sapori *(WC2)*
Spago *(SW7)*
Strada *(EC1, N1, SW11, SW13, SW4, SW5, SW6, W1, WC2)*
Wine Factory *(W11)*

SANDWICHES, CAKES, ETC

★★
Brick Lane Beigel Bake *(E1)*
Konditor & Cook *(SE1)*
Lisboa Patisserie *(W10)*

A★
Maison Bertaux *(W1)*
Smiths (Ground Floor) *(EC1)*

★
Fileric *(SW7)*
Segafredo Zanetti *(W1)*

A-
Bar Italia *(W1)*
Troubadour *(SW5)*

-
Boiled Egg *(SW11)*
Chamomile *(NW3)*
Pâtisserie Valerie *(SW1, W1, W8)*
Paul *(W1, WC2)*
Tom's *(W11)*

SOUP

-
Soup Opera *(E14, EC2, EC3, SW5, W1, WC2)*

SOUTH AMERICAN

★★
El Vergel *(SE1)*

-
La Piragua *(N1)*

AFRO-CARIBBEAN

A★
Mango Room *(NW1)*

MOROCCAN

A★
The Swan *(W4)*

★
Aziz *(SW6)*
Tajine *(W1)*

-
Adams Café *(W12)*
Maghreb *(N1)*

NORTH AFRICAN

A★★
Moro *(EC1)*

A-
So.uk *(W1, SW4)*
Souk *(WC2)*

-
Azou *(W6)*

SOUTH AFRICAN

★★
Fish Hoek *(W4)*

TUNISIAN

-
Adams Café *(W12)*

EGYPTIAN

★
Ali Baba *(NW1)*

ISRAELI

-
Solly's Exclusive *(NW11)*

KOSHER

-
Solly's Exclusive *(NW11)*

LEBANESE

★★
Beirut Express *(W2)*

★
Phoenicia *(W8)*
Ranoush *(SW3, SW5, W2)*

-
Kaslik *(W1)*

MIDDLE EASTERN

★
Abu Zaad *(W12)*
Aziz *(SW6)*

A-
Levant *(W1)*

-
Gaby's *(WC2)*
Shish *(EC1, NW2)*
Solly's Exclusive *(NW11)*

PERSIAN

★
Alounak *(W14, W2)*
Mohsen *(W14)*

-
Kandoo *(W2)*
Yas *(W14)*

TURKISH

★★
Mangal *(E8)*

A★
Gallipoli *(N1)*
Ozer *(W1)*

★
Haz *(E1)*
Raks *(W1)*

A-
Kazan *(SW1)*
Tas *(SE1)*
Tas Pide *(SE1)*

-
Efes Kebab House *(W1)*
Sedir *(N1)*

AFGHANI

★
Afghan Kitchen *(N1)*

BURMESE

★★
Mandalay *(W2)*

CHINESE

A★★
Yming *(W1)*

★★
Mandarin Kitchen *(W2)*
Royal China *(E14, W1)*
Royal China *(NW8, W2)*
Sakonis *(HA0)*

A★
Hakkasan *(W1)*
Opera *(NW3)*

★
The Four Seasons *(W2)*
Good Earth *(SW3)*
Jenny Lo's *(SW1)*
Joy King Lau *(WC2)*
Mr Kong *(WC2)*
New Mayflower *(W1)*
Singapore Garden *(NW6)*
Stick & Bowl *(W8)*
ZeNW3 *(NW3)*

A-
Shanghai *(E8)*

-
Chuen Cheng Ku *(W1)*
Golden Dragon *(W1)*
Gung-Ho *(NW6)*
Harbour City *(W1)*
New World *(W1)*
Poons *(WC2)*
Poons, Lisle Street *(WC2)*
Wong Kei *(W1)*

CHINESE, DIM SUM

★★
Royal China *(E14, W1)*
Royal China *(NW8, W2)*

★
Joy King Lau *(WC2)*

A-
Shanghai *(E8)*

-
Chuen Cheng Ku *(W1)*
Golden Dragon *(W1)*
Harbour City *(W1)*
Khew *(W1)*
New World *(W1)*

FRENCH-VIETNAMESE

A★
Bam-Bou *(W1)*

INDIAN

A★★
Vama *(SW10)*

★★
Geeta *(NW6)*
Kastoori *(SW17)*
Lahore Kebab House *(E1)*
Madhu's *(UB1)*
Mirch Masala *(SW16, SW17)*
The Parsee *(N19)*
Rasa *(N16, W1)*
Sakonis *(HA0)*
Sarkhel's *(SW18)*
Vijay *(NW6)*

A★
Malabar *(W8)*
Malabar Junction *(WC1)*
Veeraswamy *(W1)*

★
Anglo Asian Tandoori *(N16)*
Babur Brasserie *(SE23)*
Bengal Clipper *(SE1)*
Brilliant *(UB2)*
Chowki *(W1)*
Chutneys *(NW1)*
Diwana B-P House *(NW1)*
Indian Ocean *(SW17)*
Jashan *(HA0, N8)*
Kasturi *(EC3)*
Khan's *(W2)*
Khan's of Kensington *(SW7)*
Ma Goa *(SW15)*
Mela *(WC2)*
Ophim *(W1)*
Rani *(N3)*
Sree Krishna *(SW17)*
Tandoori Lane *(SW6)*
Tandoori of Chelsea *(SW3)*
Woodlands *(SW1, W1, W4)*

A-
Zamzama *(NW1)*

-
Anarkali *(W6)*
Chula *(W6)*
Gopal's of Soho *(W1)*
Great Nepalese *(NW1)*
India Club *(WC2)*
Khyber Pass *(SW7)*
Masala Zone *(W1)*
Nayaab *(SW6)*
Noor Jahan *(SW5, W2)*
Standard Tandoori *(W2)*

INDIAN, SOUTHERN

★★
Geeta *(NW6)*
Kastoori *(SW17)*
Rasa *(N16, W1)*
Sabras *(NW10)*
Sagar *(W6)*
Vijay *(NW6)*

A★
Malabar Junction *(WC1)*

★
Chutneys *(NW1)*
Coromandel *(SW11)*
Ragam *(W1)*

Rani *(N3)*
Rasa Travancore *(N16)*
Sree Krishna *(SW17)*
Woodlands *(SW1, W1, W4)*

-

India Club *(WC2)*

INDONESIAN

-

Melati *(W1)*

JAPANESE

★★

Inaho *(W2)*
Jin Kichi *(NW3)*
K10 *(EC2)*
Kulu Kulu *(SW7, W1, WC2)*
Tsunami *(SW4)*
Yoshino *(W1)*

A★

Benihana *(NW3, SW3, W1)*

★

Abeno *(WC1)*
Bar Japan *(SW5)*
Bu San *(N7)*
Café Japan *(NW11)*
Ikkyu *(W1)*
Itsu *(E14, SW3, W1)*
Noto *(EC2)*
Sushi-Say *(NW2)*
Tokyo City *(EC2)*
ZeNW3 *(NW3)*

Fujiyama *(SW9)*
Moshi Moshi *(E14, EC2, EC4)*
Satsuma *(W1)*
Taro *(W1)*
Tokyo Diner *(WC2)*
Wagamama *(E14, EC2, EC4, NW1, SW1, W1, W8, WC1, WC2)*

KOREAN

★

Bu San *(N7)*

MALAYSIAN

★

Mawar *(W2)*
Singapore Garden *(NW6)*

-

Café de Maya *(NW3)*
Melati *(W1)*

PAKISTANI

★★

Lahore Kebab House *(E1)*
Mirch Masala *(SW16, SW17)*

A★

New Tayyab *(E1)*

-

Nayaab *(SW6)*

PAN-ASIAN

★★

Uli *(W11)*

A★

Zimzun *(SW6)*

★

Pan-Asian Canteen *(SW1)*
Southeast W9 *(W9)*

-

Apium *(EC1)*
Just Oriental *(SW1)*
Khew *(W1)*
O'Zon *(TW1)*
Oriental City *(NW9)*

THAI

★★

Chiang Mai *(W1)*
Talad Thai *(SW15)*
Thailand *(SE14)*

A★

Amaranth *(SW18)*
Blue Elephant *(SW6)*
Churchill Arms *(W8)*
Thai on the River *(SW10)*
Yum Yum *(N16)*

★

Bangkok *(SW7)*
Chada *(SW11, W1)*
Lan Na Thai *(SW11)*
Latymers *(W6)*
The Papaya Tree *(W8)*
Tawana *(W2)*
Thai Bistro *(W4)*
Thai Corner Café *(SE22)*

A-

Busaba Eathai *(W1, WC1)*
Café 209 *(SW6)*
The Pepper Tree *(SW18, SW4)*
Thai Noodle Bar *(SW10)*
The Walmer Castle *(W11)*

-

Ben's Thai *(W9)*
Blue Jade *(SW1)*
Blue Lagoon *(W14)*
Café de Maya *(NW3)*
Elephant Royale *(E14)*
Krungtap *(SW5)*
Kwan Thai *(SE1)*
Little Basil *(NW3)*
Old Parr's Head *(W14)*
Sabai Sabai *(W6)*
Thai Café *(SW1)*
Thai Canteen *(W6)*
Thai Garden *(SW11)*
Yelo *(N1)*

VIETNAMESE

★★

Huong-Viet *(N1)*

-

Viet Hoa *(E2)*
Viet-Anh *(NW1)*

AREA OVERVIEWS

Where the ratings for a restaurant appear in brackets, eg *(A★)*, you can usually keep expenditure within our £20-a-head budget only at certain times of the day, or by sticking to a particular menu. Eating at other times or from the à la carte menu may be much more expensive.

CENTRAL

Soho, Covent Garden & Bloomsbury (Parts of W1, all WC2 and WC1)

£20	Bank Aldwych	*British, Modern*	(A★)
	Aurora	*"*	(A)
	The Endurance	*British, Traditional*	★
	J Sheekey	*Fish & seafood*	(A★★)
	Incognico	*French*	(★★)
	Balans	*International*	
	Luigi's	*Italian*	A
	Mela	*Indian*	★
£15+	Café du Jardin	*British, Modern*	(A★)
	Le Deuxième	*"*	(★)
	The Easton	*"*	
	Smithy's	*"*	
	Maggiore's	*French*	(A★)
	Café Emm	*International*	A
	Gordon's Wine Bar	*"*	A
	Sarastro	*"*	(A)
	Shampers	*"*	(A)
	Boulevard	*"*	
	Aperitivo	*Italian*	A
	Rusticana	*"*	
	Sapori	*"*	
	Strada	*"*	
	Mildred's	*Vegetarian*	★
	World Food Café	*"*	
	North Sea Fish	*Fish & chips*	★
	Ask!	*Pizza*	
	So.uk	*North African*	A
	Souk	*"*	A
	Kaslik	*Lebanese*	
	Gaby's	*Middle Eastern*	
	Yming	*Chinese*	(A★★)
	Joy King Lau	*"*	★
	Mr Kong	*"*	★
	New Mayflower	*"*	★
	Chuen Cheng Ku	*"*	
	Golden Dragon	*"*	
	Harbour City	*"*	
	New World	*"*	
	Chowki	*Indian*	★
	Ophim	*"*	(★)
	Gopal's of Soho	*"*	
	Kulu Kulu	*Japanese*	★★
	Itsu	*"*	★
	Satsuma	*"*	
	Wagamama	*"*	
	Melati	*Malaysian*	
	Busaba Eathai	*Thai*	A
£10+	Mon Plaisir	*French*	(A★)
	Exotika	*International*	
	Star Café	*"*	

	La Porchetta Pizzeria	*Italian*	★
	Bistro I	*Mediterranean*	
	Food for Thought	*Vegetarian*	★
	Paul	*Sandwiches, cakes, etc*	
	Poons	*Chinese*	
	Poons, Lisle Street	"	
	Wong Kei	"	
	India Club	*Indian*	
	Masala Zone	"	
	Taro	*Japanese*	
	Tokyo Diner	"	
	Chiang Mai	*Thai*	(★★)
£5+	Red Veg	*Vegetarian*	★
	Fryer's Delight	*Fish & chips*	
	Maison Bertaux	*Sandwiches, cakes, etc*	A★
	Bar Italia	"	A
	Pâtisserie Valerie	"	
	Soup Opera	*Soup*	

Mayfair & St James's (Parts of W1 and SW1)

£20	Fortnum's Fountain	*British, Modern*	(A)
	Deca	*French*	(A★)
	Hard Rock Café	*Burgers, etc*	A
	Hakkasan	*Chinese*	(A★)
	Veeraswamy	*Indian*	(A★)
	Khew	*Pan-Asian*	
£15+	Running Horse	*International*	
	Strada	*Italian*	
	Rocket	*Mediterranean*	A
	Ask!	*Pizza*	
	Gourmet Pizza Co.	"	
	Levant	*Middle Eastern*	(A)
	Rasa	*Indian*	(★★)
	Yoshino	*Japanese*	(★★)
	Benihana	"	(A★)
	Wagamama	"	
£10+	Raks	*Turkish*	(★)
	Woodlands	*Indian*	(★)
£5+	Soup Opera	*Soup*	

Fitzrovia & Marylebone (Part of W1)

£20	Sherlock's Grill	*British, Modern*	(★)
	La Rueda	*Spanish*	(A)
	Tajine	*Moroccan*	★
	Royal China	*Chinese*	(★★)
	Malabar Junction	*Indian*	(A★)
£15+	La Brasserie Townhouse	*British, Modern*	(★)
	Cabanon	*French*	★
	La Galette	"	
	Tapa Room (Providores)	*Fusion*	(A★)
	Hellenik	*Greek*	(A★)

	Giraffe	*International*	
	Cristini	*Italian*	★
	Carluccio's Caffè	*"*	
	Strada	*"*	
	Italian Kitchen	*"*	
	Eagle Bar Diner	*Burgers, etc*	A
	Ask!	*Pizza*	
	Ozer	*Turkish*	(A★)
	Efes Kebab House	*"*	
	Bam-Bou	*French-Vietnamese*	(A★)
	Ikkyu	*Japanese*	★
	Wagamama	*"*	
	Chada	*Thai*	★
£10+	Bistro 1	*Mediterranean*	
	Segafredo Zanetti	*Sandwiches, cakes, etc*	★
	Paul	*"*	
	Woodlands	*Indian*	(★)
	Ragam	*Indian, Southern*	★
	Abeno	*Japanese*	(★)
£5+	Govinda's	*International*	★
	Pâtisserie Valerie	*Sandwiches, cakes, etc*	

Belgravia, Pimlico, Victoria & Westminster (SW1, except St James's)

£20	Bank Westminster	*British, Modern*	(A★)
	Blue Jade	*Thai*	
£15+	Ebury Street Wine Bar	*British, Modern*	
	Grumbles	*International*	
	Royal Court Bar	*"*	
	Pizza on the Park	*Italian*	A
	Uno	*"*	
	Ask!	*Pizza*	
	Kazan	*Turkish*	A
	Wagamama	*Japanese*	
	Pan-Asian Canteen	*Pan-Asian*	★
	Just Oriental	*"*	
	Thai Café	*Thai*	
£10+	Grenadier	*British, Traditional*	(A)
	Brahms	*International*	
	Jenny Lo's	*Chinese*	★
£5+	Pâtisserie Valerie	*Sandwiches, cakes, etc*	

WEST

Chelsea, South Kensington, Kensington, Earl's Court & Fulham (SW3, SW5, SW6, SW7, SW10 & W8)

Price	Restaurant	Cuisine	Rating
£20	The Builder's Arms	*British, Modern*	𝔸
	The Ifield	*"*	𝔸
	Lots Road	*"*	𝔸
	The Abingdon	*"*	(𝔸)
	The Chelsea Ram	*"*	
	Le Metro	*"*	
	Vingt-Quatre	*"*	
	Ffiona's	*British, Traditional*	
	Stratford's	*Fish & seafood*	(★)
	Le Colombier	*French*	(𝔸)
	Balans West	*International*	
	Balans	*"*	
	Aglio e Olio	*Italian*	★
	Made in Italy	*"*	★
	Riccardo's	*"*	𝔸
	La Rueda	*Spanish*	(𝔸)
	Noor Jahan	*Indian*	
	Bangkok	*Thai*	★
£15+	Orangery	*0*	𝔸
	The Phoenix	*British, Modern*	𝔸
	White Horse	*"*	
	Lundum's	*Danish*	(𝔸★★)
	Lou Pescadou	*Fish & seafood*	(★)
	Nicolas Bar à Vins	*French*	★
	Wine & Kebab	*Greek*	(★)
	Coopers Arms	*International*	𝔸
	The Windsor Castle	*"*	𝔸
	Chelsea Bun Diner	*"*	
	Giraffe	*"*	
	Palms-on-the-Hill	*"*	
	Giá	*Italian*	𝔸★
	Pappa e Ciccia	*"*	𝔸★
	Frantoio	*"*	(𝔸★)
	Pellicano	*"*	(★)
	Bersagliera	*"*	𝔸
	Buona Sera	*"*	𝔸
	Il Pagliaccio	*"*	𝔸
	Carpaccio's	*"*	(𝔸)
	Spago	*"*	
	Strada	*"*	
	Il Falconiere	*"*	
	Meridiana	*"*	
	The Atlas	*Mediterranean*	𝔸
	Wódka	*Polish*	(𝔸★)
	Ognisko Polskie	*"*	(𝔸)
	Daquise	*"*	
	Tendido Cero	*Spanish*	★
	Lomo	*"*	𝔸
	Rôtisserie Jules	*Steaks & grills*	
	Café Crêperie	*Crêpes*	
	Le Shop	*"*	

	Basilico	*Pizza*	★★
	Pucci Pizza	*"*	(A)
	Ask!	*"*	
	Calzone	*"*	
	Troubadour	*Sandwiches, cakes, etc*	A
	Phoenicia	*Lebanese*	(★)
	Good Earth	*Chinese*	(★)
	Vama	*Indian*	(A★★)
	Malabar	*"*	A★
	Khan's of Kensington	*"*	★
	Tandoori Lane	*"*	★
	Tandoori of Chelsea	*"*	★
	Nayaab	*"*	
	Kulu Kulu	*Japanese*	★★
	Benihana	*"*	(A★)
	Itsu	*"*	★
	Bar Japan	*"*	(★)
	Wagamama	*"*	
	Zimzun	*Pan-Asian*	A★
	Blue Elephant	*Thai*	(A★)
	Thai on the River	*"*	(A★)
	The Papaya Tree	*"*	★
	Thai Noodle Bar	*"*	A
£10+	La Bouchée	*French*	(A)
	Gourmet Burger Kitchen	*Burgers, etc*	★
	La Delizia	*Pizza*	★
	Ranoush	*Lebanese*	★
	Aziz	*Middle Eastern*	★
	Stick & Bowl	*Chinese*	★
	Khyber Pass	*Indian*	
	Churchill Arms	*Thai*	A★
	Café 209	*"*	A
	Krungtap	*"*	
£5+	The Mall Tavern	*British, Modern*	(★)
	Fileric	*Sandwiches, cakes, etc*	★
	Pâtisserie Valerie	*"*	
	Soup Opera	*Soup*	

Notting Hill, Holland Park, Bayswater, North Kensington & Maida Vale (W2, W9, W10, W11)

£20	Paradise, Kensal Green	*British, Modern*	A
	Golborne House	*"*	(A)
	Raoul's Café	*"*	
	Café Laville	*International*	A
	Osteria Basilico	*Italian*	(A★)
	The Red Pepper	*"*	★
	Royal China	*Chinese*	(★★)
	Noor Jahan	*Indian*	
£15+	Dakota	*American*	
	Formosa Dining Room	*British, Modern*	A★
	The Station	*"*	★
	The Vale	*"*	(★)
	The Prince Bonaparte	*"*	

	The Cow	*Fish & seafood*	(A)
	Père Michel	*French*	
	Café 206	*Italian*	A
	Wine Factory	"	
	Mediterraneo	*Mediterranean*	(A★)
	Galicia	*Spanish*	
	Rôtisserie Jules	*Steaks & grills*	
	Ask!	*Pizza*	
	Tom's	*Sandwiches, cakes, etc*	
	Beirut Express	*Lebanese*	★★
	Alounak	*Persian*	★
	Mandarin Kitchen	*Chinese*	(★★)
	The Four Seasons	"	★
	Inaho	*Japanese*	(★★)
	Uli	*Pan-Asian*	★★
	Southeast W9	"	★
	Tawana	*Thai*	★
	The Walmer Castle	"	A
	Ben's Thai	"	
£10+	Ranoush	*Lebanese*	★
	Kandoo	*Persian*	
	Mandalay	*Burmese*	★★
	Khan's	*Indian*	★
	Standard Tandoori	"	
	Mawar	*Malaysian*	★
£1+	Lisboa Patisserie	*Sandwiches, cakes, etc*	★★

Hammersmith, Shepherd's Bush, Olympia, Chiswick & Ealing (W4, W5, W6, W12, W14)

£20	The Havelock Tavern	*British, Modern*	A★
	The Anglesea Arms	"	★
	Popeseye	*Steaks & grills*	★
	The Gate	*Vegetarian*	★★
	Azou	*North African*	
£15+	The Brackenbury	*British, Modern*	(A★)
	Bush Bar & Grill	"	A
	Stone Mason's Arms	"	A
	The Thatched House	"	A
	The Crown & Sceptre	"	
	The Pilot	"	
	Giraffe	*International*	
	Carluccio's Caffè	*Italian*	
	The Swan	*Mediterranean*	A★
	Patio	*Polish*	(A)
	Rôtisserie	*Steaks & grills*	(★★)
	Blah! Blah! Blah!	*Vegetarian*	★★
	Ask!	*Pizza*	
	Adams Café	*Moroccan*	
	Fish Hoek	*South African*	(★★)
	Alounak	*Persian*	★
	Mohsen	"	★
	Yas	"	
	Madhu's	*Indian*	★★

	Brilliant	"	★
	Chula	"	
	Thai Bistro	*Thai*	★
	Sabai Sabai	"	
£10+	Lowiczanka	*Polish*	
	Abu Zaad	*Middle Eastern*	★
	Woodlands	*Indian*	(★)
	Anarkali	"	
	Sagar	*Indian, Southern*	★★
	Latymers	*Thai*	★
	Old Parr's Head	"	
	Thai Canteen	"	
	Blue Lagoon	"	

NORTH

Hampstead, West Hampstead, St John's Wood, Regent's Park, Kilburn & Camden Town (NW postcodes)

£20	William IV	*British, Modern*	(𝔸★)
	Bradley's	*"*	(★)
	The Green	*"*	𝔸
	Lansdowne	*"*	(𝔸)
	The Chapel	*"*	
	The Salusbury	*Italian*	
	The Gate	*Vegetarian*	★★
	Mango Room	*Afro-Caribbean*	𝔸★
	Solly's Exclusive	*Israeli*	
	Royal China	*Chinese*	(★★)
	ZeNW3	*"*	(★)
	Jin Kichi	*Japanese*	★★
	Café Japan	*"*	★
£15+	The Lord Palmerston	*British, Modern*	𝔸★
	The Highgate	*"*	(★)
	Dartmouth Arms	*"*	𝔸
	Queen's Pub & Dining Rm	*"*	
	Le Petit Prince	*French*	
	Lemonia	*Greek*	𝔸
	Daphne	*"*	
	Giraffe	*International*	
	La Brocca	*Italian*	𝔸
	Marine Ices	*"*	
	Zamoyski	*Polish*	
	Troika	*Russian*	
	Don Pepe	*Spanish*	𝔸
	Nautilus	*Fish & chips*	★
	Seashell	*"*	★
	Basilico	*Pizza*	★★
	Ask!	*"*	
	Ali Baba	*Egyptian*	★
	Shish	*Middle Eastern*	
	Opera	*Chinese*	(𝔸★)
	Gung-Ho	*"*	
	Chutneys	*Indian*	★
	Great Nepalese	*"*	
	Sabras	*Indian, Southern*	★★
	Benihana	*Japanese*	(𝔸★)
	Sushi-Say	*"*	★
	Wagamama	*"*	
	Singapore Garden	*Malaysian*	(★)
	Little Basil	*Thai*	-
£10+	Brew House	*0*	𝔸
	Vegia Zena	*Italian*	(★)
	The Little Bay	*Mediterranean*	𝔸
	Gourmet Burger Kitchen	*Burgers, etc*	★
	Chamomile	*Sandwiches, cakes, etc*	
	Geeta	*Indian*	★★
	Sakonis	*"*	★★
	Vijay	*"*	★★

	Diwana B-P House	"	★
	Jashan	"	★
	Zamzama	"	A
	Oriental City	*Pan-Asian*	
	Café de Maya	*Thai*	
	Viet-Anh	*Vietnamese*	

Hoxton, Islington, Highgate, Crouch End, Stoke Newington, Finsbury Park, Muswell Hill & Finchley (N postcodes)

£20	Frederick's	*British, Modern*	(A★★)
	Chez Liline	*Fish & seafood*	(★★)
	Vrisaki	*Greek*	★
	Banners	*International*	
	Banners on the Hill	"	
	Cantina Italia	*Italian*	
	The Parsee	*Indian*	★★
£15+	Tartuf	*Alsatian*	★
	Café Mozart	*East & Cent. European*	A
	Petit Auberge	*French*	
	The Real Greek	*Greek*	(A★)
	Giraffe	*International*	
	Pizzeria Oregano	*Italian*	★
	Carluccio's Caffè	"	
	Strada	"	
	Rôtisserie	*Steaks & grills*	(★★)
	Two Brothers	*Fish & chips*	★
	Furnace	*Pizza*	★
	Ask!	"	
	La Piragua	*South American*	
	Maghreb	*Moroccan*	
	Gallipoli	*Turkish*	A★
	Sedir	"	
	Rasa	*Indian*	(★★)
	Anglo Asian Tandoori	"	★
	Rani	"	★
	Rasa Travancore	*Indian, Southern*	★
	Bu San	*Korean*	★
	Yum Yum	*Thai*	A★
	Yelo	"	
£10+	Le Sacré-Coeur	*French*	(A)
	Bar Mezé	*Greek*	
	La Porchetta Pizzeria	*Italian*	★
	Toff's	*Fish & chips*	
	Afghan Kitchen	*Afghani*	★
	Jashan	*Indian*	★
	Huong-Viet	*Vietnamese*	★★

SOUTH

South Bank (SE1)

£20	Tate Modern (Café 7)	*International*	A
	La Lanterna	*Italian*	
£15+	Konditor & Cook	*British, Modern*	★★
	Bankside	*"*	
	Butlers Wharf Chop-house	*British, Traditional*	(A★)
	Film Café	*International*	
	Baltic	*Polish*	(A)
	Meson don Felipe	*Spanish*	A
	Pizzeria Castello	*Pizza*	★
	Ask!	*"*	
	Gourmet Pizza Co.	*"*	
	Tas	*Turkish*	A
	Tas Pide	*"*	A
	Bengal Clipper	*Indian*	(★)
	Kwan Thai	*Thai*	
£10+	El Vergel	*South American*	★★

Greenwich, Lewisham & Blackheath (All SE postcodes, except SE1)

£20	The Trafalgar Tavern	*British, Traditional*	A
	Spread Eagle	*French*	(A★)
	Babur Brasserie	*Indian*	★
£15+	Kennington Lane	*British, Modern*	(★)
	The Sun & Doves	*"*	A
	Lobster Pot	*Fish & seafood*	(A★)
	Arancia	*Italian*	A
	Zero Degrees	*Pizza*	A
£10+	Thai Corner Café	*Thai*	★
£5+	Thailand	*"*	(★★)

Battersea, Brixton, Clapham, Wandsworth Barnes, Putney & Wimbledon (All SW postcodes south of the river)

£20	The Stepping Stone	*British, Modern*	(A★★)
	Phoenix	*"*	(A★)
	Willie Gunn	*"*	A
	Balham Kitchen & Bar	*"*	-
	Alma	*International*	A
	Hudson's	*"*	A
	La Rueda	*Spanish*	(A)
	Popeseye	*Steaks & grills*	★
	Polygon Bar & Grill	*"*	(A)
	Coromandel	*Indian, Southern*	★
	Tsunami	*Japanese*	(★★)
	Lan Na Thai	*Thai*	(★)

£15+	Cinnamon Cay	*Australian*	(A★)
	The Depot	*British, Modern*	(A★)
	The Abbeville	*"*	★
	The Castle	*"*	
	Rick's Café	*"*	
	Gastro	*French*	(A)
	Bread & Roses	*International*	A
	Chelsea Bun Diner	*"*	
	Giraffe	*"*	
	Ost. Antica Bologna	*Italian*	A★
	Pappa e Ciccia	*"*	A★
	Antipasto e Pasta	*"*	(★)
	Buona Sera	*"*	A
	Antipasto & Pasta	*"*	
	Strada	*"*	
	Rocket Riverside	*Mediterranean*	A
	Café Portugal	*Portuguese*	A
	Rebato's	*Spanish*	A
	Brady's	*Fish & chips*	★
	Basilico	*Pizza*	★★
	Eco	*"*	★
	Eco Brixton	*"*	★
	Ask!	*"*	
	So.uk	*North African*	A
	Sarkhel's	*Indian*	★★
	Indian Ocean	*"*	★
	Ma Goa	*"*	★
	Chada	*Thai*	★
	Thai Garden	*"*	
£10+	Bar Mezé	*Greek*	
	Cantinetta Venegazzú	*Italian*	(★)
	Fish in a Tie	*Mediterranean*	A
	Bar Estrela	*Portuguese*	★
	Gourmet Burger Kitchen	*Burgers, etc*	★
	Boiled Egg & Soldiers	*Sandwiches, cakes, etc*	
	Kastoori	*Indian*	★★
	Mirch Masala SW16	*"*	★★
	Sree Krishna	*"*	★
	Fujiyama	*Japanese*	
	Talad Thai	*Thai*	★★
	Amaranth	*"*	A★
	The Pepper Tree	*"*	A

Outer western suburbs
Kew, Richmond, Twickenham, Teddington

£15+	Ma Cuisine	*French*	★★
	White Cross	*International*	A
	A Cena	*Italian*	(A★)
	don Fernando's	*Spanish*	A
	O'Zon	*Pan-Asian*	
£10+	Chez Lindsay	*French*	(A★)

EAST

Smithfield & Farringdon (EC1)

£20	Alba	*Italian*	(★)
	Hope & Sir Loin	*Steaks & grills*	
£15+	The Quality Chop House	*British, Modern*	(★)
	St John	*"*	(★)
	Fox & Anchor	*British, Traditional*	
	The Real Greek Souvlaki	*Greek*	A★★
	Carluccio's Caffè	*Italian*	
	Strada	*"*	
	The Eagle	*Mediterranean*	A★
	Don Pedro	*Spanish*	A
	Carnevale	*Vegetarian*	(★)
	Ask!	*Pizza*	
	Smiths (Ground Floor)	*Sandwiches, cakes, etc*	(A★)
	Moro	*North African*	(A★★)
	Shish	*Middle Eastern*	
£10+	Bar Mezé	*Greek*	
	The Little Bay	*Mediterranean*	A
	Apium	*Pan-Asian*	

The City (EC2, EC3, EC4)

£20	The Fox	*British, Modern*	A★
	The Evangelist	*"*	A
	Sosho	*"*	A
	The Wine Library	*British, Traditional*	A
£15+	Simpson's Tavern	*"*	A
	Cantaloupe	*Mediterranean*	
	Bar Capitale	*Pizza*	★
	Kasturi	*Indian*	★
	K10	*Japanese*	★★
	Noto	*"*	★
	Tokyo City	*"*	★
	Moshi Moshi	*"*	
	Wagamama	*"*	
£10+	Sweetings	*Fish & seafood*	(A)
	The Place Below	*Vegetarian*	A★
£5+	Futures	*"*	★
	Soup Opera	*Soup*	

East End & Docklands (All E postcodes)

£20	Royal China	*Chinese*	(★★)
£15+	LMNT	*British, Modern*	A
	Frocks	*"*	(A)
	Carluccio's Caffè	*Italian*	
	Arkansas Café	*Steaks & grills*	
	Faulkner's	*Fish & chips*	★★
	Gourmet Pizza Co.	*Pizza*	
	Haz	*Turkish*	★

	Shanghai	*Chinese*	A
	Itsu	*Japanese*	★
	Moshi Moshi	"	
	Wagamama	"	
	Elephant Royale	*Thai*	
£10+	Lahore Kebab House	*Indian*	★★
	New Tayyab	*Pakistani*	A★
	Viet Hoa	*Vietnamese*	
£5+	Soup Opera	*Soup*	
	Mangal	*Turkish*	★★
£1+	Brick Lane Beigel Bake	*Sandwiches, cakes, etc*	★★

MAPS

MAP 1 – LONDON OVERVIEW

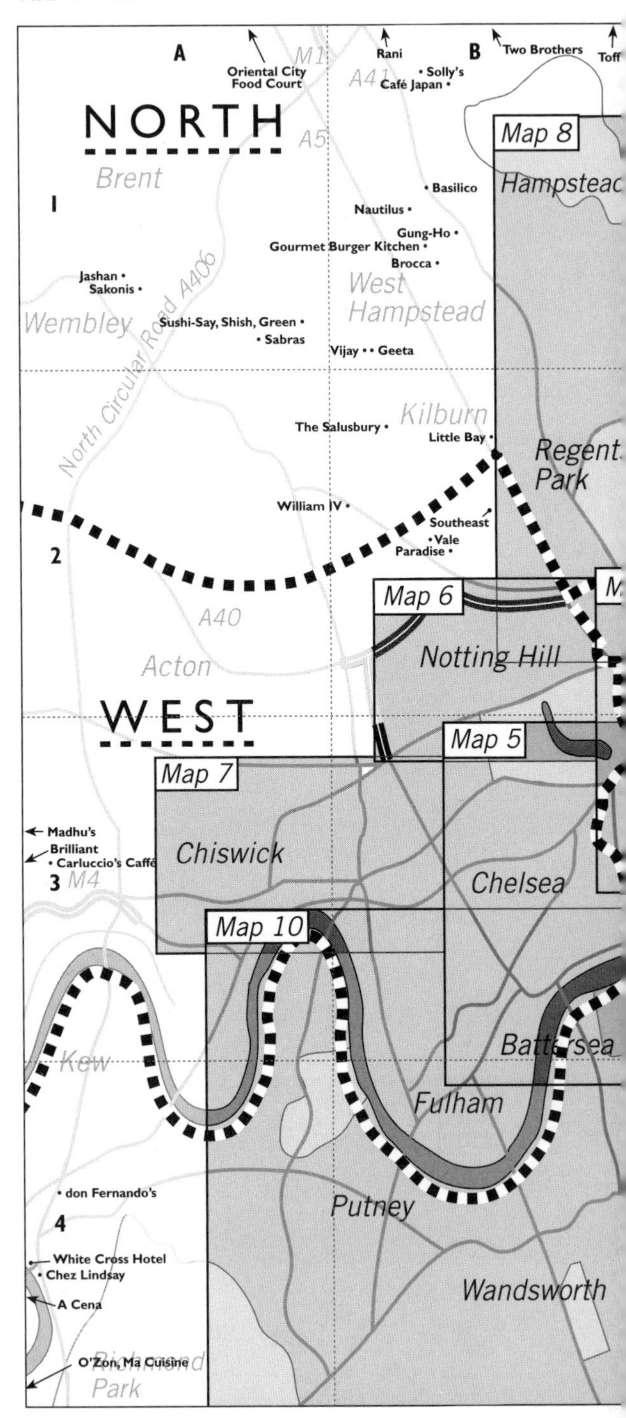

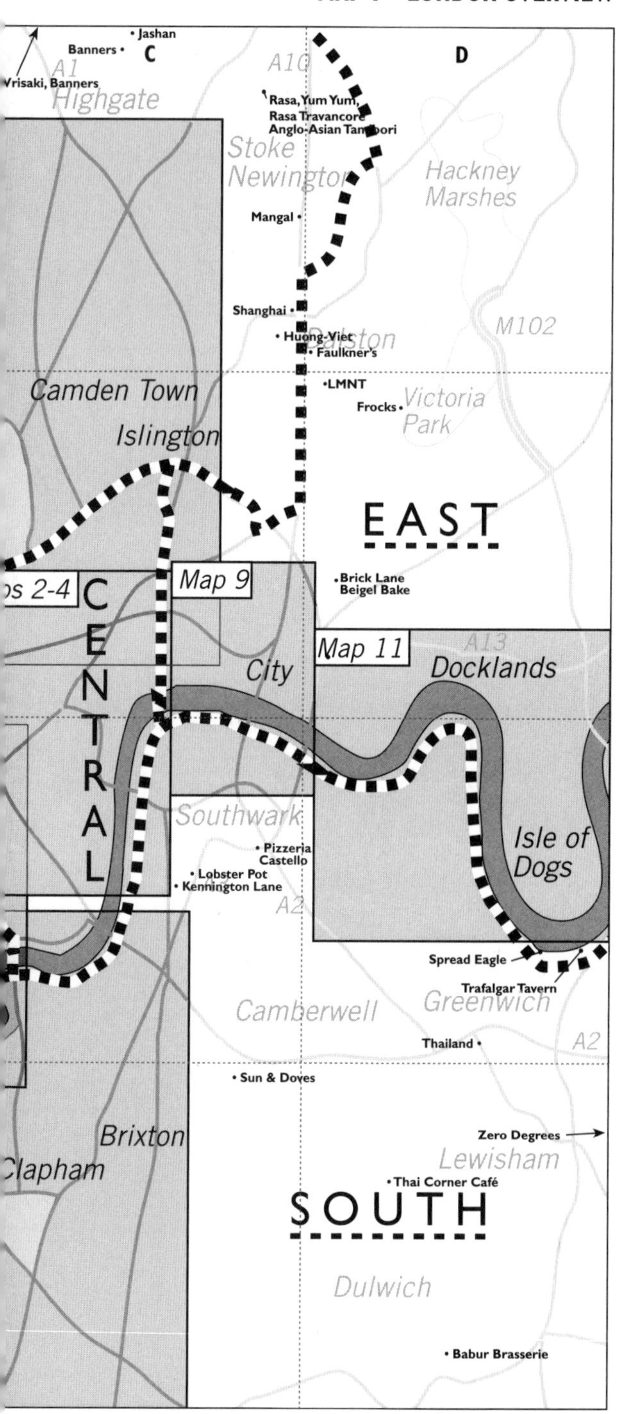

C
D
Jashan
Banners
Vrisaki, Banners
A1
Highgate
A10
Rasa, Yum Yum,
Rasa Travancore
Anglo-Asian Tandoori
Stoke Newington
Hackney Marshes
Mangal
Shanghai
Huong-Viet
Faulkner's
Dalston
M102
Camden Town
LMNT
Frocks
Victoria Park
Islington
EAST
Map 9
Brick Lane Beigel Bake
CENTRAL
Map 11
A13
City
Docklands
Southwark
Pizzeria Castello
Lobster Pot
Kennington Lane
Isle of Dogs
A2
Spread Eagle
Trafalgar Tavern
Camberwell
Greenwich
Thailand
A2
Sun & Doves
Zero Degrees
Brixton
Lewisham
Clapham
Thai Corner Café
SOUTH
Dulwich
Babur Brasserie

MAP 2 – WEST END OVERVIEW

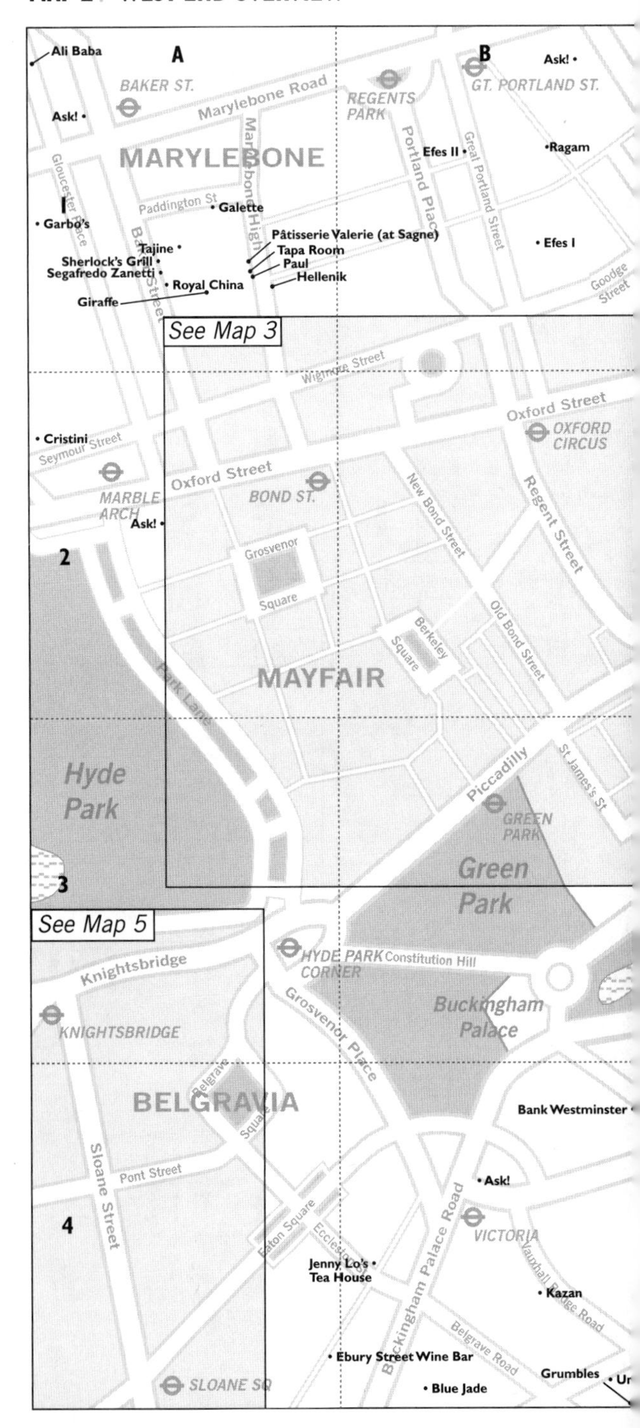

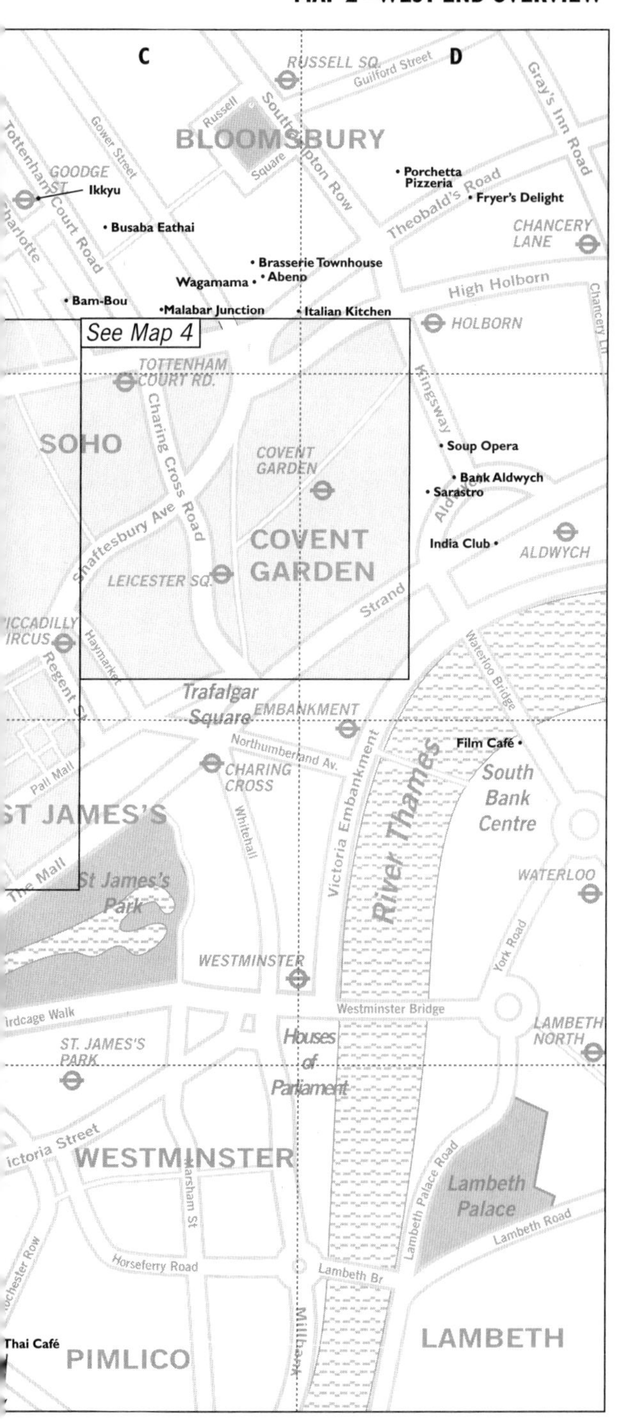

C
D
RUSSELL SQ.
Guilford Street
Gray's Inn Road
Russell Square
Southampton Row
BLOOMSBURY
Gower Street
Tottenham Court Road
GOODGE ST.
Ikkyu
Charlotte
Busaba Eathai
Porchetta Pizzeria
Theobald's Road
Fryer's Delight
CHANCERY LANE
Brasserie Townhouse
Abeno
Wagamama
High Holborn
Bam-Bou
Malabar Junction
Italian Kitchen
HOLBORN
See Map 4
TOTTENHAM COURT RD.
Kingsway
SOHO
Charing Cross Road
COVENT GARDEN
Soup Opera
Bank Aldwych
Sarastro
Shaftesbury Ave
COVENT GARDEN
India Club
ALDWYCH
LEICESTER SQ.
Strand
PICCADILLY CIRCUS
Haymarket
Regent St
Waterloo Bridge
Trafalgar Square
EMBANKMENT
Northumberland Av.
Film Café
CHARING CROSS
South Bank Centre
Pall Mall
ST JAMES'S
Whitehall
Victoria Embankment
River Thames
The Mall
St James's Park
WATERLOO
York Road
WESTMINSTER
Westminster Bridge
Birdcage Walk
LAMBETH NORTH
ST. JAMES'S PARK
Houses of Parliament
Victoria Street
WESTMINSTER
Marsham St
Lambeth Palace Road
Lambeth Palace
Lambeth Road
Horseferry Road
Lambeth Br
Millbank
LAMBETH
Thai Café
PIMLICO

MAP 3 – MAYFAIR, ST JAMES'S & WEST SOHO

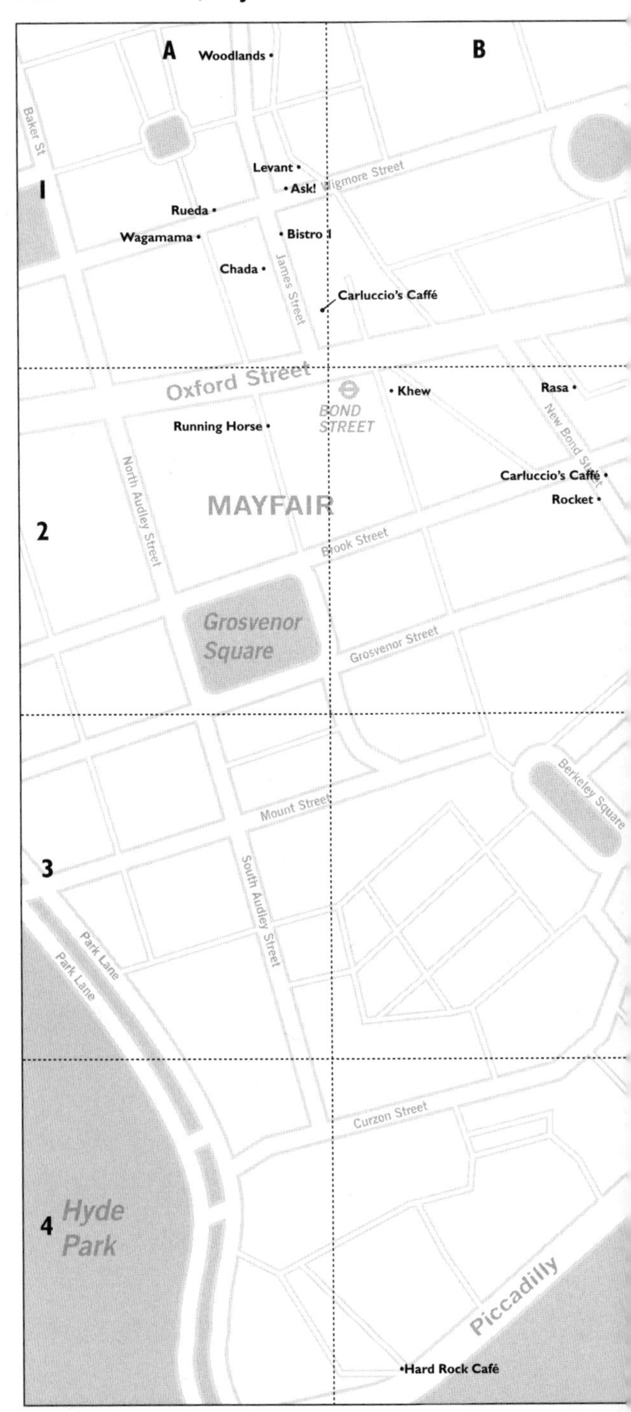

MAP 3 – MAYFAIR, ST JAMES'S & WEST SOHO

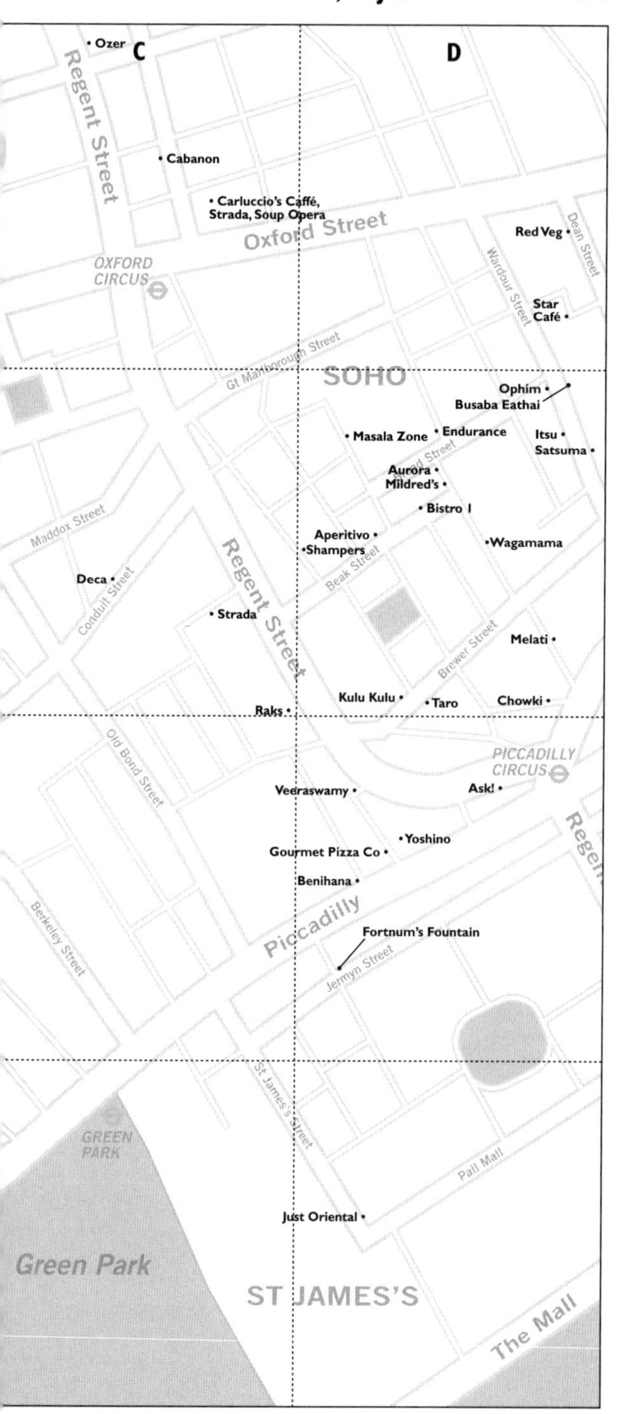

MAP 4 – EAST SOHO, CHINATOWN & COVENT GARDEN

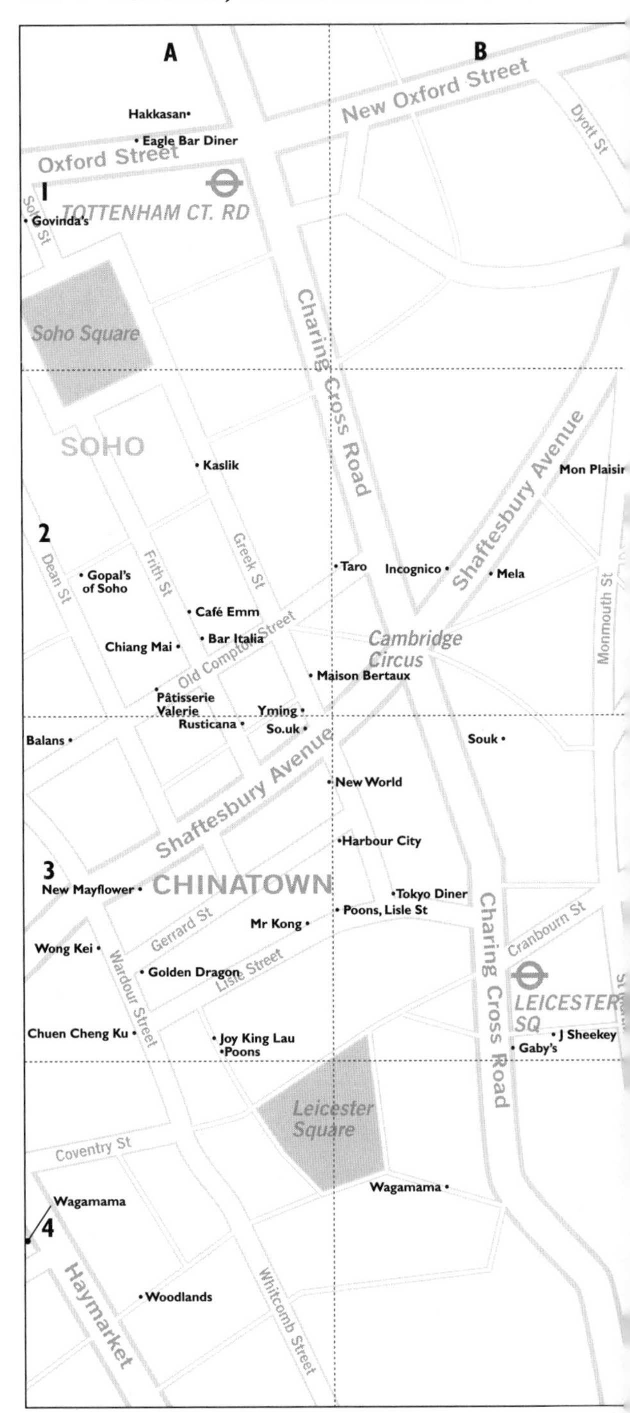

MAP 4 – EAST SOHO, CHINATOWN & COVENT GARDEN

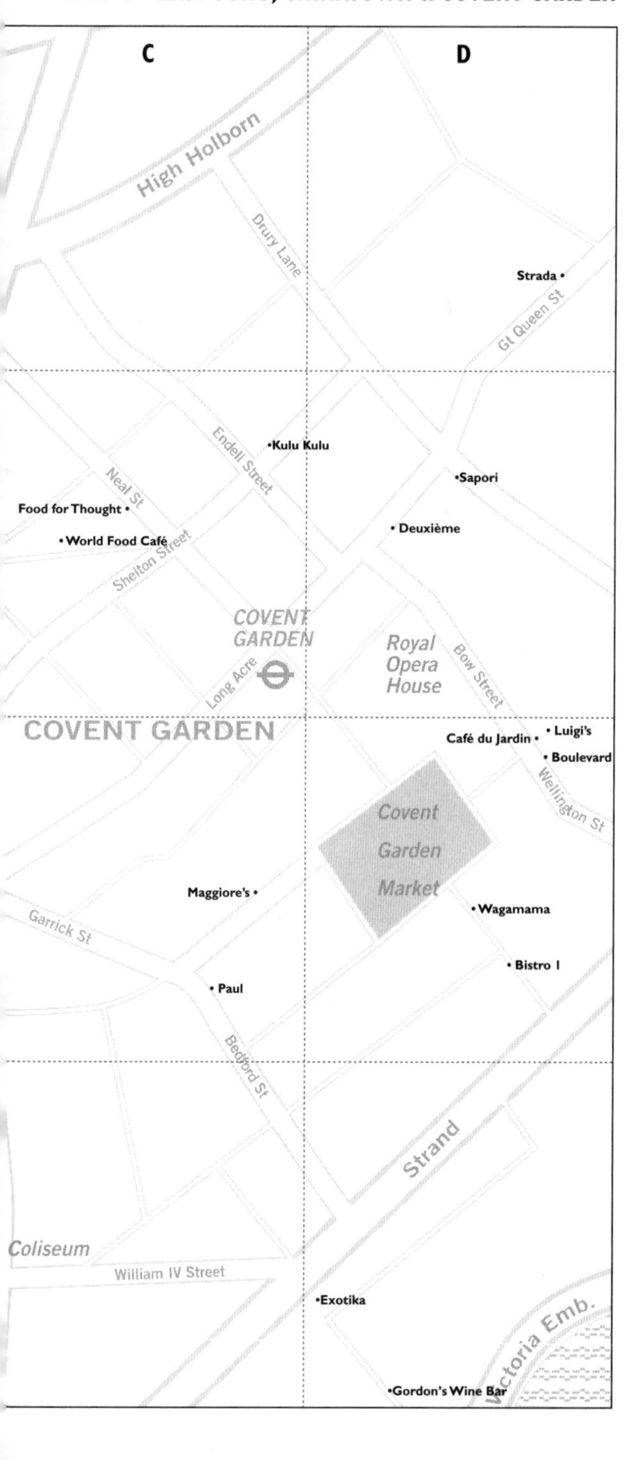

MAP 5 – KNIGHTSBRIDGE, CHELSEA & SOUTH KENSINGTON

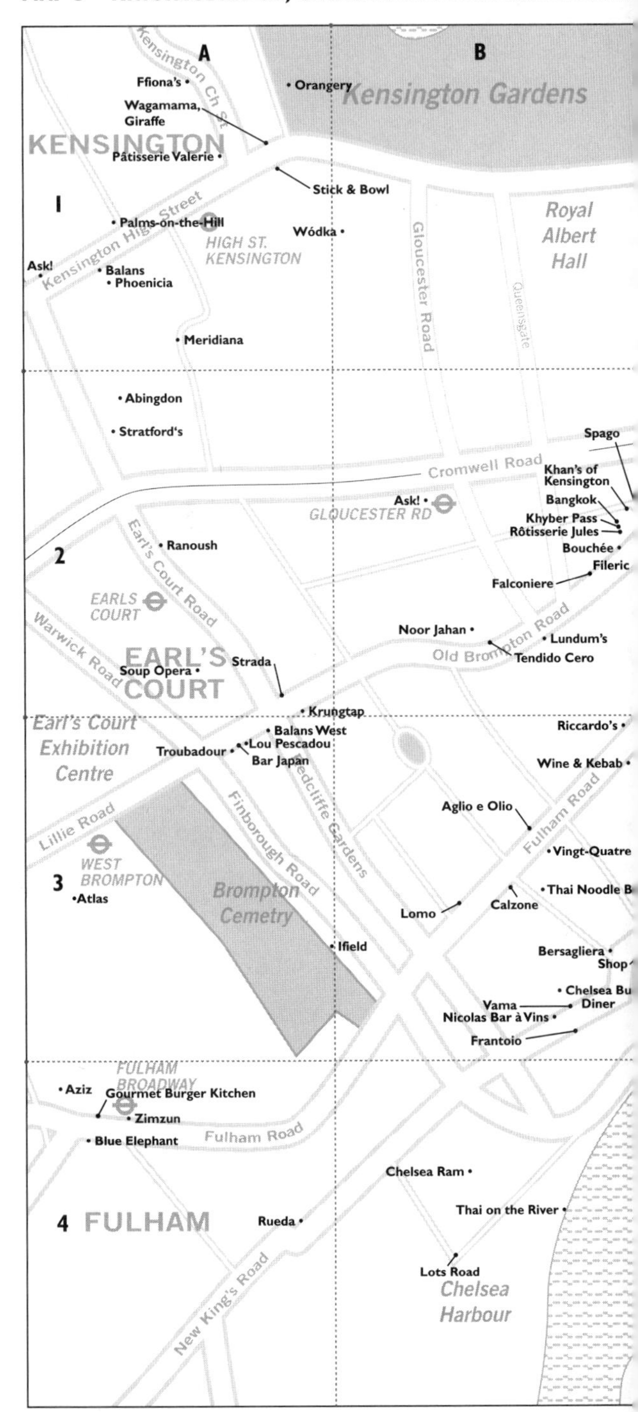

MAP 5 – KNIGHTSBRIDGE, CHELSEA & SOUTH KENSINGTON

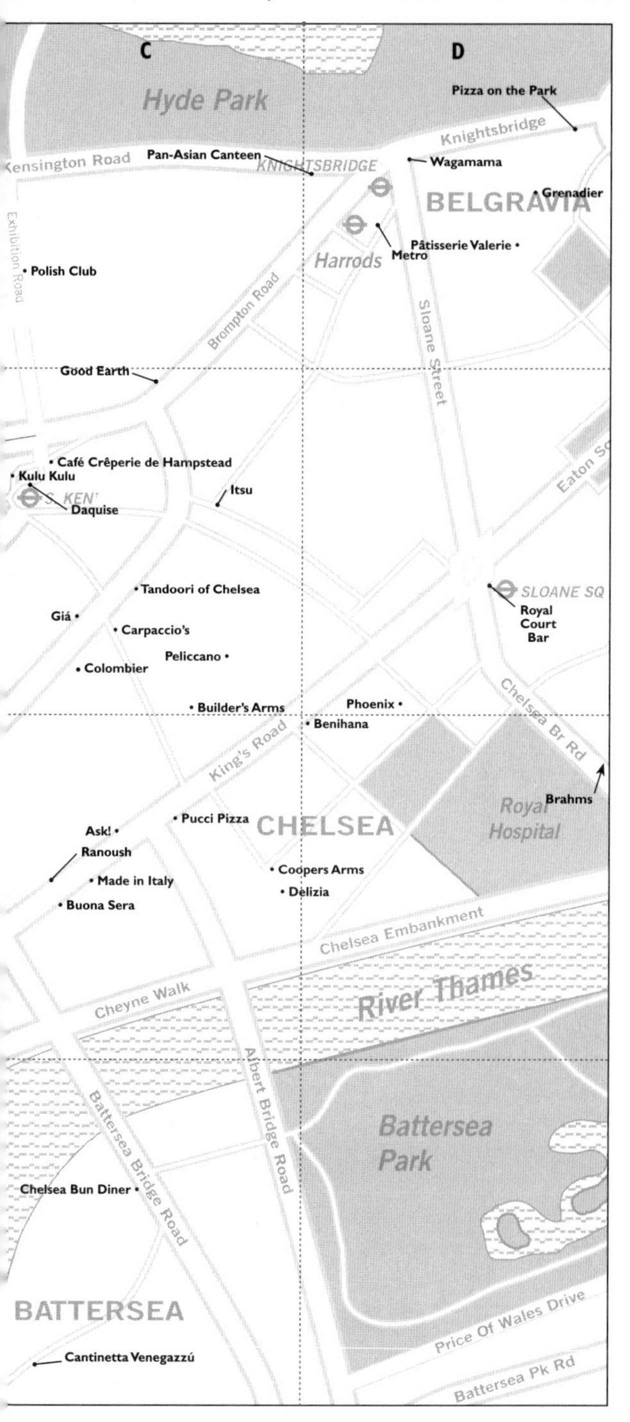

MAP 6 – NOTTING HILL & BAYSWATER

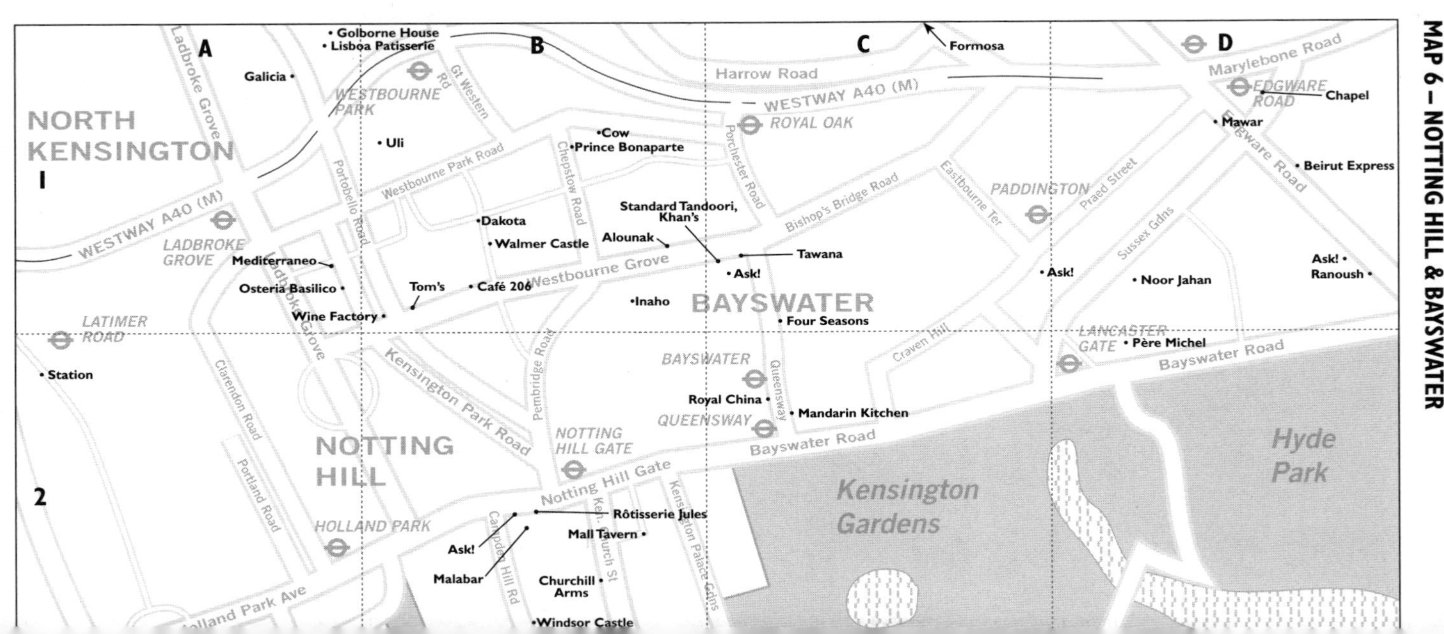

MAP 7 – HAMMERSMITH & CHISWICK

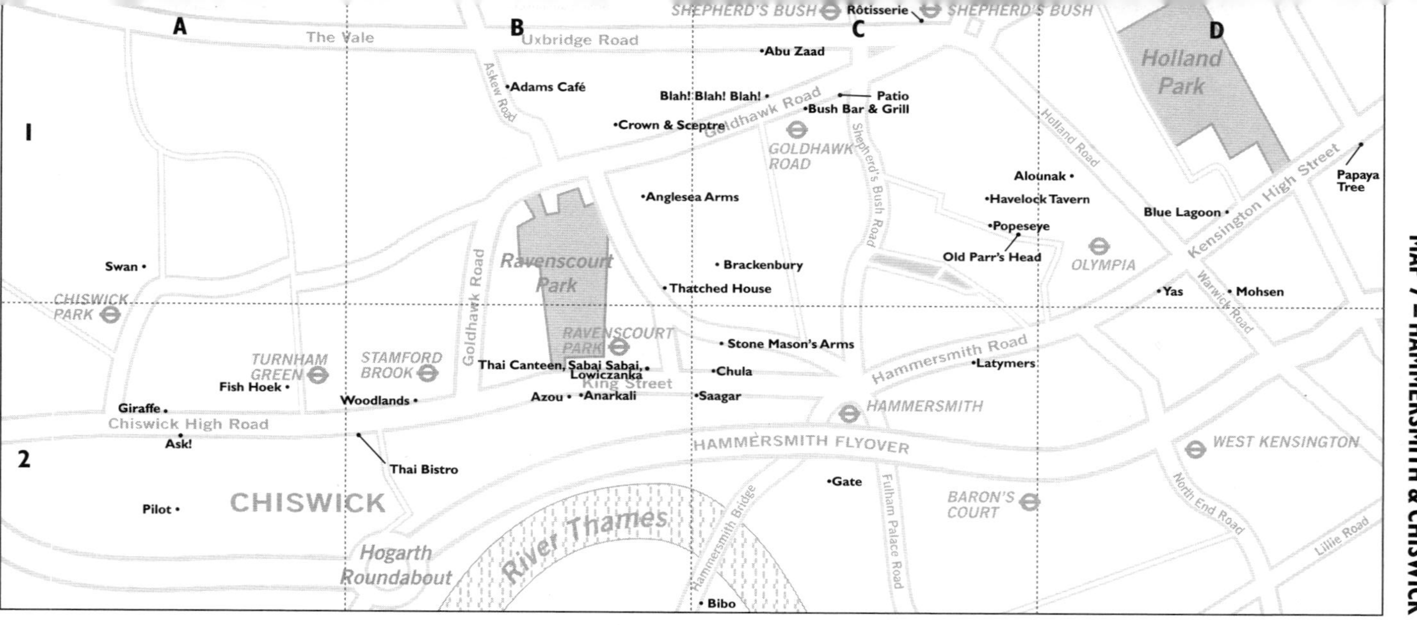

MAP 8 – HAMPSTEAD, CAMDEN TOWN & ISLINGTON

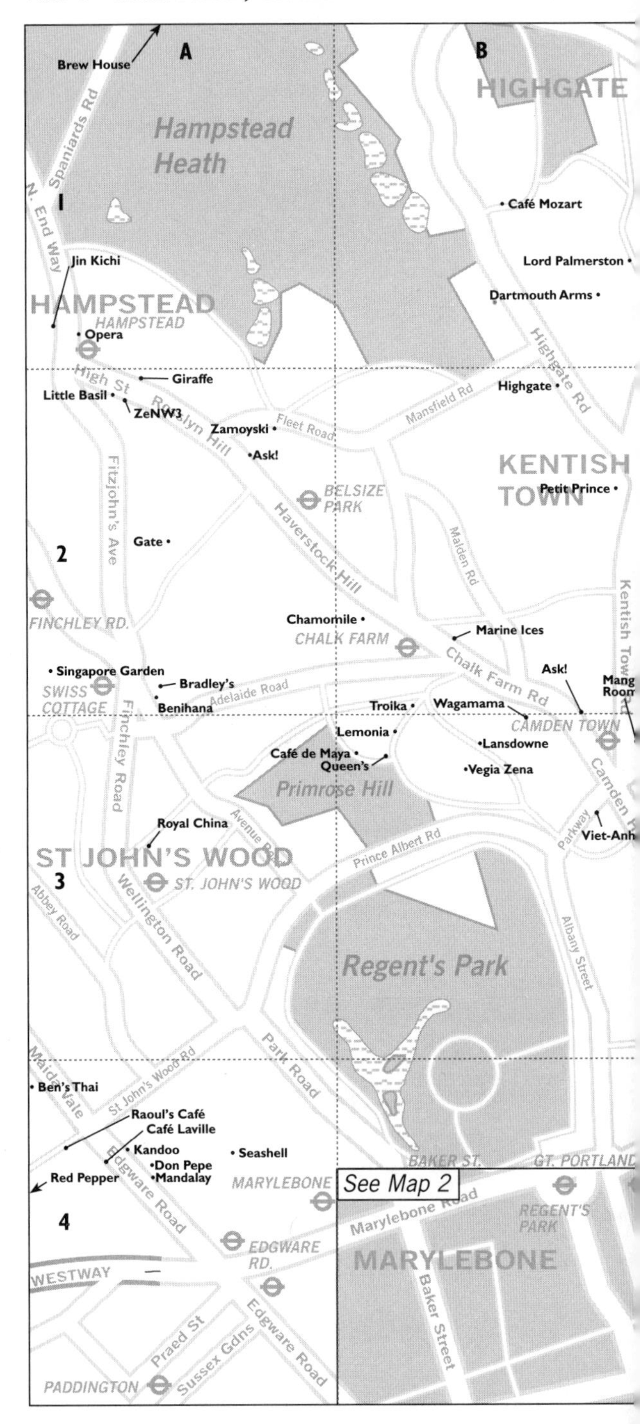

MAP 8 – HAMPSTEAD, CAMDEN TOWN & ISLINGTON

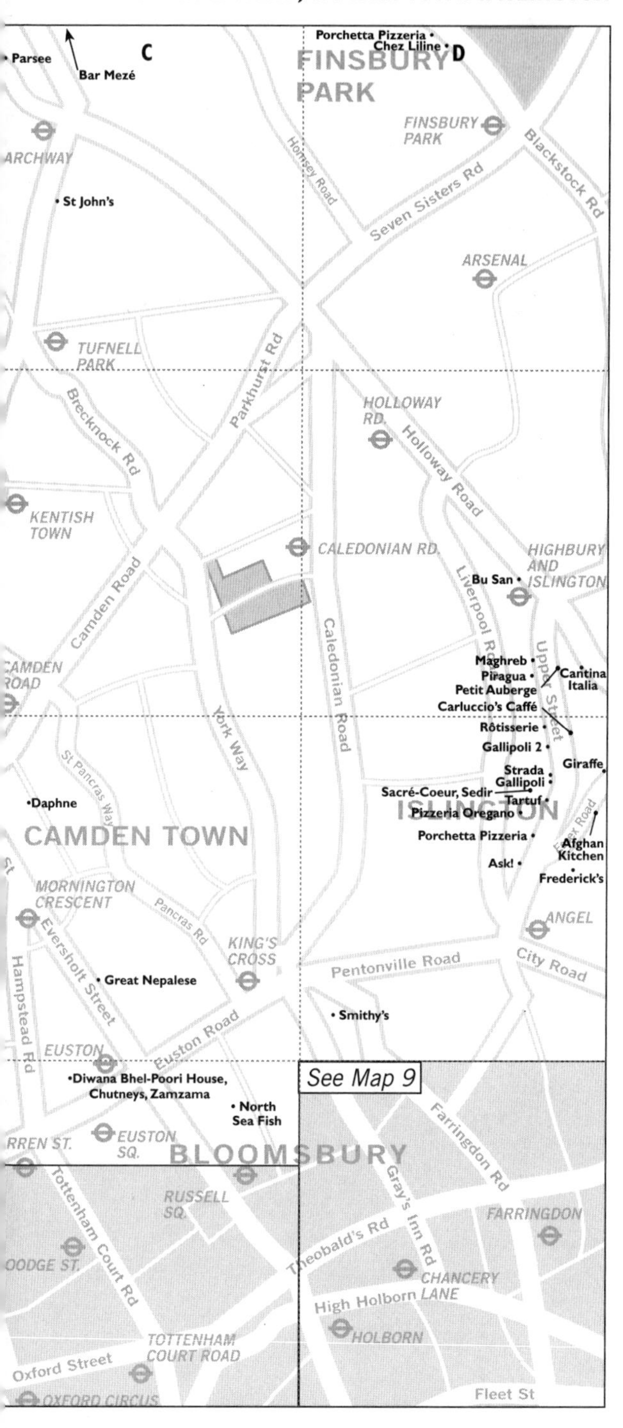

MAP 9 – THE CITY

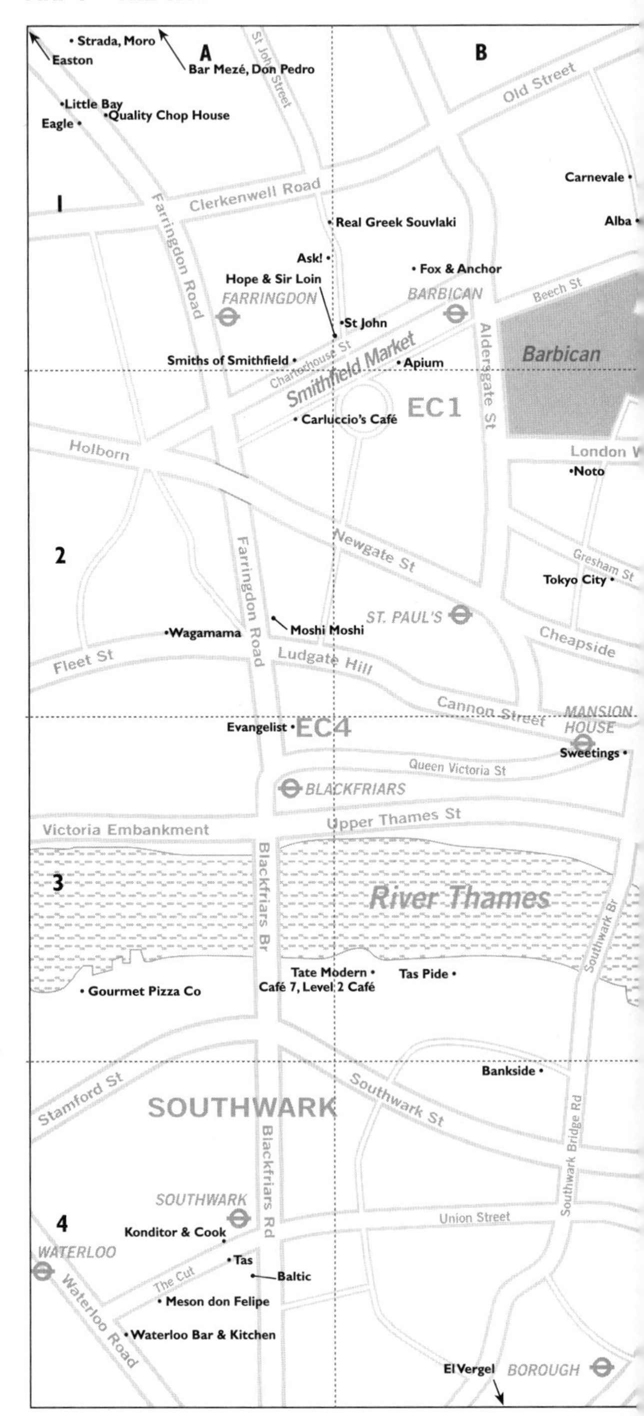

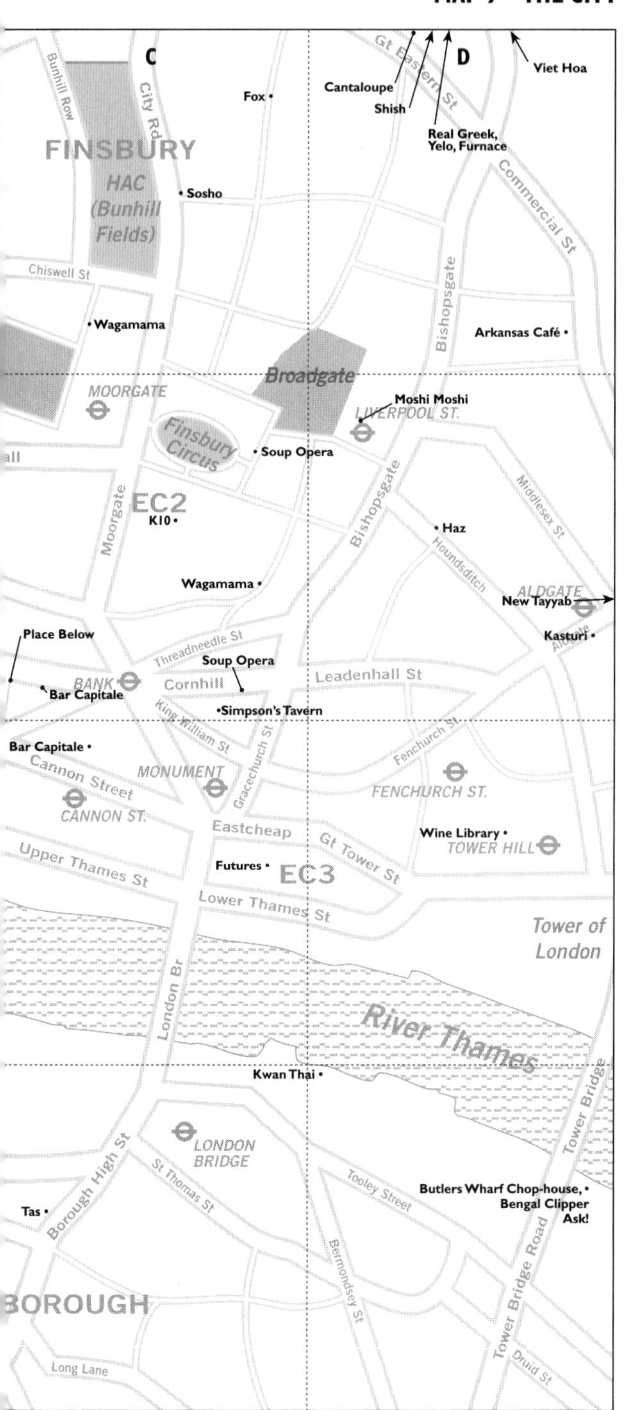
C
D
Viet Hoa
Cantaloupe
Shish
Real Greek, Yelo, Furnace
Fox
FINSBURY
HAC (Bunhill Fields)
Sosho
Bunhill Row
City Rd
Gt Eastern St
Commercial St
Chiswell St
Wagamama
Bishopsgate
Arkansas Café
Broadgate
MOORGATE
Moshi Moshi
LIVERPOOL ST.
Finsbury Circus
Soup Opera
EC2
K10
Moorgate
Haz
Middlesex St
Houndsditch
Wagamama
ALDGATE
New Tayyab
Kasturi
Place Below
Threadneedle St
Soup Opera
BANK
Bar Capitale
Cornhill
Leadenhall St
Simpson's Tavern
King William St
Fenchurch St
Bar Capitale
Cannon Street
MONUMENT
Gracechurch St
FENCHURCH ST.
CANNON ST.
Eastcheap
Wine Library
TOWER HILL
Upper Thames St
Futures
EC3
Gt Tower St
Lower Thames St
Tower of London
London Br
River Thames
Kwan Thai
Tower Bridge
LONDON BRIDGE
St Thomas St
Tooley Street
Butlers Wharf Chop-house, Bengal Clipper Ask!
Tas
Borough High St
Bermondsey St
Tower Bridge Road
BOROUGH
Druid St
Long Lane

MAP 10 – SOUTH LONDON (& FULHAM)

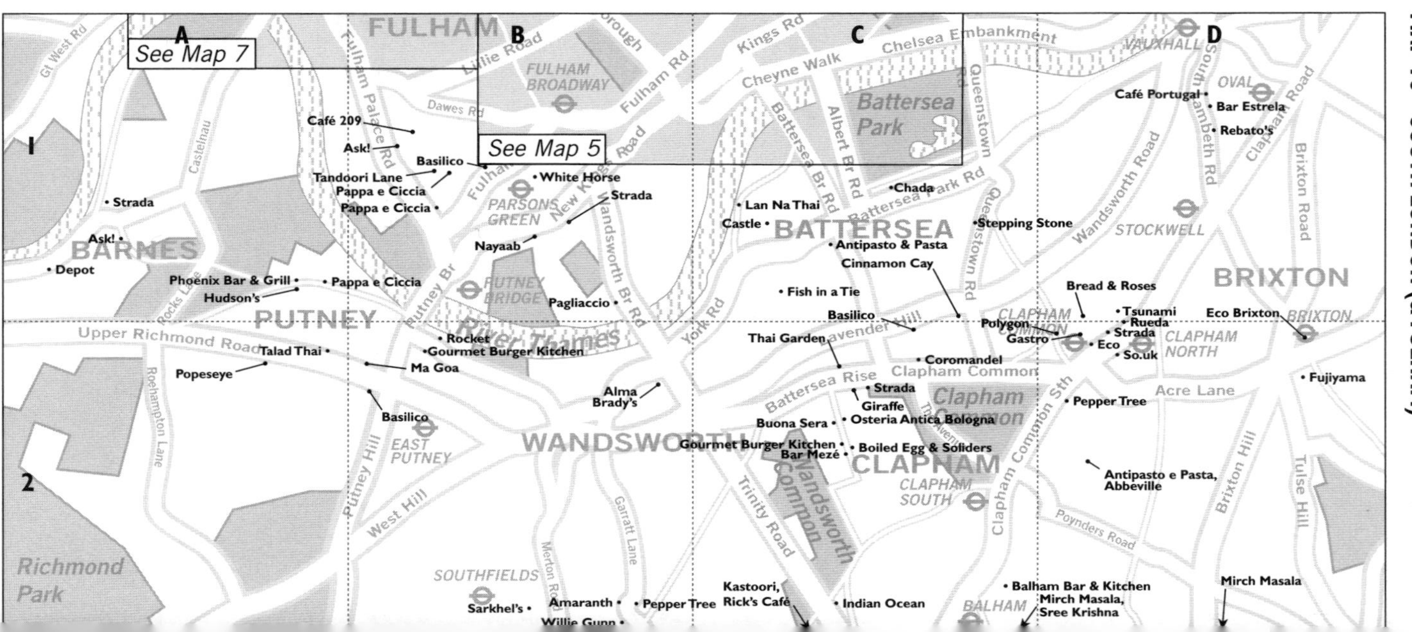

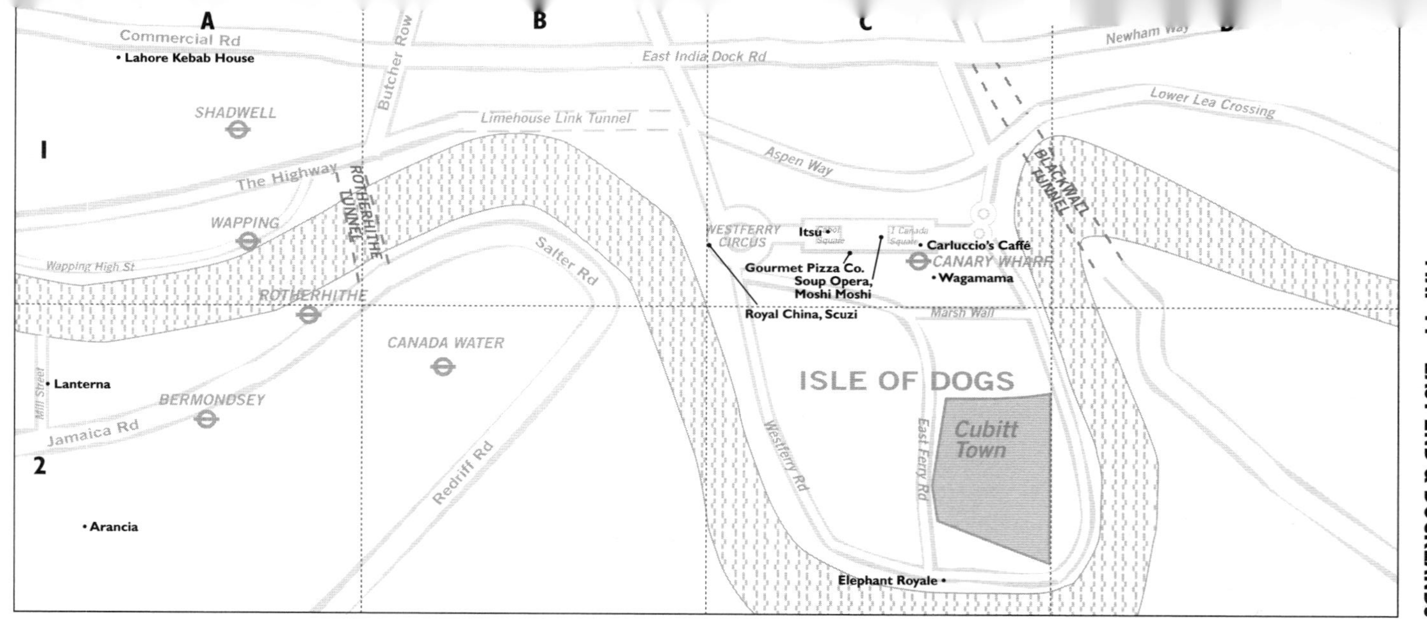
A
B
C
1
2
Commercial Rd
Lahore Kebab House
Butcher Row
East India Dock Rd
Newham Way
SHADWELL
Limehouse Link Tunnel
Lower Lea Crossing
The Highway
ROTHERHITHE TUNNEL
Aspen Way
BLACKWALL TUNNEL
WAPPING
WESTFERRY CIRCUS
Itsu
1 Canada Square
Carluccio's Caffè
CANARY WHARF
Wagamama
Wapping High St
Salter Rd
Gourmet Pizza Co.
Soup Opera, Moshi Moshi
ROTHERHITHE
Royal China, Scuzi
Marsh Wall
CANADA WATER
ISLE OF DOGS
Mill Street
Lanterna
BERMONDSEY
Jamaica Rd
Westferry Rd
East Ferry Rd
Cubitt Town
Redriff Rd
Arancia
Elephant Royale

NOTES